Palliative Care, Social Work and Service Users

of related interest

Dealing with Death
A Handbook of Practices, Procedures and Law
Second Edition
Jennifer Green and Michael Green
ISBN 978 1 84310 381 3

Supporting the Child and the Family in Paediatric Palliative Care
Erica Brown with Brian Warr
Foreword by Dr. Sheila Shribman
ISBN 978 1 84310 181 9

Nearing Death Awareness
A Guide to the Language, Visions, and Dreams of the Dying
Mary Ann Sanders
ISBN 978 1 84310 857 3

The Psychology of Ageing
An Introduction
Fourth Edition
Ian Stuart-Hamilton
ISBN 978 1 84310 426 1

Making Sense of Spirituality in Nursing and Health Care Practice
An Interactive Approach
Second Edition
Wilfred McSherry
Foreword by Keith Cash
ISBN 978 1 84310 365 3

The Inspiration of Hope in Bereavement Counselling
John R. Cutcliffe
Foreword by Ronna Jevne
ISBN 978 1 84310 082 9

Relative Grief
Parents and children, sisters and brothers, husbands, wives and partners,
grandparents and grandchildren talk about their experience of death and grieving
Clare Jenkins and Judy Merry
Foreword by Dorothy Rowe
ISBN 978 1 84310 257 1

Social Work and Dementia
Good Practice and Care Management
Margaret Anne Tibbs
Foreword by Murna Downs
ISBN 978 1 85302 904 2

Palliative Care, Social Work and Service Users

Making Life Possible

Peter Beresford, Lesley Adshead and Suzy Croft

Foreword by Dorothy Rowe

Jessica Kingsley Publishers
London and Philadelphia

First published in 2007
by Jessica Kingsley Publishers
116 Pentonville Road
London N1 9JB, UK
and
400 Market Street, Suite 400
Philadelphia, PA 19106, USA

www.jkp.com

Copyright © Peter Beresford, Lesley Adshead and Suzy Croft 2007
Foreword copyright © Dorothy Rowe 2007

Library of Congress Cataloging in Publication Data
Beresford, Peter.
  Palliative care, social work, and service users : making life possible / Peter Beresford,
Lesley Adshead, and Suzy Croft ; foreword by Dorothy Rowe.
    p. cm.
  Includes bibliographical references and index.
  ISBN-13: 978-1-84310-465-0 (pbk. : alk. paper)
  ISBN-10: 1-84310-465-2 (pbk. : alk. paper) 1. Social work with the terminally ill. 2.
Palliative treatment. 3. Care of the sick. I. Adshead, Lesley, 1953- II. Croft, Suzy. III.
Title.
  HV3000.B47 2007
  362.17'5--dc22
                                                          2006020067
British Library Cataloguing in Publication Data
A CIP catalogue record for this book is available from the British Library

ISBN 978 1 84310 465 0

Printed and bound in Great Britain by
Athenaeum Press, Gateshead, Tyne and Wear

In memory of my dear sister Maureen (1942–2000)
and to Maria, my great friend
at Springfield Hospital, who sadly died

To the memory of Jack Fisher,
a loyal and much missed friend

To Sally Ager, an inspiration
from whom I learned much about living and dying

CONTENTS

Foreword *by Dorothy Rowe*   9

Acknowledgements   11

Introduction   13

Part One: The Background
to Palliative Care Social Work   19

Chapter 1:   Palliative Care: A New Perspective   21

Part Two: What Service Users Say   39

Chapter 2:   Becoming Involved with Palliative Care   41

Chapter 3:   Starting the Palliative Care Social Work Journey   52

Chapter 4:   What Does the Social Worker Do?   68

Chapter 5:   What Service Users Value Most   88

Chapter 6:   Working with Difference   105

Chapter 7:   Exploring Outcomes: Evaluating Specialist
             Palliative Care Social Work   114

Part Three: Developing the Discussion   131

Chapter 8:   Accessing Specialist Palliative Care Social
             Work: A Broader Image Problem?   133

Chapter 9:   The Problem of Referral   139

Chapter 10: **The Nature, Strengths and Weaknesses**
of Practice   154

Chapter 11: **Theory and Practice**   174

Chapter 12: **Specialist Palliative Care Social Work:**
A Service in the Shadows?   189

Chapter 13: **Issues for the Future**   208

Appendix 1: How We Carried Out the Research   227

Appendix 2: The Interview Schedule   247

References   252

Subject Index   261

Author Index   266

List of Tables

4.1   Range of social work interventions reported by service users   69
4.2   Range and nature of issues identified by service users   69
A1.1 Profile of service users interviewed by age and gender   237
A1.2 Profile of service users interviewed by type and gender   237
A1.3 Profile of service users interviewed by type and age   237

FOREWORD

As I get older I receive many reminders of my own death. Like most of my contemporaries, I find that what troubles me most is not death itself but what comes before that, not just the possibility of pain, infirmity and intense discomfort but being helpless and in the hands of others. If you are old when you die you already have had many experiences of being treated as an object of no importance, so you know how immensely unpleasant that is. This book is a great comfort to me because it assures me that there are at least some social workers who would treat me the way I wish to be treated.

What I fear is those people whom I regard as being the most dangerous people in the world; that is, the ones who believe that they know what is best for other people. Dangerous people like this have always flourished in the health and social services. Because they believe that they know what is best for others they see no need to enquire how the recipients of their ministrations feel about what they receive. Perhaps they are wise to refrain from asking because they might not be best pleased with what they are told. In this study, where recipients (service users) were actually asked their opinion about the work of social workers in palliative care, they revealed their distrust of social workers generally. Either from their direct personal experience or from media reports they had become profoundly distrustful of the way social workers can use their power against their clients' interests. When the service users discovered that their own social worker in palliative care didn't operate in the traditional 'I know best' way they were relieved and delighted. A frequent comment was that their social worker was 'not like a professional'. Their social worker listened to them, supported them helped them sort out practical problems, and worked in the times and places that best suited the clients.

However, this informal way of working is under great threat from those who believe that they know what is best for other people; that is, those people called managers. Managers like strict, exclusive categories and time sheets. They don't like people, because people ruin theories and systems by not behaving in the way the managers think they should behave. The mental health services now have far too many managers who think that therapy can be prescribed in the way that drugs are prescribed. Such managers would destroy everything which is best in social work in palliative care.

This is why this book should be read not just by social workers in palliative care and other palliative care workers, but by all social workers whatever their speciality, and by managers, especially those managers responsible for social work policy. Theories and systems should be made to fit people, and people shouldn't be forced to fit the theories and systems of those who believe, quite erroneously, that they know what is best for other people.

Dorothy Rowe

ACKNOWLEDGEMENTS

We have many people to thank for making this book and the project it is based upon possible. First, David Oliviere for his initial role in helping to get the project off the ground. Then the Joseph Rowntree Foundation, without whose support it would not have been possible. We would particularly like to thank Alex O'Neil for his constant commitment, enthusiasm and reassurance, especially when we encountered real difficulties. We would also like to acknowledge the administrative support given so diligently and calmly by Hilary Everitt who worked behind the scenes at Brunel University to make sure that everything flowed smoothly.

We would like to thank all members of the Advisory Group for all the help, experience and encouragement they gave us. The group was made up of Fiona Broughton (service user), Karen Wilman (service user), Linda Bell (Middlesex University), Jabeer Butt (Race Equality Unit), Pam Firth (Isabel Hospice), Gloria Gifford (service user), Judith Hodgson (Dove House Hospice, Hull), Nic MacManus (Dove House Hospice), Eileen McLeod (University of Warwick) and Michael Turner (Shaping Our Lives).

We want to thank the service users who were members of steering groups held at St Joseph's Hospice, London; the Isabel Hospice, Hertfordshire; the Sussex Beacon, Brighton; and the Nottinghamshire Hospice. We valued their ideas, insights, observations and questions and would like to thank them for giving so freely of their time. We would also like to thank the colleagues at each venue who helped us set up these groups and their meetings.

We would like to thank those individual specialist palliative care social workers and their professional association (the Association of Palliative Care Social Workers) who helped us make contact with service users to take part in our project. This book truly would not have been possible without them. They welcomed us to their hospices and palliative care units and worked hard to ensure that service users who wanted to meet us and take part in our project were able to in privacy and comfort. We valued the time and energy that they put into this. We would like to mention the particular contribution of Sue Taplin and Heather MacMillan. We would also like to thank managers and chief executives of services who supported their social workers to contribute to the project. We want to add our thanks to all palliative care services that offered us help and support. We have greatly valued their contribution and collaboration. We also have thanks to give Steve Jones, Jessica Stevens and Jessica Kingsley for all their help in preparing this book for publication.

Finally, and perhaps most important, we want to thank all the service users who agreed to take part in individual interviews and in discussion groups. We appreciate the time that they gave us so generously, often welcoming us into their own homes. We want to thank them for willingness to share their personal experiences in such an open way. We want to thank them for contributing their unique expertise and knowledge. On a personal level we have felt privileged to meet with these service users at what we know were frequently very difficult and distressing times. We know that some service users have died since we started this work and we would like to say to their families and friends how much we have valued the contribution that their loved ones made and how important we feel it will be for the future.

INTRODUCTION

This book is concerned with life and death and what people value to help them deal with both. It focuses specifically on what people want from specialist palliative care social work. Specialist palliative care social work is key to providing the personal and social support needed by people who are facing life-limiting illnesses and bereavement. It also plays a central role in helping people navigate the palliative care and broader health and welfare service systems. That is why this book is likely to be relevant to all who are concerned with life-limiting illnesses and conditions and supporting people when life may be ending or at risk.

The book aims to be part of a process of improving the help and support people get from such services, by providing new information to develop policy and practice, drawing on people's direct experience of support and services. It connects the detail of day-to-day professional practice and its improvement with broader social, policy, ethical and philosophical issues that relate to it. Specialist palliative care social work is concerned with offering support to two (potentially overlapping) groups of people. These are people with life-limiting illnesses and conditions and people experiencing bereavement through the loss of someone close to them. They, of course, face many other problems in their lives, from poverty to poor housing, from discrimination to child-care difficulties – problems which have always been the stuff of *all* social work. Of course there is more to life than death and loss, but these are among the pivotal issues which we all have to grapple with, as individuals and societies, if we are to make the most of our and other people's lives.

THE BACKGROUND TO THE BOOK
Death, dying and loss

Death, dying and loss are constants in the human condition. They are always there and they hang over our lives, experience and understanding. A few people would see themselves as outside this equation and have fantasies of cryogenesis: freezing their bodies to be regenerated when science is sufficiently advanced. For the rest of us, birth, ageing and death remain the only certainties of life. For a long time in western societies, death and dying have been highlighted as areas of taboo, which people are generally reluctant to consider or talk about. People who have been bereaved talk about people who know them crossing the road to avoid having to speak to them.

There is no doubt though that personal and political responses to death and dying have been changing. Many changes are taking place in both objective and subjective understandings of death, dying and loss. More recently there have been suggestions that people are more prepared to talk about sex and death than they are about money, income and their mortgages. Death is no longer 'the last taboo'. Other people's deaths are regular subjects of television news and increasingly the stuff of television documentary and drama. We live in a period of constant war and political killing, the images of which are routinely beamed into our homes. Television programmes have now examined most areas relating to death, including terminal illness, post-mortems, the construction of artworks from corpses and even the process of physical decomposition.

However, it is not only that we hear more about death. In the western world, in some senses, it is *further* from us. Death does not knock on most people's door as often or as early as it did a century ago. Conventional medical science has undoubtedly changed understandings of the relationship between disease, death and dying. Diseases which once routinely killed millions, such as TB and diphtheria, in the West have now been reduced to much more manageable and, in some cases, marginal levels (even though their capacity to strike back should never be forgotten). Many people increasingly assume everything is curable. Thus the fundraising for surgery abroad, the language of 'beating illnesses' and the commitment to drastic diets, regimes and remedies – which have no evidenced track record of success – for life-threatening diseases.

A growing proportion of deaths can now be seen to have broader political, social and economic relations, as human beings have learned how to control natural forces and overcome disease and want. We can see this clearly when we compare mortality rates for HIV/AIDS in the West with those in the majority world. Major killers such as cancer and heart disease are increasingly being shown to be closely related to environmental and cultural factors. Whether deaths and disease are a result of pollution, unequal distribution of wealth and resources, the creation of natural hazards, crime, inequality, oppression, discrimination or, of course, war and genocide, they can increasingly be traced to how societies, groups, corporations and governments behave, rather than to isolated individual behaviour or random accidents of nature.

Just as human beings gained greater control over fertility and life during the twentieth century, they now seem to be seeking greater control over death and dying in the twenty-first. In the UK and other western societies, this has become a significant focus for public discussion. It has become a political issue with demands for legislation and in some cases the introduction of new laws to control death and dying. Interest has mainly centred on the *hows* and *whens* of death. Advances in medical science have blurred traditional distinctions between natural life and death. But current debates and developments also demarcate the convergence of medical science's limits and advances. Medical science has the capacity to maintain life, but it is also seen to pose questions about the quality of the life it sustains. These are being raised in relation to:

- foetuses and babies who would formerly not have lived
- disabled people (with both inherited and non-inherited impairments)
- the capacity to keep people alive who would formerly have died.

Focuses for discussion have been abortion, euthanasia, advance directives, assisted suicide and 'do not resuscitate' (DNR) orders. So far, debate has mainly been framed in terms of a 'good death' – *euthanasia* – rather than a 'good life'. The emphasis has been placed on people having the right to a 'good death', rather than the right to support to enable a good life. 'Quality of life' has tended to be defined in medicalized individual, rather than social or experiential, terms. Discussion has been overlaid by conflicting ideological views about the right to life and death, as well as religious and secular ethical concerns.

There are still big divides over death and dying. The religious beliefs, spirituality and faith of some can mean that, for them, dying is a prelude, just a stage that they are going through. For others death is an absolute end. In a multi-faith western society like the UK, attitudes to death and dying are defined by more than matters of faith and non-faith. Christians, Muslims, Jews, Buddhists, Sikhs, Hindus and others all approach death and dying differently.

This, then, is the context of human efforts to do the most for people, including both adults and children, facing life-limiting illnesses and conditions and bereavement. It is a complex, changing and contentious context for palliative care and there can be no question that it is affecting palliative care and our understandings of it. Palliative care is having to position itself and develop its own responses in relation to all these issues. They can come close to home. One of the authors, for example, has worked with someone who subsequently went abroad to secure their own assisted suicide.

Social work

In addition, specialist palliative care social work has its own complex and contentious background. It is just one area of social work, and social work itself is a controversial field of professional activity. Because of this, specialist palliative care social work offers some particularly helpful insights for understanding and advancing social work in general. Social work is a profession with many critics, limited status and a relatively short history, whose workforce has traditionally been made up mainly of women. When things go wrong in social work, people can and sometimes do die. All these factors have made social work a regular candidate for hostile political and media criticism. In addition, palliative care itself, as a medical specialism which is not framed in terms of treatment and cure, has traditionally carried less status than many other areas of health care. Specialist palliative care social work may offer many insights for palliative care more generally, as well as for both health care and social work overall.

THE APPROACH OF THE BOOK

There are many studies of both palliative care and social work. There are also a small but growing number of discussions about specialist palliative care social work. What distinguishes this book is that it focuses on what *service users* – the people on the receiving end – have to say about the subject. This is unusual. Traditionally, explorations of health and welfare policy and practice have been based on what outside experts have to say. These have tended to be policy-makers, managers, service providers, professionals, academics and researchers. Generally their perspectives are in some way bound up with and socialized into the values, traditions and approaches which they discuss. Often the experts are associated with the very services they critique. All will have something to offer, but they cannot provide the full picture. Historically the people whose rights and needs such policy and provisions are meant to serve – health and welfare service users, a key stakeholder group – who have been left out of the discussion. This book seeks to address this gap. Thus it is the first book to examine what service users think of a specialist palliative care service and specifically what they think of specialist palliative care social work. For the first time the book explores what they feel it offers and what they want from it.

In this sense the book represents a break from the paternalistic past of health and welfare policy, practice and study. As such it is part of a broader development and movement, both to include service users in the formation, development and control of health and social welfare, and to recast them as active participants in the policy process. In this way they can make a positive contribution to the construction and development of services and support, rather than remain passive recipients of public services. In countries like the UK, governments, service systems and service users themselves are increasingly committed to such a shift in philosophy and practice. This is now embodied in legislation and reflected in government priorities and strategies. It has led to changes in the nature and process of policy, practice, research and knowledge development.

In this book we have sought to be sensitive to and address all of these domains. This has led us to adopt a different approach to research which seeks to involve service users on equal terms. It has led us to try to challenge the traditional 'them' and 'us' of the policy process, which drew a distinction between 'consumers' and 'producers' of health and welfare, placing them on opposite sides of a counter and sometimes on opposite sides in calculations of net 'givers' and net 'takers'. As a research team we include people with experience both as service workers and service users, with affiliations to service user as well as service worker organizations. Thus while this book takes account of conventional expert judgements and assessments of palliative care and specialist palliative care social work, its primary contribution is to bring together and access more widely what service users' themselves have to say.

THE STRUCTURE OF THE BOOK

The book is organized in three parts. In Part One, the shortest, we set the scene, exploring the context of palliative care social work more fully and looking at how we undertook the research study on which the book is based. We set out the background, aims and methods of the study. We discuss why we adopted an approach based on user involvement and user involvement in research and the issues that such an approach raises, particularly in relation to palliative care service users.

Part Two of the book reports what service users have to say. We hear their views and ideas about specialist palliative care social work, in their own words, based on their own direct experience. This part of the book is organized in terms of service users' journey through palliative care social work, both as people facing life-limiting illnesses and conditions and people facing bereavement. This includes how they became involved with palliative care, their former views of social work and social workers and how they came into contact with palliative care social work. We learn how they were assessed, what social workers did, what service users particularly valued and how social workers worked with different groups of service users. Finally we look at what evaluation of services takes place, where service users feel practice can be improved and what they feel they gained from palliative care social work.

In Part Three, we offer our own discussion of what service users have to say about specialist palliative care social work. We connect their comments with both theoretical work and broader debates going on within social work and palliative care. We look at a range of issues and themes emerging from what service users say. This part of the book explores their views of palliative care social work and examines how people actually access the service and some of the problems associated with this. It considers what the particular contribution of specialist palliative care social work may be, examines some of the challenges facing it and considers some of the implications for the future.

Our examination of palliative care social work and the issues of death, dying and loss with which it daily grapples have drawn us in this book to the most personal of issues as well as much broader political and ideological concerns. It has also required us to consider the policy process, at both micro and macro levels. This has confronted us with fundamental questions. Can such a policy process really connect adequately with the kind of complex, sensitive and subtle experiences and emotions that go with such difficult times of life and death – or is it inevitably a blunt instrument? Can support for people facing life-limiting illnesses and loss really be converted into an area of 'professional competence and practice' from acts of love and affiliation? If so, what should it look like and how is it to be achieved? Does social work have a future and what insights might specialist palliative care social work offer it?

These are big issues to address. However, this is a time of great debate about health and welfare. The message for some time in the UK and beyond has been that there must be radical change in health and welfare. We are told there is a need to 'think the unthinkable' and challenge traditional assumptions and arrangements. Who should fund and provide health and welfare – state or market? Who should be responsible for people's well-being – the individual or society? We have seen big changes in these areas. But perhaps the most radical proposal to emerge in recent years has also been the most hesitant in its development. This is the call to equalize roles and relationships and redistribute power in health and welfare. This has prioritized a more participatory process of policy production and more egalitarian relationships between service users and workers. If policy-makers are serious in these aspirations, then what service users say in this book may offer a starting point for taking these aspirations forward in the context of death, dying and loss. The book brings together the experience of those on the receiving end of such issues. It provides an experiential knowledge base for building more participatory policy and practice to support people moving towards the end of life.

Part One
The Background to Palliative Care Social Work

The first part of the book puts specialist palliative care social work into its broader ideological, political, policy and professional context. It discusses the history and aims of specialist palliative care social work. It pays particular attention to current interest in improving the quality of health and social care policy and services and increasing public, patient and service user involvement in them. It sets out how the participatory research project on which this book is based focuses on this agenda in the context of palliative care and specialist palliative care social work.

CHAPTER 1

PALLIATIVE CARE: A NEW PERSPECTIVE

THE NATURE AND PURPOSE OF PALLIATIVE CARE

The term *palliative care* is one that many people are unfamiliar with. Yet there was a time when much if not most medical and health care was probably palliative in purpose and effect, because so little curative treatment was available. In the Middle Ages, the word *hospice* was used for what we might now describe as a hospital. Perhaps that is why the word 'hospice' has come to be associated with palliative care and is the term through which people in the UK and some European countries are most familiar with palliative care. The dictionary definition of *palliate* is to 'alleviate without curing' (Fowler and Fowler 1970, p.875). Palliative care is care that does not claim to offer curative treatment for diseases and conditions but to offset their ill effects, to improve people's quality of life and to support them in the process of change which they are undergoing. As the *Hospice and Palliative Care Directory* puts it, palliative care 'is for those whose illness may no longer be curable… It enables them to achieve the best possible quality of life especially during the final stages of their illness' (Hospice Information 2005, p.iii).

Palliative care is defined by the World Health Organization as:

> An approach that improves the quality of life of patients and their families facing the problems associated with life-threatening illness, through the prevention and relief of suffering by means of early identification and impeccable assessment and treatment of pain and other problems, physical, psychosocial and spiritual. (Cited in Davies and Higginson 2004, p.14)

Palliative care places an emphasis on an *holistic* approach to people, which takes account of their wide range of needs: physical, psychological, social, cultural and material. (Davies and Higginson 2004, p.14).

In western societies like the UK, health and welfare support were historically provided first by religious orders and religious organizations and then by charities and the state. The modern hospice movement, which has greatly influenced modern specialist palliative care, has strong religious origins and inspirations. Two key starting points of this movement, St Joseph's and St Christopher's Hospices, both had such Christian origins. They are linked through the person of Dame Cicely Saunders, who is often identified as the founder of the movement. The hospice movement is a surprisingly recent development: St Christopher's was only founded in 1967. The first purpose-built day care facility was built by St Luke's Hospice in Sheffield in 1975; the first hospital- based palliative care team established at St Thomas's in 1977.

SPECIALIST PALLIATIVE CARE SERVICES

A distinction is sometimes drawn between palliative care (meaning general care, where the expectation is palliation rather than cure, in mainstream health settings) and *specialist* palliative care. Specialist palliative care services are provided by specialists in palliative care who work in multi-professional teams where palliative care is the core activity of the team. They work in independent (charitable) hospices, NHS hospices, and specialist palliative care teams and NHS specialist palliative care teams working in hospitals. Care and support are provided for patients and families, friends and loved ones. Specialist palliative care is provided at home, in hospices and palliative care centres, in hospice day centres and in hospitals. A wide range of services are available, including medical and nursing care; symptom control; social, creative and occupational provision; spiritual support; counselling and practical advice; physiotherapy; lymphoedema service; bereavement support; respite care; and a sitting service for patients at home (Hospice Information 2005, p.iii). A wide range of professions provide specialist palliative care services including doctors, nurses (including Macmillan and Marie Curie specialist nurses), chaplains, and art, occupational, physio and complementary therapists.

A time of change

While an outsider coming to the world of hospice and specialist palliative care can be struck by its focus on its history, founding myths and founding personnel, this emphasis on its past has recently been overtaken by the broader, more urgent issues with which it is now confronted. What was for a long time the relatively small and separate world of hospice and specialist palliative care has now been drawn much more closely into the mainstream world of health and public policy. Crucially it has been faced with a wide range of broader changes which have been taking place, which it is having to address.

This is a time of massive change in and for specialist palliative care. This change relates to perceptions of the role of specialist palliative care, broader social change, developments in medical care, the funding of independent hospices, change in the provision and funding of health and welfare and changes in the role of the state and market in public services. We will look at the wider changes in health and welfare shortly, but first we will examine these other developments a little more closely.

Changing perceptions of palliative care

The hospice movement has historically been associated with supporting people with terminal cancer. This gave it a particular identity and status; cancer is a much-feared disease that can be seen to affect anyone, regardless of class or status. This association helped lead to hospices being seen as a particularly deserving cause. The provision of specialist palliative care is still largely restricted to people with cancer, AIDS and motor neurone disease. Yet there are many other conditions, for example pulmonary and coronary conditions, for which particularly at their end stage an equal case could be made for specialist palliative care support. There are now growing public and political pressures for such support to be available. It is not clear, however, how specialist palliative care could meet this need, given its existing limited resources.

Broader social change

Other demographic changes also impact on palliative care, with people living longer, the emergence of a multi-racial society, different patterns of living, increasing inequalities of income and a massive increase in single-person households. These raise other issues of access and equity relating to ethnicity, gender, age, geographic location and class which have yet to be addressed in the provision of specialist palliative care.

Developments in medical care

Historically, the focus of hospices on people with 'terminal' cancer generally meant that support was needed for a relatively short period before people died, allowing valued but limited resources to be spread relatively widely. But, more recently, with pressure for specialist palliative care support to be available for people with a wider range of conditions and with the life expectancy of people with non-curative cancer and with AIDS being much greater because of new medical developments, the picture has become much more complex. Support may be needed over a much longer period, with people coming in and out of hospices and facing the prospect of much longer periods of both sickness and active life.

One point that does need to be added is that, in the UK at least, the emphasis in health policy is still on illness and care, rather than prevention and well-being, although there is beginning to be official recognition of the need for this to change (see, for example, Department of Health 2006). While there has been much more talk of public health, this has mainly taken the form of individualized approaches encouraging people to take more personal responsibility for their health, rather than policies effectively addressing social factors relating to ill health (including life-limiting conditions), such as poverty, pollution, occupational stress, food production and tobacco and alcohol consumption. Indeed some public policies, like transport and food production, have received adverse criticism for heading in the opposite direction.

The funding of independent hospices

Hospices were traditionally funded on the basis of charitable giving. With the sophistication and expense of modern treatment, technology and support and a commitment to core services 'free at the point of delivery', this is no longer a viable means of maintaining such services – although this may continue to be the public perception. Instead independent hospices are significantly reliant on state funding, through either individual contracts or broader funding arrangements, which makes them much more dependent on government policy and priorities.

While so far a for-profit sector does not seem to have developed in palliative care (at the time of writing there was one private palliative care consultant), it is no longer only the province solely and primarily of the voluntary sector. The state through the National Health Service has become a large-scale provider and commissioner of palliative care services. In 2005, the NHS managed about 26 per cent of inpatient palliative care and provided funding for about 28 per cent of the cost of voluntary hospices overall (Hospice Information 2005, p.150). This is likely to have significant implications for the future and nature of palliative care more generally and indeed for the independent hospice sector. It is questionable whether primary care trusts as commissioning organizations will continue to purchase voluntary provision as before in preference to expanding and using their own (lower-cost) palliative care services. Searching for additional markets, both the voluntary disability sector, notably Sue Ryder Care, and private nursing homes are developing their provision of palliative care beds.

SOCIAL WORK: THE BROADER CONTEXT

One of the services offered as part of specialist palliative care is *social work*. A distinct area of social work, specialist palliative care social work has developed with its own professional organization, training, literature and body of knowledge. Yet interestingly there is often little or no mention of specialist palliative care social work in mainstream social work literature and discussions (see, for example, Adams, Dominelli and Payne 2002; Davies 2002).

The role and nature of social work

Social work has a complex and ambiguous history. Historically its origins have most often been traced to the Charity Organization Society and the housing reformer Octavia Hill. Both of these were expressions of nineteenth-century charitable philanthropy and the utilitarian ideology which underpinned the harsh new Poor Law of 1832. Both based their interventions on moral judgements about 'the poor' and disadvantaged. Some commentators, however, have identified other sources for social work which they see as more progressive, including the settlement movement and provincial guilds of help (Adams et al. 2002, p.333; Laybourn 1997). Social work's portrayal has tended to be polarized. On the one hand, it has been presented as an expression of humanitarianism and altruism, ameliorating people's poverty and powerlessness in a mixed economy. On the other, it has been condemned as an agent of social control, taking the edge off the worst excesses of a capitalist economy, while still serving as a 'soft cop' to keep oppressed people in order. Certainly social work has historically been associated with interventions into the lives of poor and disadvantaged people.

Social work in the UK and internationally has been applied to a wide range of groups. These include older people, people with physical and sensory impairments, mental health service users, young people, people with learning difficulties and, more recently, people living with HIV/AIDS. But it is most often associated with work with 'children and families', particularly with 'child protection' work. This has been the most high-profile area of social work practice and the area where in the UK it has most come in for criticism. It has been associated with a long series of child care tragedies and scandals stretching from the 1950s to the twenty-first century. These have been influential both in shaping social work policy and practice and in influencing public attitudes towards social work. While it is in the fields of child care and child protection that social work seems to have experienced the most difficulties, this has tended to be a preferred area of practice among many social workers; other groups, such as older and disabled people, have tended to be seen as less interesting and attractive.

In the 1970s social work experienced a renaissance, with the creation of 'social services departments', the emergence of 'radical social work' and a new commitment to community-based working and renewed links with 'the grass-roots' (Langan and Lee 1989). However, child-care tragedies and scandals and growing managerialist pressure from the 1980s onwards led to a pattern of constant reorganizations and restructurings. Most recently this has resulted in the ending of social services departments, the shift of child-care responsibilities to the Department for Education and pressure for the integration of adult social work services with health. During the 1990s, social work came in for growing criticism for having an increasing role as a means of state control, reinforcing broader pressures to economic individualism and social division and for its weakening concern with social justice and equality (Jordan 1997; Parton 1994, 1996; Williams 1996).

There have been many social work approaches, from individual casework, heavily based on psychiatric models, to community-based and groupwork approaches, that highlight collective action and local involvement. Now the state, charitable and for-profit organizations provide social work services and employ social workers.

Social work has long sought to associate itself with principles of supporting independence, self-determination and autonomy. It also highlights the need to take into account both the individual and the society in which they live. It may do this with varying emphasis, but what makes social work *social work* is that it is inherently concerned – in theory at least – with the social as well as the personal. The tension for much social work has been, of course, that often it is only seen to have the capacity to intervene in the personal, rather than the social. Nonetheless, this consciousness of both aspects of people's lives – the personal and the social – and their complex interactions and interrelations – lies at the heart of formal conceptions of social work.

SPECIALIST PALLIATIVE CARE SOCIAL WORK

The history of specialist palliative care social work, like that of modern specialist palliative care, is a relatively short one. A small group of hospice social workers first met together at St Christopher's Hospice in Sydenham in 1982. In 1986 the Association of Hospice Social Workers was founded (Franklin 1996). By the early 1990s, it had about 100 members. At the time of writing this book the number has increased to about 260 – although no reliable data are available for the overall number of social workers now working in palliative care.

It is worth quoting at length what its professional association says about palliative care social work:

> Social work is an integral part of the multi-disciplinary team within palliative care, offering an holistic service to patients and families. Unlike many fields of social work, specialist palliative care social work is potentially a universal service and we are used to working with a diverse range of people in terms of age, diagnosis, class, ethnicity, sexual orientation, religion and culture. Palliative care social work involves working with two groups of people – direct service users with life threatening or terminal conditions and those who are bereaved. Social workers are skilled at balancing the different and sometimes competing needs of the two groups.
>
> Specialist palliative care social work is provided in a range of settings, including independent hospices, day hospices, NHS specialist palliative care units, oncology wards and in home care teams... Specialist palliative care social workers are used to working across the fields of health and social care and often provide a link between the two. They are also used to working with both children and adults and in working with people in their own homes.
>
> Specialist palliative care social workers offer a wide range of support to patients and families from practical help and advice around income maintenance, debt counselling, help with housing and accessing other services, through to advocacy, individual counselling and group support. This will

include bereavement work with adults and children both as individuals and in group settings. Key to specialist palliative care social work is the desire and ability to see people as whole people and not as a set of problems, to understand the connections of their lives and to seek to act on, rather than ignore, the constraints and discrimination they experience in society. As Napier has observed: 'Social work places ideas about crisis, loss, grief and bereavement within an appreciation of people's diverse and unequal social circumstances' (Napier 2003, p.154). (APCSW 2006, p.6)

The formal definition of specialist palliative care social work, as of all social work, is that it should:

> [promote] social change, problem solving in human relationships, and the empowerment and liberation of people to enhance well-being. Utilising theories of human behaviour and social systems, social work intervenes at the point where people interact with their environments. Principles of human rights and social justice are fundamental to social work. (IFSW 2001)

The General Social Care Council, which is responsible for the regulation of social work and social care in England, has developed a code of practice for social care workers, including specialist palliative care social workers. This states that they must:

- protect the rights and promote the interests of service users and carers
- strive to establish and maintain the trust and confidence of service users and carers
- promote the independence of service users while protecting them as far as possible from any danger of harm
- respect the rights of service users while seeking to ensure that their behaviour does not harm themselves or other people
- uphold public trust and confidence in social care services and
- be accountable for the quality of work and take responsibility for maintaining and improving knowledge and skills.

(General Social Care Council 2002, p.23)

A set of 'national occupational standards' for social workers have also been established by Skills for Care, formerly the Training Organization for Personal Social Services. The key purpose and roles of social work are identified as:

1. Prepare for and work with individuals, families, carers, groups and communities to assess their needs and circumstances.

2. Plan, carry out, review and evaluate social work practice with individuals, families, carers, groups, communities and other professionals.

3. Support individuals to represent their needs, views and circumstances.

4. Manage risk to individuals, families, carers, groups and communities.

5. Manage and be accountable, with supervision and support, for own social work practice.

6. Demonstrate professional competence in social work practice.
   (Training Organisation for the Personal Social Services 2004, p.12)

These codes of practice and set of standards lay down the basis for all social work practice and underpin professional training and qualification.

A CHANGED APPROACH TO HEALTH AND WELFARE

As we indicated earlier, wider changes in health and welfare have also had profound implications for palliative care and palliative care social work. These are still in process of being worked through. The shift to the political right in the UK in the 1970s, embodied in the election of Thatcher governments, represented a watershed in public policy both domestically and internationally which has had enduring consequences for health and welfare services, including palliative care. The political new right was committed to reduced state intervention and expenditure and opposed state provision of services as inefficient, bureaucratic and centralizing, reducing individual freedom and encouraging dependency. Instead it sought a greater role for the market in public policy and a pluralist approach to the supply of health and welfare services. It argued for individual responsibility rather than collective support, scapegoated 'benefit scroungers', emphasized the value of 'informal', unpaid 'care' and support from friends and family and prioritized the introduction of market-based models of management into public services (Deakin 1994; Hayek 1982; King 1987; Marsland 1992).

Not only was the approach to public and social policy of the political new right ideological, based on a commitment to the market, it also highlighted market values, particularly relating to choice and quality. Now the talk began to be of *customers* and *consumers* in public services, rather than *clients* and *claimants*, as it had been before. A new age of consumerism had dawned in health and welfare policy and provision. Whatever may be thought of the applicability of such a model to the public sector – which often deals with the most powerless and disadvantaged people – or the reality of the new consumerist rhetoric associated with it, the fact of the matter is that such market sector values and language began to assume a central importance in government thinking, policy and practice. Although there have been significant political changes since – with the election from 1997 of New Labour governments – this approach to public policy continued. It has assumed particular importance in the field of health care and the NHS, which have continued to be politically sensitive and high-priority areas of public policy. The emphasis in government statements and policy has been on 'putting the patient at the centre of health', a patient-driven NHS and 'the expert patient'.

User involvement

A related concept that has developed in public policy over this period has been that of service *user involvement*. The idea of participation is as old as that of democracy, but the recent emphasis on user involvement has specific origins. The first of these is undoubtedly the shift to the market in public policy and the desire to give it popular appeal by highlighting its association with the direct engagement of patients, public and service users. As a result what might be called a managerialist/consumerist model of involvement has become a significant feature of social policy and legislation. It is reflected in requirements for consultations, participatory forums and the involvement of user/patient representatives and bodies in the development and process of policy. The second development which has underpinned the modern emphasis on user involvement has been the rise of movements of health and social care service users from the 1970s onwards. These include movements of disabled people, older people, people with learning difficulties, mental health service users/survivors, people living with HIV/AIDS and so on. The impetus for their interest in user involvement has been a democratic one, seeking a more active involvement in policies and services which affect their lives and a desire to have more say in their development and decision-making processes (Campbell 1996; Campbell and Oliver 1996; Oliver and Barnes 1998).

Social care has made a particular contribution in the development of user involvement, particularly in the fields of disability and mental health policy. It has developed new approaches and worked to include marginalized groups. Such involvement became a requirement in social care in the early 1990s for both adults and children, with the introduction of the 1990 NHS and Community Care Act and the 1989 Children Act. Social work, as part of social care, has placed an emphasis on user involvement over this period in its organizations, structures, practice, education and training. In addition, service user movements, particularly the disabled people's movement, have developed new approaches to support, including direct payments schemes, putting service users in control of the 'package of care' they receive, user-controlled services provided by centres for independent living and other service user led organizations and non-medicalized schemes for support for mental health service users/survivors.

Improving quality

Over this same period, the concern with improving quality has developed in health and social care. The new rhetoric is immediately apparent in the policy process. In the NHS this has particularly been framed in terms of developing the 'choice agenda'. This has been a strongly ideologically based development linked to government's commitment to an increasing role for the private sector. The individual citizen/consumer is presented with the argument that improved quality of service will be forthcoming because they will have a 'choice' of service, service supplier, clinician and so on. This has been a contentious and highly politicized development in public policy. It has also been associated with an increasing focus on quality standards by which such service providers might be judged.

Thus, in relation to 'quality', government has established National Service Frameworks to establish standards for key policy areas and service user groups, including mental health, cancer, long-term conditions, and young and older people. It established a *'quality strategy* for social care' which emphasized the importance of policy and practice being knowledge- or evidence-based. There is a new language of 'quality standards', 'performance indicators' and 'outcome measures'. In the last few years, new Care Standards Commissions were established to monitor and safeguard quality in social care which culminated in the creation of the Commission for Social Care Inspection. A General Social Care Council was set up to identify and maintain standards of occupational practice and conduct, a training organization for personal social services (TOPSS, subsequently Skills for Care) established to improve the quality of the workforce and a Social Care Institute for Excellence created to develop the knowledge base for improving quality (Beresford 2003a, 2004; Beresford et al. 1997).

The 'quality agenda' and ideas of user and patient involvement have become central in health and social care and can be seen as expressions of the shift in political and ideological interest over recent decades. But a significant issue is that these two strands of development have tended to be treated separately. Thus quality standards have predominantly been based on professional and bureaucratic approaches to standard setting, rather than involving service users. Yet it cannot be assumed that what service providers and purchasers would value and prioritize as good quality would necessarily coincide with what service users would want. Indeed there is evidence to indicate the opposite (Beresford 2003a, 2004; Evers et al. 1997; Harding and Beresford 1996).

It was in order to explore this issue that the national independent user-controlled organization, Shaping Our Lives, was first set up. Its aim was to unify so far unrelated interests in user involvement and quality standards. Since 1996, it has been exploring with health and social care service users the idea and practice of *user-defined* outcome measures – that is to say measures of what people want from services and support which they themselves identify and develop – to add to the managerial and professional measures that have so far tended to predominate (Balloch *et al.* 1998; Beresford *et al.* 1997; Schalock 1995; Shaping Our Lives National User Network *et al.* 2003; Turner 1997, 1998). It has carried out development work with a range of different service users to explore the feasibility and nature of such quality measures. Shaping Our Lives encountered some reluctance on the part of service agencies to adopt service user led quality standards, but at the same time established that such standards made sense to and could be developed by service users.

This book builds on and connects with that work. The aim of the project on which the book draws was to inform discussion, policy and practice about user-defined outcomes in palliative care by exploring what service users want from specialist palliative care social work. Thus it is an expression of the developing interest there now is both in improving the quality of health and social care provision and in user involvement. It also embodies a concern to combine the two.

PALLIATIVE CARE AND PARTICIPATION

The Calman Hine Report in 1995 paved the way for user involvement in palliative care by recommending that cancer services should be patient centred (Department of Health 1995). The National Health Service Cancer Plan (Department of Health 2000) encouraged user involvement in the context of recognizing the quality of cancer services as a national priority. These specific developments have taken place within a wider context of government emphasis on user involvement and service users being at 'the centre' of health and social care services. In 2003, for example, the government established a major NHS consultation, Choice, Responsiveness and Equity in the NHS and Social Care, which placed a specific emphasis on patient and user involvement and which directly involved service users in eight officially appointed task groups, including one focusing on 'long-term conditions' which addressed palliative care issues (Department of Health/NHS 2003).

There are, however, some important and interesting contradictions about user involvement in palliative care. Palliative care, particularly as reflected in the hospice movement, has always emphasized the centrality of the patient or service user and its own 'holistic' approach to provision and practice. It has highlighted its concern with the individual's physical, social, psychological and spiritual needs. It has traditionally placed an emphasis on 'voice and choice', ideas which have subsequently gained a key place in health and care more generally. As Dame Cicely Saunders said, one of its key and explicit aims was to provide a 'voice for the voiceless' (Oliviere 2000).

Yet it can be argued that hospice and palliative care have been slow to address service user involvement. Apart from the development of 'patient satisfaction surveys', whose helpfulness as a form of user involvement is questionable, it was not until the late 1990s that user involvement really emerged as an issue in palliative care, with the beginning of public discussion, organized events, publications and the commissioning of research (Beresford, Croft and Oliviere 2001; Kraus, Levy and Oliviere 2003; Monroe and Oliviere 2003; National Hospice Council 2001; Oliviere 2001b). By contrast, as we have seen, user involvement was a legislative requirement in social care from the early 1990s and participatory developments in that field can be traced back to the early 1980s.

Pressures against participation

While it is not clear why palliative care has been slow to take user involvement forward as rapidly as some other policy areas, some possible reasons are apparent. One explanation seems to be the feeling that 'we are doing it anyway'; the sense that patients are involved routinely, following from the longstanding commitment in this field to listen to the patient/service user and to act as an advocate for them. However, offering a voice is not the same as accessing people's *own* voices. Another explanation may be that while being multidisciplinary and committed to a holistic way of working, palliative care has tended to be medically led. The health field more generally has been slower to address issues of participation than has that of social care, which is now acknowledged to have had a pioneering role in this field. But this still would not explain why palliative care came later to participation than some other areas of health specialism, such as mental health.

It is a third possible explanation that seems the most likely. Palliative care services work with two groups of people who are seen as particularly vulnerable in our society. These are people with life-limiting illnesses who may be facing death and people who are either facing bereavement or have been bereaved. Thus palliative care service users are at very difficult times in their lives, having to cope with massive change, fears for the future and possibly financial uncertainty. For some it may mean having little time and feeling weak and very ill; for others coping with loss and perhaps the prospect of loneliness and isolation.

It would not be surprising, therefore, if workers and services were reluctant to place additional burdens on service users who can already be seen to have other difficulties and preoccupations. Death, dying and loss are also still areas of taboo in western societies to at least some extent. Workers and managers do express particular concerns about involving palliative care patients and service users. Issues are raised about how meaningful such involvement may be at the 'end of life stage' of people's illness. There has also been a significantly pessimistic strand in academic/research discussions of user involvement in palliative care. Fears have been raised about such involvement being stressful, unhelpful and coming to be seen as an obligation (Gott 2004; Payne 2002; Small and

Rhodes 2000). These are important issues and need to be addressed. So far, however, they have not followed from research findings and there is not a strong evidence base for them. Research work done so far has also been based on very small numbers.

More positive experience

In contrast, where efforts have been made to involve service users with careful planning and preparation, there has been a positive response. User involvement in palliative care emerges as a much more practical possibility. This has included involving people with different conditions, who are very ill and who have little time to live. There have been some significant recent developments. Thus, in 1999, a national seminar on Improving Quality and Developing User Involvement in palliative care was held (Beresford *et al.* 2000). This was jointly organized with current palliative care service users and attended by a majority of service users. User involvement was made the subject of the National Council for Palliative Care Annual Awards scheme in 2001. This led to the establishment of a User Involvement Panel, jointly hosted with Help the Hospices and composed of palliative care service users and others, which developed and ran a series of educational regional seminars on user involvement, culminating in the first national conference on this subject held in 2003. In 2005, Help the Hospices established a national user involvement initiative, led by a group of palliative care service users. In 2005 at an international conference organized by Help the Hospices, a panel of service users involved in this initiative provided a highly rated question-and-answer session on user involvement.

Progress in developing user involvement in palliative care is unquestionably being made. However, these activities have also highlighted – through contact with a wide range of managers, practitioners and service users – that this is still at an early stage, is patchy in implementation and is raising a number of concerns and uncertainties from service providers.

At the same time, most of the large independent palliative care and related organizations, including Marie Curie, Macmillan Cancer Relief, Help the Hospices, the National Council for Palliative Care and Sue Ryder Care, have variously developed their own policies and schemes for user involvement. It is important at this stage neither to over- nor to understate the progress that has been made. What is likely to be most helpful is to develop some critical consideration of key issues currently being raised in relation to this issue (see, for example, Carr 2004). The aim here is to explore user involvement in palliative care in the broader context of theoretical and practical developments drawing on a wider range of policy areas.

People's feelings about involvement need to be put in context. There is no doubt that participation can be a negative and unhelpful activity (Cooke and

Kothari 2001). Arnstein's development of a ladder of participation in the 1960s has long highlighted this. Her ladder descended from 'citizen power', through 'placation' to 'manipulation' (Arnstein 1969). But such deficiencies may be less to do with the inherent nature of participation itself, than with what it constitutes and what purpose it is put to in any given situation.

Palliative care service users who get involved generally seem to value it. However, so far it appears likely that only a small proportion of such service users have responded to invitations to get involved. But this is true of most groups – both of 'service users' and of other people. We are likely to need to look to broader structural issues for an understanding of this. We live in a representative, not participatory, democracy, where many people do not expect and are not accustomed to 'getting involved' in formal public policy or state-related activities and where these processes are often opaque and excluding.

Equally reservations have traditionally been raised about the involvement not only of palliative care service users, but also of many 'vulnerable' groups. This has frequently been the case in relation to people with learning difficulties, particularly those seen as having profound or multiple 'handicaps' or who do not communicate verbally. But there are a few groups in relation to whom this has not been raised during the course of the modern development of participation policy and practice, including children and young people, mental health service users/survivors and others who have experienced long-term institutionalization (Dowson 1990; Thompson 1991; White et al. 1988). Concerns have been raised that such groups would not be able to contribute, would be liable to manipulation, and would be left exposed and experience distress as a result. No body of evidence has developed to support these concerns, influential though they have been. It is helpful to recognize that they are not new issues, but have frequently been identified and applied to many groups and individuals.

They have also often been associated with traditions of 'protecting' (vulnerable) service users, issues of 'gatekeeping' by service providers and paternalistic health and welfare cultures. This is in sharp contrast to more recent thinking that patients and service users should have the chance to be 'co-producers' of their own welfare. It is also now established that a wide range of groups which previously would not have been seen as able to 'get involved' have since demonstrated both their interest in being involved and the feasibility of them having an effective involvement in issues which concern them. This includes people with dementia (Allen 2001) and people with aphasia (Parr et al. 1998), as well as people with 'profound' learning difficulties and without verbal communication.

USER INVOLVEMENT IN RESEARCH

User involvement has not only developed in policy, planning and practice. There has been similar pressure in recent years for user involvement in research and evaluation. As with user involvement more generally, such pressure for user involvement has come from more than one source and as a result has taken different expressions, based on different philosophies. Two key sources for this development can be identified: first, the service user movements, particularly the disabled people's movement, and, second, mainstream research, government and the service system. The latter have encouraged both an interest in and requirements for service user involvement in research and participatory approaches to research. The former has encouraged the development of new research approaches which place an emphasis on changed, more equal relationships between research, researchers and research participants and on research for change linked with the rights and demands of service users, rather than research primarily and solely concerned with producing new knowledge (Barnes and Mercer 1997; Kemshall and Littlechild 2000; Lowes and Hulatt 2005).

Three overall approaches to such research can be identified. These are:

1. *User involvement research* – where service users are actively involved in research, research projects and research processes.

2. *Collaborative research* – where service users and/or their organizations undertake research jointly and collaboratively in association with conventional researchers.

3. *User-controlled research* (also identified as survivor researcher, emancipatory disability research) – where service users initiate run and control research projects and activities.

The research approach adopted in the project on which this book was based comes into the first category; that is to say the aim was fully to involve palliative service users. It is not claimed that it is an example of either collaborative or user-controlled research. This is because while the inspiration for this project came from what service users themselves said – both in the course of the user-controlled research and development work of Shaping Our Lives and previous work with palliative care service users in which two of the authors were involved – due to the length, scale and nature of this project, a decision was made, mostly for practical reasons, to undertake a participatory project which sought to enable as much service user involvement as possible. A group of palliative care service users did not exist to take the lead on the work themselves and nor was there such a group to collaborate with. This is not to say that either user-controlled or collaborative projects with palliative care service users are not feasible, but rather at this relatively early stage in the development of service user involvement in palliative care research, the approach adopted seemed the most honest, realistic and achievable one.

Questions have been raised from traditional research perspectives about whether the involvement of service users (or other groups) in research undermines the independence and rigour of such research. These arguments have in turn been challenged. Supporters of user involvement research, like qualitative, feminist and action researchers before them, call into question the positivist premises of traditional research which emphasizes 'neutrality', 'objectivity' and 'distance' and also point to gains that they see user involvement offering research (Barnes 2003; Barnes and Mercer 1997; Barton and Oliver 1997; Baxter, Thorne and Mitchell 2001; Beresford 2003b; Mercer 2002; Reason and Rowan 1981; Turner and Beresford 2005; Wallcraft 1998; Winter and Munn-Giddings 2001).

These gains include:

- addressing and including key previously neglected perspectives and experience
- encouraging trust and openness from research participants
- gaining fuller and more reliable information from service users because research is more sensitive to them
- equalizing research relationships
- improving the accountability of research (Faulkner 2004; Faulkner and Layzell 2000; Hanley 2005).

THE RESEARCH PROJECT

The project we undertook was a three-year national research project, supported by the Joseph Rowntree Foundation. We report the method and methodology of this project in more detail in Appendix 1. The project's focus was service users' perspectives on specialist palliative social work: what it was like for them, what they thought of it and what ideas they had about how it could be improved. We had three aims in undertaking the project. These were:

1. to improve social work practice with people facing life-limiting illnesses and conditions and bereavement

2. to inform policy in this field

3. to develop and improve training, by building on the knowledge and experience of service users.

Participants in the project were located in the full range of settings for such social work, including independent hospices, NHS hospice units, hospital oncology units and palliative care day centres. They lived in many varied parts of the UK. The project distinguished between two groups of service users and included both those who were living with a life-threatening illness or condition and those who had been bereaved. The project adopted in-depth, qualitative methods to explore the views of both these groups. People were interviewed either as individuals or through group discussions, using a semi-structured schedule.

A total of 111 people were interviewed in the project: 61 were bereaved, and 52 had life-limiting illnesses and conditions (two people were both bereaved and patients). Most were interviewed individually. The project included 39 men and 72 women; 9 per cent of participants identified themselves as black and/or members of minority ethnic groups.

Palliative care service users were involved in both the design and management of the project. We aimed to involve specialist palliative care service users in all stages of the project, including finalizing the research focus, developing the research schedule, and analysing and disseminating findings. This involvement had a number of expressions. Palliative care and other service users were included in the Advisory Group which met regularly through the life of the project. Three steering groups of palliative care social work service users were also set up and met during the project. Their purpose was to enable there to be continuity of user involvement in the project, offering ideas and feeding back on its progress. It was expected that their membership might alter during the course of the project, given that some service users were likely to die. We also produced newsletters to keep everyone who participated in the project informed about and involved in the progress of the work.

We knew that involving service users in a project like this would raise its own complex ethical issues. The project was granted formal ethical approval, but a range of issues needed to be addressed with particular care. We sought to build these into the project. These issues included ensuring adequate and accessible information so that participants had as real opportunities for informed consent as possible, avoiding overburdening service users who might be extremely distressed, offering participants all the support that they needed and providing opportunities for follow-up support.

Some of the central questions to which we sought answers included:

- What do service users see as constituting good practice in specialist palliative care social work?
- In a context of limited resources, what priorities do service users highlight?
- How can specialist palliative care social work support the empowerment of service users?
- How can service users be more involved in the construction and practice of specialist palliative care social work?
- How might professional training be improved building on service users' views and experience?

- What are the lessons to be gained from service users' knowledge and experience for improved collaboration between health and social services in palliative care?
- What insights do the views of service users offer for social work as a profession and user involvement more generally?

In the next chapter, we begin looking at the findings emerging from what people said in the project.

SUMMARY

This chapter introduces readers to palliative care, specialist palliative care services and the wide-ranging changes currently impacting on both. It looks at the nature, history and aims of social work generally and of specialist palliative care social work both within social work and within palliative care.

Palliative care and specialist palliative care social work are then located in the changing nature of health and welfare policy over recent years. Particular attention is paid to two recent and related developments, increasing interest in the *quality* of health and welfare provision among policy-makers and a growing emphasis on 'service user involvement' in health and social care policy and practice. Service users have sought to combine these two discussions and development by developing 'user-defined' quality and outcome measures. This book builds on that work with its focus on what service users want from specialist palliative care social work.

To contextualize this, the chapter examines the development of participation in palliative care, noting that it has been slower than in many other fields. There seems to have been some reluctance to involve service users, for a variety of reasons, but early initiatives demonstrate both the feasibility of and potential benefits of user involvement in this area.

Finally the chapter describes the participatory research project whose findings this book reports and discusses. It puts this in the broader context of current interest in service user involvement in research. It briefly sets out the methodology and methods used in the project which are reported in more detail in Appendix 1 later in the book.

Part Two
What Service Users Say

In this second part of the book we report what service users have to say. We have sought to increase our and other people's understanding of specialist palliative care social work from the perspective of those who use it. As far as possible we therefore present our findings using service users' own words. For this reason, this part of the book has minimum discussion and interpretation of what they say. Here we seek to offer service users' own interpretations – although, of course, the choice and arrangement of their comments are ours. We have, however, sought to reflect as far as possible the concerns and emphases that they offer, rather than impose our own. In presenting these findings we are not setting out to measure, quantify, or state the incidence and prevalence of anything. Rather, as Clark (2001, p.63) puts it, our emphasis will be on 'sources of variation, nuances of difference, the elicitation of meaning and the understanding of processes'.

CHAPTER 2

BECOMING INVOLVED WITH PALLIATIVE CARE

As we listened to what service users told us about how they came to palliative care and specialist palliative care social work, it became clear that they had usually experienced a series of events relating to their health, their diagnosis and their treatment, each new event taking them a further step in their involvement with hospital and palliative care services. It was possible to see their experiences in terms of a journey. This is a metaphor that is commonly used in palliative care literature and sometimes by service users themselves. We felt that it offered a useful way of organizing what service users told us, which could make sense both to readers but which also followed from service users' own experience and accounts.

We wanted to see what service users had to say about their journey generally and also about their experience both before and after they had met the specialist palliative care social worker. In this part of the book, we will look in turn at each stage of the journey from first entering palliative care, through the process of involvement with the specialist palliative care social worker – including referral, assessment and intervention – through to their evaluation of the social work service in terms of its strengths and weaknesses.

THE START OF INVOLVEMENT

When we asked service users how they first became involved with specialist palliative care, many returned to a far earlier stage of their journey. They often took us back, in detailed and lengthy accounts, to the first days of their or their loved one's illness; to initial symptoms, the diagnosis and the feelings that they had experienced then. They told us about the treatments that they had received and the high and low points of remission and relapse. They told us about excellent care and sometimes of poor, even negligent treatment. Our process notes show how distressing some of these accounts were, how painful to tell and sometimes how painful to listen to.

It had not been our aim to explore these very early stages of their journeys. Our focus was on specialist palliative care social work. However, service users certainly wanted to tell us about them. They were an inseparable part of their experience. Service users tended to focus on the specific aspects that had been most significant for them personally and this meant their stories were very varied. It was difficult to identify coherent themes. However, there were some consistencies.

Most striking perhaps was how much people wanted and perhaps needed to share their accounts – from the very beginning – and in this way, to put their experiences of coming into palliative care into a more meaningful context. We saw that the referral to specialist palliative care marked a real turning point in people's journey and two strong themes emerged in relation to that referral.

Fear of palliative care

The first of these themes was the horror and dread that many service users told us they or those close to them felt when referral to a hospice was first mentioned. There were several strands within this theme of 'being horror struck'. Many patients equated the word 'hospice' with imminent death:

> Well, the nurse from the hospital suggested that I came to the hospice and be pampered and I threw my arms in the air and said, 'Hospice – no, no, no, no, no, I know I'm ill but I'm not that ill.' (Woman patient, white UK, age group 66–75)

Another woman patient referred to her husband's feelings when she decided to turn to a hospice for help. He also had cancer but had not considered hospice support for himself.

> My husband was horrified...hospice – terminal, you know, the last resort. (Woman patient, white UK, age group 66–75)

That was a view shared by many other patients:

> [The nurse] suggested I come here 'cos I was feeling pretty low after my heart operation and I didn't want to come here at all... A hospice...the word frightened the life out of me... (Man patient, white UK, age group 56–65)

> [T]hey thought it was a good idea that I go to the hospice which absolutely petrified me 'cos I only had one vision of a hospice you know, like most people, and I was very, very reluctant to go there. (Man patient, white UK, 50 years old)

A few of the service users that we spoke to had previously been employed as medical or nursing professionals and some of these individuals still shared the view that hospices were associated only with death and terminal care:

> my conception of them was that they were places for terminal care and that they didn't offer the range of services...and so initially I thought, oh, a hospice is for people who die, but that was the initial thing. (Woman, former nurse, white UK, age group 36–45)

Some service users associated referral to palliative care with giving up on attempts to 'fight' their illness:

> They gave me the telephone number for contacting the hospice to see a Macmillan nurse... I was quite anti the word hospice 'cos I wasn't going to die...and I would say, 'No, I'm fighting this and I'm doing very well.' (Woman patient, white UK, age group 26–35)

Changing attitudes

The second theme which emerged from service users was how rapidly their attitudes to palliative care changed once they had contact with it. Many service users reported that anxieties about palliative care disappeared quickly when they actually visited the hospice or palliative care unit. Many people talked about this reduction in anxiety, but different service users highlighted different reasons for this change. Some talked about increased feelings of security, of being supported:

> the moment you're through the doors of the hospice it does feel very safe. (Woman patient, white UK, age group 56–65)

Some linked the feeling of increased security to the fact that they were put fully in the picture about what was happening to them:

> the support seemed to be there from the minute I walked through that door... I never felt afraid when I had the hospice on board. Everything was explained in detail and they talked to me and to [her husband] not above us or below us...my husband died with dignity because of the hospice. (Bereaved woman, white UK, age group 26–35)

Others commented on the positive impression made by the pleasant environment. The widow of a man who died of cancer in an NHS palliative care unit told us:

> I went to look at it and I fell in love with it, it's a lovely place. (Bereaved woman, white UK, age group 36–45)

Many service users highlighted excellent standards of professional care. The male patient in his fifties we quoted who said the word 'hospice' frightened the life out of him went on to tell us:

> I fell in love with it straight away. I found the nurses here really, really seem to take care and I'm certain about it. (Man patient, white UK, age group 56–65)

It was clear that whatever misgivings or fears service users had at the outset, most of those that we spoke with saw the palliative care service and palliative care team in a very positive light after they had direct experience of them.

> I've been going now for over 12 months...and to me it's one of the best things that's happened... It's been a godsend. (Man with motor neurone disease, white UK, age group 75+)

This man's wife, at his request, was present at the interview and she was one of many who drew a distinction between hospice and hospital care. She said:

> I think the atmosphere's good when you go in there, it's a different atmosphere to going in a hospital...and the people in there are different aren't they?... They're caring, they're more caring. (Older woman, white)

Some people spoke about what hospice care had meant to the whole family. A widowed mother talking in a discussion group of bereaved people about the death of her husband said:

> I have two young daughters, well teenagers, but it was a very difficult time for us all and the hospice made it very bearable and wonderful. (Woman participant in a discussion group of bereaved people)

Service users often commented on how much better they or their family member felt physically or emotionally after receiving hospice care:

> They basically brought back my life. You know the doctors did and they are so supportive of me when I come here. You feel special and I am not praising for the sake of praising...they've given me back a lot of confidence because I was really down and now I'm on top of the world. (Man patient, white UK, age group 56–65)

> [H]e went in very down and very ill. But he came out much better, full of the joys of [the hospice] because they made him feel better and they were so good to him. And my husband was a very private person and I wondered how he would react to this but he loved it and he asked if he could go back. (Woman participant in a discussion group of bereaved people)

The woman who first said 'Hospice – no, no, no, no, no' told us that she had totally changed her opinion of palliative care:

> If anyone says, 'Are you doing anything on Wednesday?' I say, 'Yes, I'm going to the hospice and nothing is going to stop me!' (Woman patient, white UK, age group 66–75)

And the man who said he only had one (negative) vision of a hospice went on to say:

> People don't know until it's too late how special a place that is, and it's not just for dying people which I thought. (Man patient, white UK, 50 years old)

LATE REFERRAL

Some service users reported late referral. Several people said that they had only been referred for specialist palliative care very late in the day and this had presented them and their families with difficulties. One woman's husband had been ill for a very long time. She said that she felt referral to palliative care had come far too late and that she had been kept in the dark about the terminal stage of her husband's illness, so that she was unprepared for his death soon after referral:

> By the time he got to [the hospice] he was quite ill, they knew that anyway...but the doctors don't explain everything and they don't tell you how far gone they are... (Bereaved woman, black Caribbean, age group 46–55)

If people are initially reluctant to accept referral, through fears and anxiety, they might never be offered palliative care again. Although it was not mentioned often enough for it to be identified as a broader issue, a few service users made us realize how close they or their family member had come to missing out on palliative care altogether. An example of this was the woman who described how her father, a man in his eighties with a long history of mental health problems, refused to go to hospital or hospice 'without a fight'. The family felt they were unable to give him the care he needed and were becoming quite desperate.

> We didn't get any help from our GP. It only came from a passing comment from a registered nurse who came to our house. Just a passing comment she made about coming here [to the hospice]...and when he said no, she didn't bother asking again, and it wasn't until we had come to the end of our tether – right we'll go there for the day, see – we'll take him there and he can see how nice it is... (Bereaved woman, white UK, age group 46–55)

It was clear that most of the service users we spoke to were very happy about the care they or their loved ones had received from the broader specialist palliative care team and consequently their views of specialist palliative care social workers need to be seen within this wider context. For example, one man had an extremely negative view of social workers following a personal experience of social work that he described as 'horrendous', but he was specifically prepared to give the social worker at the hospice a chance:

> because of the way the hospice had treated my wife. (Bereaved man, white UK, age group 46–55)

EXISTING VIEWS OF SOCIAL WORK AND SOCIAL WORKERS

We knew that we could expect social work to be a profession that was not necessarily familiar to or even available to everyone in the same way as, for example, the services of a GP or nurse are familiar and available. We were also aware of the negative and sometimes inaccurate images of social work that are presented, particularly in the tabloid media. We therefore felt it was important to find out what people knew and thought about social work prior to their meeting with the specialist palliative care social worker, as this might impact on the nature of their involvement with specialist palliative care social work.

What service users thought of social work

We asked service users to tell us their views of social work or social workers before they met the specialist palliative care social worker. A small minority of service users described positive experiences of social work prior to meeting the palliative care social worker. One woman, for instance, had found her husband's social worker from the local authority care management team exceptionally helpful:

> She couldn't do enough for him… (Bereaved woman, white UK, age group 36–45)

However, many people were initially reluctant to respond to our question, and comments like 'you wouldn't want to know' were common. We found that, when pressed for an answer, there was a strongly consistent theme to the replies. Service users were overwhelmingly negative about social work and social workers. There were two categories of response. These reflected people's previous relationship with social work and came from:

- a position of ignorance – the service user had no direct prior experience of social work
- direct personal and/or professional experience of social work.

It is important to note that the majority of service users fell into the first category: they had no previous personal experience of social workers and so relied heavily on media reporting and other accounts for their information. A number of different strands appeared within the general theme of negativity towards social work. These can be summed up as:

- Social work is not for people like me.
- Social workers are only there for one thing.
- Social workers intrude and take over.
- Social workers don't help much anyway.
- They're hard to get, these social workers.

SOCIAL WORK IS NOT FOR PEOPLE LIKE ME!

Many people said that they believed that social work had no relevance to 'people like them'.

> It wasn't something that crossed my mind that when people, well with cancer, or people in hospices, that they had social workers…it just never crossed my mind. (Bereaved woman, white UK, age group 19–25)

Service users often seemed to equate social work with people who did not want to be 'independent' and some saw needing social work support as demeaning and a last resort.

> I just thought people were very sad you know, I couldn't understand why anyone wants to go and talk to anyone about a problem and that was very adamant in my mind, very clear... I didn't see why anyone had problems, when I had more problems than most, I suppose. I just didn't deal with them. (Man patient, white UK, 50 years old)

> Really and truly I suppose it was a last ditch stand, you know, to get in touch with her because there was nothing else we could do. (Bereaved man, white UK, 68 years old)

> [I]f we've not had any money – we've never gone on benefits or anything, always worked...we've just managed on what we have had. So I've never gone into the depths of needing a social worker before...no, in our day we were brought up very independent. (Woman patient, white UK, age group 56–65)

Some service users were quite clear that they only associated social workers with people they saw as socially marginalized:

> I thought social work was for the down and outs, people that, you know, lived on the streets and things like this. (Woman patient talking in a discussion group)

SOCIAL WORKERS ARE ONLY THERE FOR ONE THING!

Whilst many people said they associated social workers with children, it was clear that a number of these saw the social worker in a predatory rather than a protective role. Some parents told us how they had actively resisted referral because of this view and the anxieties associated with it.

> I thought that's it, they want to come in and take the kids because they know I'm not going to be able to look after them... I was frightened, I was very frightened at first. Because I thought not only am I losing [her husband], I'm now going to lose the kids as well. That's what I initially thought. I did feel that for quite a long time. (Bereaved woman, white UK, age group 26–35)

Many of those service users who did see the social worker as being in a protective role felt that they only heard about those that failed to fulfil their responsibilities. Many volunteered that their judgement was totally based on media horror stories and they said that they were not necessarily getting an unbiased perspective.

Some service users were, however, talking from experience. A father talked about how dealings with an adoption team had 'scarred me for life' and that this meant that he felt reluctant to ask for support for his young daughter on the death of her mother. Another man said that he had a poor opinion based on personal experience prior to meeting the palliative care social worker.

> My honest opinion was that I didn't think much of them because of an incident that happened years ago, but I have changed my opinion. (Man patient from a minority ethnic group, age group 56–65)

SOCIAL WORKERS INTRUDE AND TAKE OVER!

As well as seeing social workers as being for people who did not themselves want independence, it was apparent that some service users saw social workers as actively using their power in a threatening or undermining way which restricted people's independence:

> I was a bit wary of them, can I put it that way, I think we are very influenced by what we read in the press... I thought they might be a bit intrusive into my life. (Woman patient, white UK, age group 56–65)

> [T]he impression we had was that social workers just go into a home and sit there...and order the people they are supposed to look after about... (Bereaved woman, white European, age group 66–75)

> I've found them a little bit overbearing sometimes, not all of them, I'm not generalizing. But I have found that – I worked in a children's home...but I found it a little bit of a battleground, and they were taking control away basically. (Bereaved woman, white UK, age group 75+)

SOCIAL WORKERS DON'T HELP MUCH ANYWAY!

Either from personal or from professional experience, some service users had reached the conclusion that social workers often failed to be supportive. Some people, like this woman, felt that there were structural constraints limiting their effectiveness:

> In my job, I came in contact with social workers all the time. I think their hands are tied. I think some of them are excellent, but there's a lot left to be desired with some... I think possibly it's because they haven't either got the time or they are too busy to do the things that I would think are part of their job... (Woman patient, white UK, age group 75+)

Those service users who had personal experience of working as social workers gave a similar picture:

> I have a pretty poor view of our profession, I'm afraid, and what we are able to offer, because of the structures that we have, that we don't have any control over...we were allowed to do less and less things than I was trained to do. (Bereaved man, white UK, age group 46–55)

Some service users had been let down as promises had not been kept. This woman had seen a non-specialist social worker earlier in her illness:

> I will do this for you [she said] but it never transpired, and I'll get that going for you and it still never transpired. (Woman patient, white UK, age group 46–55)

A small minority of service users felt that social workers were likely to be of little value because it wasn't possible for any professional to make a difference:

> I really didn't think anyone could sort anybody else out, I thought you'd got to sort yourself out. (Bereaved woman, white UK, age group 36–45)

THEY'RE HARD TO GET, THESE SOCIAL WORKERS!

As we have reported, a small number of service users, prior to meeting the specialist palliative care social worker, did have positive views of social workers and actively sought their support but had found that accessing a social worker was difficult. Service users' own definitions of need were sometimes ignored. One patient recalled how her desperate request for social work support was met with refusal when her husband was sectioned under the Mental Heath Act shortly after her own diagnosis of cancer:

> they didn't really recommend a social worker, because I asked…because I said I got children, and I said I got, you know, a child with special needs and I was ill, you know, with cancer, but I didn't get a social worker. They said it wasn't needed… I said, 'What about me, what about the kids? Will we have a social worker please?' Oh no!…they didn't think it was necessary…even the GPs didn't. (Woman patient, white UK, age group 36–45)

Another couple described repeatedly asking for help at the hospital where the husband was seen, as both an inpatient and an outpatient, over a period of several months:

Wife:	[We asked] can we see someone…a social worker because we need help, and they went 'Yeah we'll send someone up' and they never did.
Husband:	They never did.
Wife:	And they never did and it got to the point where I just couldn't take it any more and I thought what is the point of going on, you know, because no one's helping, they've written him off, they just don't want to know, they don't care.
Interviewer:	So it just felt hopeless really?
Wife:	I felt totally out of my depth and I've always been in control and I felt completely out of it and that is the most awful feeling when you can't control nothing. (Man patient, white UK, age group 46–55, interviewed with his wife)

This patient's wife had gone on to make a suicide attempt at which point the referral was made to the specialist palliative care social worker.

It was clear that some service users held not just one of these negative images but several of them, and they said how surprised they were when the social worker turned out to be different to the image.

> You only hear the problems with social workers if something goes wrong, don't you? Like if a child is killed, or something like that. I think you have pre-conceived ideas – oh they meddle, or they're not going to help you, they're going to delve into your finances, they're going to do this, they are going to do that. [The specialist palliative care social worker] didn't do any of that. She was just there and was nice – I have to say I was surprised…she was what probably we actually needed. (Bereaved woman, white UK, age group 46–55)

Lack of information about social work

Our question about people's pre-existing views of social work and social workers revealed another strong theme. This was people's lack of information about social work . A number of service users made the point that they thought it was difficult to have any view about social work and social workers because they felt they were kept in the dark as to what social workers actually did in practice. Many stated that everything they knew about social work came from newspapers. This patient found his lack of information and knowledge about the role inhibited him in his first meetings with the specialist palliative care social worker:

> I had no idea what the role was… I had absolutely no idea what I could say or couldn't say or could ask or what they actually did, to what extent… (Man patient, white UK, age group 26–35)

There were a small number of people who already knew about and had positive views of specialist palliative care social work prior to entering palliative care. These tended to be professionals working in either medical or social work fields. For example the social worker quoted above, who felt he had little control in his own area of social work, told us that:

> I think hospice and hospital social workers are the last outpost – one of the last outposts – of proper social work… (Widowed father of young children, white UK, age group 46–55)

And this former nurse told us:

> I don't think you can call yourself a proper multidisciplinary team without a social worker… (Bereaved woman, white UK, age group 56–65)

SUMMARY

People's attitudes to palliative care

- Many service users described their feelings of horror and dread when referral to a hospice was first mentioned.

- They said they had equated the word 'hospice' with imminent death and with giving up on the fight against their illness.

- However, service users reported extremely positive feelings about the hospice or palliative care unit once they had direct experience of it. Views often changed rapidly and dramatically after actual contact.

- Service users frequently mentioned experiencing a feeling of safety in the palliative care setting. High standards of care and pleasant environments were appreciated.

- Many service users said that their health and sense of well-being actually improved after they entered specialist palliative care.

- A minority of service users mentioned very late referral to specialist palliative care and felt this had been detrimental.

People's views of social work and social workers

- Service users' views of social work generally mainly came from the media. In a minority of cases it was based on previous experience of social work.

- Service users held overwhelmingly negative views of social work and social workers *prior* to meeting the specialist palliative care social worker.

- Social workers were seen as being for other types of people and social work was linked with a lack of independence.

- Social workers were strongly linked with taking children into care and also with failing to protect children.

- Social workers were seen as intrusive, bossy and controlling.

- Social workers were seen as ineffectual.

- Social work was seen as difficult to find out about and social workers as difficult to access.

- Only a very small number of people had prior knowledge of specialist palliative care social work and this was often linked to their own related work experience.

CHAPTER 3

STARTING THE PALLIATIVE CARE SOCIAL WORK JOURNEY

The next stage in the service user's journey is meeting the specialist palliative care social worker. We were keen to find out more about service users' experiences of this first meeting. We wanted to know how this had come about and how it felt. We wanted to know whether it was service users themselves who had instigated this contact, or whether someone else had prompted the referral and whether there were any obvious barriers to it being made.

MAKING CONTACT: THE PROCESS OF REFERRAL

We asked service users to tell us how they first came to see the specialist palliative care social worker. A number of service users were very vague and could not say how they had first come into contact with the specialist palliative care social worker. It seemed that either they had simply forgotten or they had been unaware of any formal referral process although, of course, this may have been happening behind the scenes, for example in multidisciplinary meetings of which they were not aware.

The first clear issue to emerge was that there were few self-referrals for social work support. Only a small minority of patients and bereaved people had initiated the contact themselves. Those who referred themselves were likely to be individuals who already had positive personal or professional experience of social work. For example:

> having two young children at the time, and struggling, I just thought I needed some – we both needed some help. (Bereaved father, white UK, age group 46–55, who was a social worker in another field)

A bereaved woman in her fifties told us that she had been a nurse in palliative care herself and when faced with the death of someone very close she realized that she needed the support of a specialist palliative care social worker. This was one of the prime reasons she wanted her mother to be cared for in a hospice:

> I wanted help from a proper social worker and…if she goes into the hospice we will have the resources of the hospice, which I will need. (Bereaved woman, white UK, age group 56–65)

But among other service users, as we have already indicated, there was widespread ignorance about social work in general and many told us that it had simply not occurred to them that there was such a thing as a specialist palliative care social work service. Few therefore knew to ask directly for it. For example:

> I really didn't think there was a social worker there, within the hospice, I didn't know about that... I was quite surprised actually. (Bereaved woman, black Caribbean, age group 46–55)

> I wasn't aware that the support service was there till that nurse told me. So it's letting people know... (Man patient, white UK, age group 26–35)

The value of informal contact

A further strong issue to emerge was that service users liked informal contact by the specialist palliative care social worker and found it reassuring. A significant minority of service users told us that the palliative care social worker had approached them without them being aware of any formal request or referral process. It appeared that some social workers tried to meet all new patients and this was particularly common in day-care settings.

> [T]hat's the first thing she does when a new person comes in, she goes and makes herself known to them. (Service user in discussion group)

Service users told us that they appreciated these informal introductions and had been reassured and put at their ease by the social worker as a result.

> I suppose it was maybe the second day he was here and she [the social worker] said if there was anything she could do, you know, I was to speak to her... I felt it was a very reassuring thing for people in my position... (Bereaved woman, white UK, age group 56–65)

> [S]he came and introduced herself...she actually said, 'I'd like to come and have a little talk to you'...we went and had a little cuppa that day or else it was the next. (Bereaved woman, white UK, age group 56–65)

We quoted one woman in Chapter 2 who had a wholly negative picture of social workers prior to meeting the specialist palliative care social worker. Yet, when she told us how the hospice social worker had approached her and her family, she said:

> We were in with my father. She came in, introduced herself. And she was very nice, and was there anything she could do? And we got talking and one thing led to another and she realized how fraught we were as a family. (Bereaved woman, white UK, age group 46–55)

This raises the question of whether this particular woman would have ever voluntarily sought referral or agreed to it if the option had just been suggested and what the implications might have been for her had she not.

Some service users felt that being given too much choice about seeing the specialist palliative care social worker was not always helpful. One service user said he hadn't requested to see the social worker but the idea had been put to him and he had agreed. He told us that, while it was important that nothing was forced onto him, it had also been essential that he wasn't left too much to himself, as he wasn't really aware of what he needed or what was available. His comments sum up his ambivalence:

> they didn't leave it up to me; they did leave it up to me...whilst it was entirely up to me they still, you know, made it, kept me aware that they were there... (Man patient, white UK, age group 26–35)

Another patient, who said that he had been deeply distressed, was not asked if he wanted to see the social worker. She simply turned up at his bedside. He thought he might have refused had he been asked. He was the man who, in Chapter 2, said he thought people were 'a bit sad' if they wanted to talk about their problems:

> I just remember coming out of a black hole and that's how I described it and seeing her face, and that was the first contact. And I don't know why, you know, I just don't know why, I just felt I had to talk to this person and it was just like somebody's brought me from a dark hole to make me talk to this person, that's exactly how it was. (Man patient, white UK, 50 years old)

It is difficult to be certain if there were significant gender differences. However, it did seem that this view – that it was not always helpful to be given too much choice about seeing the social worker – was perhaps more prevalent amongst the men to whom we spoke.

One 70-year-old man who had lost his wife felt that it would have been better if the social worker had just called in 'for a cup of tea and a chat' rather than ringing him first and asking him whether there was anything he wanted to talk to her about. He had told her he was okay and did not want to see her. A district nurse manager had simply called to see him:

> She just popped in, on her own. Had a cup of tea and a chat. That was it. That was worth a million dollars... (Bereaved man, white UK, 70 years old)

This same man told us, however, that he really had needed to talk and with hindsight regretted turning the social worker down:

> When my wife was ill, at that time that's when you could have done with [support]...you know you get nothing much from doctors – they flit in and out – and 'Here's a prescription'. Nurses come on a daily basis to treat the ill... We maybe could have done with someone in between, who wasn't a nurse, who wasn't a doctor, who I could have sat and talked to downstairs...generally about anything, just me and the social worker, that was away from my family, that I could say 'I feel like this' or 'I feel like that'. That might have been a big help.

Fortunately this service user had been offered social work support once again after bereavement. This time he accepted. He told us that it had been of considerable help.

The picture of how service users first came to see the specialist palliative care social worker was, however, a confusing one. There was, for instance, evidence of inconsistency on occasions even within the same unit. Sometimes one service user told us that the social worker had been very proactive in offering support, while another service user of the same hospice or palliative care team gave an opposing story of how they had needed to be very active in seeking out support. We gradually realized that there were definite patterns emerging in how patients, as compared to people who were bereaved, talked about first meeting the social worker.

The inconsistency of referrals

A pattern began to emerge of inconsistent referrals of patients and their families to specialist palliative care social work. The evidence did not suggest that specialist palliative care social work was being offered to patients and their families in a systematic and consistent way prior to the death of the patient.

SLIPPING THROUGH THE NET

Some service users voiced their anxieties that people might slip through the net and this appeared to be a valid concern. A bereaved woman, for example, told us how, despite frequent visits to the hospice *before* the death of her family member, she did not recall being asked if she wanted to meet with a social worker:

> Whilst she was actually ill I don't remember being introduced to them... I think it would have been easier if we had met them properly before she died. (Bereaved woman, white UK, age group 19–25)

A few people felt they had needed to be very assertive in order to see the social worker for bereavement support.

> I kind of knew that [social work support] was going to be there, that the service was available but I had to go looking for it. Other people might not know it was there. (Bereaved man, white UK, age group 26–35)

However, it should be said that this was not a general view.

Offering bereavement support more proactively

While support for patients and their loved ones appeared to be offered in an inconsistent manner, many of the bereaved service users had been approached by the social workers in a proactive and systematic way – but only after the death. A number of people referred to receiving letters advising them of bereavement groups and one-off meetings for bereaved people. Service users who were bereaved were often conscious that other bereaved people had received similar letters and they referred to these approaches being routinely offered. Sometimes though these letters arrived many months after the death (ten months in one case). Some of these people expressed sadness at not having met the social workers earlier and some said they did not know whether the person whom they had lost had had the opportunity to talk with a social worker before he or she died.

This service user reflected wider comments when she talked about the way support had been offered in bereavement:

> My feeling was that, you know, the whole thing was just so proactive... I feel that they thought very carefully about, you know, what happens. And they have these sorts of safety nets which are built in...my feeling is they think very carefully about keeping that momentum up without being pushy, if that's the right way of putting it. (Bereaved woman talking in a discussion group with other bereaved people)

The importance of early referral

Service users saw early contact with the specialist palliative care social worker as very important. They expressed a strong wish that they had met the palliative care social worker earlier. This emerged as a recurrent theme. Sometimes the delay in seeing the social worker seemed to relate to the inconsistent referral patterns to the social worker within the palliative care setting itself, as we have already highlighted, but, more often, it reflected the fact that service users were not being referred for palliative care itself until very late in their diagnosis.

A patient described how her husband had approached the local hospice to see if they could offer support to his wife as he was concerned about how she was coping:

> I felt it was almost an accident...someone else who maybe didn't have someone to speak for them like I had my husband... He was determined he was going to get me some help, [they] might not have known that you could have that kind of help. (Woman patient, white UK, age group 56–65)

No one, either in the primary care team or when they were using the hospital inpatient and outpatient facilities, seems to have picked up on some service users' concerns and need for support. One man was very angry because he felt he had been denied full and truthful information about the severity of his dead wife's illness until very near the end of her life when she went into the hospice. He said:

> And [the specialist palliative care social worker] has been marvellous, no doubt. If it hadn't been for her, we wouldn't have known why she [his wife] had actually died – she has been marvellous. No doubt about it. But she's one person at the end of a very long chain, isn't she? I think we should have her at the beginning.

> If I'd had a palliative care social worker for six months, I would have known what were happening when I came here [to the hospice] and I could have used it more, I could have actually got more out of the system. (Bereaved man talking in a discussion group)

Many other service users made it clear that they would have welcomed much earlier contact. These comments were typical:

> [I]n hindsight looking back it would have been better to have earlier contact but you just don't know where you are. I think it [specialist palliative care social work] would have been helpful as soon as you find out that you've got the tumour, you've got the lump and it's been diagnosed as cancer, I think that's when you need the great support. (Woman patient, white UK, 45 years old)

> I just wish that maybe that there'd been someone like [the specialist palliative care social worker] around right from the word go...maybe through fault of our own, not knowing or not asking... (Bereaved woman, white UK, age group 26–35)

This second woman went on to emphasize that she had seen a social worker right from the beginning but wished that the *specialist palliative care social worker* had been involved earlier:

> It's not like an ordinary social worker... I think it's so important that the palliative social worker is there from the beginning when the trauma starts...through the consultation period, you know the diagnosis...you feel so alone...

Another service user, a woman who had only been referred for palliative care long after diagnosis, echoed this desire for specialist palliative care to have been involved earlier:

> I've found I've got the support I need [now], which I needed for a long time. But till it got to this point, it seemed as though you was diagnosed and left dangling and that was horrendous...that was terrifying... (Woman patient, white UK, age group 46–55)

One woman had many longstanding problems when she was first seen by the specialist palliative care social worker. She said:

> gorblimey I wish I'd got this long ago... I still wish I'd got this long ago, I suffered for seven years.

She went on to say how the specialist palliative care social worker had been the first professional to pick up on her many difficulties and losses:

> when she found out all the things I had had to cope with, I was coping with, I lost my daughter, I had cancer, I had two of her children to bring up...and I was still feeling vulnerable myself but I never had time for myself. And then everything got on top of us so [the specialist palliative care social worker]

picked up the pieces, it's just unfortunate that it went on so long because nobody picked up even when I was homeless, not even like the council, we lost our home and everything. (Woman patient, white UK, 67 years old)

Turning down support

Sometimes service users had come to feel that they needed support at an earlier stage, but had not sought it or had turned it down. One woman, for example, whose husband had died of a long-term condition, said she had found it difficult to access support for herself during his illness because he did not understand why she needed counselling, as he did not expect to die. She said:

> I didn't really understand how important a social worker was until after-wards, unfortunately... I guess it's very difficult at the time because...you're at your wits' end and you don't want to admit this to anybody. (Bereaved woman, white UK, age group 56–65)

Another woman had chosen not to see the social worker earlier:

> But I shut my door and my eyes and my ears and didn't really want to know. Big mistake. If I had come in a lot sooner things would have been far better, quicker. (Bereaved woman in discussion group)

Some people had received specialist palliative care social work early and had found this very helpful. One bereaved man was very clear that this had been essential to him, as his wife had changed so dramatically during the course of her illness. He felt the social worker would have been redundant if she had only become involved later.

> I think they should know or try to get to know the people before the drastic changes of whatever disease it is, occurs... I don't think there's any point in, like I said, somebody from the social workers coming to visit me to talk to me about my wife's death when they've no conception of how she was. (Bereaved man, white UK, 68 years old)

Only one person specifically said that she would not have welcomed earlier contact – that she would have felt it was being offered too soon. She was a young woman who had been bereaved at the age of 18, the youngest person we spoke to. She said:

> When my mum died I just went through this numb period where, although I knew I felt these issues, I just... I couldn't put them into words so much and I felt really awkward talking about it and I just wanted to basically get back into my life... You know, to go to school, learn to drive, to go out with my friends, to have a laugh, just do stuff like that, but the realization dawned... (Bereaved woman, white UK, 18 years old)

She felt that the timing of bereavement support might be a very important issue for teenagers. She felt that their emotions were perhaps *stronger* and were *buzzing about* and that they might perhaps need time for these to settle before they could accept counselling.

Relying on other professionals for referral

Frequently referrals to the specialist palliative care social worker came through other professionals, and it was clear that these had been appropriate and welcomed; but there was some evidence from individuals that other professionals were not always helpful. One service user was shocked by the attitude of a hospice nurse to the social worker:

> They actually said to me, 'Well we've got a social worker here but I don't actually think that you'll like her and get on with her very well'…but actually having had contact with her I found her extremely good. (Woman patient, white UK, 45 years old)

This patient had not been put off seeing the social worker, but she raised the question of whether other patients had been told the same thing and acknowledged that the comment had troubled her:

> It has put a burden on me and it's a burden I don't like.

A few service users also questioned how much other professionals knew about specialist palliative care social work. This same woman felt that if they did know, they did not always share the information:

> no one else tells us anything, so we weren't told. Hospitals don't tell you. We'd never heard of her.

Repeating the offer of support

There seemed to be value in repeating the offer of specialist palliative care social work support. A small number of service users had turned down support from the social workers before the death of someone close, but said how much they appreciated being offered the support again at a later date.

> I didn't want to address it beforehand because there were an awful lot of emotions spraying around and I just wanted to focus on giving her support and trying to keep everything together…and then deal with the aftermath after the events. (Man who had lost his partner, white UK, age group 26–35)

The value of written information

Being able to access written information about local specialist palliative care social work support could also provide a useful line of communication. Some service users had contacted the social workers themselves having earlier received a leaflet about how to get support. One woman, who was experiencing suicidal thoughts, remembered that she had been given just such a leaflet and turned to the social worker for help.

> Well I was depressed and I didn't want, I didn't want to go on without him...
> I thought...someone has got to help me out of this rut. (Bereaved woman in
> discussion group)

Having no one to turn to

The lack of someone else to turn to for support within family or friends was a
very strong theme in the interviews and discussions and was picked up in the
steering groups.

Assumptions are sometimes made that service users who are surrounded
by what seem like loving partners, family and friends have sufficient support
and do not need referral to a social worker. However, we were told very frequently by service users that they were glad of a meeting with the social worker
because they felt that in reality they didn't have anyone to whom they could turn
within their own network of family or friends. Even service users who told us
that they came from large, loving and supportive families and had a network of
good friends said that, at times, they felt extremely isolated and alone. They
gave a number of reasons for this. First, many felt that they had to protect their
family members from their difficult or painful feelings.

> All my sisters are wonderful and we can talk...but...you don't want to worry
> family... I know that somebody else outside the family can take it...
> (Bereaved woman, white UK, age group 56–65)

Some service users made it clear that they wanted to be 'normal' with their
family and friends:

> then I can go back to these other people in my life and actually just try and
> behave as I see it, in a normal fashion. That's not to say I don't talk to them
> about my loss but I don't rely on them. (Bereaved man, white UK, age group
> 26–35)

Others felt they had exhausted the supply of support that was available from
those close to them.

> My husband was also on a low ebb...this is one reason why I agreed to go to
> the counselling because he had come through all this with me and I just felt
> he couldn't take any more. You know he had got me through most of it, we'd
> gone through it together and my friends up the road that had nursed me right
> through the illness and everything, they'd always been there for me. But I'd
> found I'd reached a point where I didn't need to worry or pressurize them
> any more... (Woman patient, white UK, age group 56–65)

Some felt that family or friends might not understand their needs.

> [A] family they'll give you all the sympathy you don't want...[the social
> worker] gives you every sympathy but she gives it in a different way alto-
> gether. (Woman service user in discussion group)

> I feel embarrassed talking to my friends about my problems…because they don't understand and I don't want to bore them with it… (Bereaved woman, white UK, 18 years old)

> I'm a fairly young widow and none of my friends have lost their partners and consequently I've nobody of my own age to discuss various things with and this [bereavement] group has enabled us to talk. (Woman service user in discussion group)

Sometimes family or friends avoided the service user or refused to talk about issues of concern. This woman with a life-limiting condition said:

> since I got diagnosed, it's as though I can give them this disease…every time that I am not feeling well they won't see me…they think they are going to get this… (Woman patient, white UK, age group 46–55)

This was especially a problem for people who had been bereaved. We were told time and again about friendships that were lost following the death of someone close.

> I found after [my wife] had died I couldn't speak to people, I found that people tried to avoid me…they don't know what to say to you… I'd be walking down the street and people would cross the road so they didn't speak to me… (Bereaved man, white UK, age group 46–55)

> I don't know whether they were keeping their distance because they didn't know how to talk to me or not… I found that very, very, very strong and other people who had lost their partners…they were telling me the same thing…they said they can't believe it… (Bereaved man in discussion group)

Some service users felt that family or friends were themselves *too* involved and wanted something else.

> It's [the social worker] someone outside the situation and I think that's the most important thing. (Man patient, white UK, age group 26–35)

THE SOCIAL WORK ASSESSMENT

Next we look at what service users said about social work assessment. We wanted to find out how the patient or bereaved person had experienced this part of their contact with the specialist palliative care social worker. We wanted to see whether they had felt informed and involved; whether they had felt that their views had been heard and their experiences valued. In particular we wanted to know whether service users had felt able to talk to the specialist palliative care social worker about the things that really mattered to them.

Assessment has come to be seen as a key element and stage in social work practice. It is described as 'the process that controls the nature, direction and scope of social work interventions' and is seen as important because of 'its potential to initiate or influence life-changing decisions in relation to vulnerable individuals' (Jackson 2000, p.20). Assessment is also seen to 'involve the formation of a judgement concerning the needs of a [service user] which may result in their requirements being met by social care provision' (Griggs 2000, p.22).

The informality of assessment

We asked service users to tell us how it was decided what the specialist palliative social worker would do to help them. It quickly became clear that assessments were generally carried out informally.

One of the most striking issues to emerge was that service users presented very little evidence of the social workers carrying out written or formalized assessments and certainly nobody mentioned filling in forms or seeing check-lists. One service user actually commented that there was no checklist:

> it's not as though they come with a list and say we do this, this, and this, you know, they don't. (Man patient, white UK, age group 26–35)

What we seemed to be seeing from service users was a picture not of a formal, pre-structured, step-like assessment process where all the issues were immediately identified, articulated and options offered, but of a more subtle process where the emphasis was placed as much on building the relationship between the social worker and service user as on finding out the 'facts'. Within this broad picture a number of specific themes emerged.

BEING PUT AT EASE

Many service users felt that the social worker had been able to engage with them right from the beginning. They reported a sense of being put at ease by the social worker. These comments were typical:

> [S]he really made me feel at ease…you're trying to speak to somebody that you've never met before and that can be quite awkward but I really felt quite at ease sitting speaking to her… (Bereaved man, white UK, 52 years old)

> I rejected all help from social workers until [the specialist palliative care social worker] appeared on the scene and then she just seemed to be the other side, the other face of the social worker. (Woman patient, white UK, age group 46–55)

One woman talked about having felt powerless in her relationship with her doctor who, she felt, was oppressive, and she contrasted this with her experience of the specialist palliative care social worker.

> I'm still scared of people in authority… I never ever felt any fear or nervousness with her you know…which I did feel with some people. (Bereaved woman, white UK, 56 years old)

Others articulated very similar views:

> [Y]ou've got some who work in an office and you're frightened of approaching them – she hasn't got that attitude. (Woman service user in discussion group)

THE SENSE OF BEING LISTENED TO

Service users emphasized the importance of being listened to by the specialist palliative care social worker. They stressed, time and time again, that being listened to was a central part of what happened during the initial assessment.

> [T]here wasn't anything really decided... I think I was in such a state, and she just sort of let me talk...how I wanted to...and she just sat and listened basically. (Woman patient, white UK, age group 56–65)

> [S]he was just a really nice person, quite quiet, and listened to me and I really liked that... (Bereaved woman, white UK, age group 15–18)

> [S]he was prepared to listen... (Woman patient, white UK, age group 66–75)

SHAPING THE AGENDA

Service users felt they could determine their own agenda. It was apparent that many service users felt that they were able to shape the direction of the assessment. For example:

> she wanted to see, you know, what my needs were and we just discussed that. We sorted it out between us, I think, and I was happy with that... I was glad that I'd had sort of a little bit of input over it rather than just what is going to happen taken away from me and I was pleased with that... (Man patient, white UK, age group 36–45)

> I don't think anybody had preconceived ideas [about] what I needed... (Woman patient, white UK, age group 56–65)

> [S]he doesn't take over and she...feeds the options for you... I always had a very strong sense that if I wanted to negotiate something else, another kind of service, then that would be entirely possible, there was certainly no kind of sense that the power was there. (Bereaved man, white UK, age group 26–35)

> She didn't railroad me into anything I didn't want to do. (Bereaved woman from a European background, 76 years old)

> She was there and she was just there to listen to me and I was the one that did most of the talking and I kind of led the actual meeting... (Woman patient, white UK, age group 56–65)

Power used appropriately

Service users didn't always feel able to shape the agenda because of the difficult times they were having. Social workers were able to be flexible where this was the case. Professionals intervening in people's lives at vulnerable times can exert significant power over service users. Service users stressed that specialist palliative care social workers used power and authority appropriately and supportively. It was clear that many service users had appreciated it when social workers had used their authority in a supportive way and had sometimes taken charge of proceedings, assuming a degree of control in a situation that was threatening to overwhelm service users. Sometimes this authority had been needed from very early on in the relationship. For example, a bereaved father of a young family, talking of his first meeting with the social worker, said that he had felt that the social worker needed to take a high degree of control so that the family felt a sense of support and direction.

> [S]he was there [for us] to tell us what she thought we needed. (Bereaved man, white UK, age group 46–55)

Another bereaved person talked about handing responsibility for many matters over to the social worker following the death of her husband. She felt she could not cope at that time with anything else:

> Just when I needed it, she took control. She actually took control for me, and handled it all. (Bereaved woman, white UK, age group 26–35)

A woman patient in her eighties described how she had asked the social worker, whom she had only just met, to sort out a move to a nursing home. She was very conscious of how much authority she had passed to the social worker, but she felt very positive about this:

> I depended on [the social worker] because I was very, very weak, I couldn't make my own decisions and I depended on her so much that I knew it would be a good decision… I trusted her…she explained everything to me so in my weaker state I never, ever doubted her. (Woman patient, white UK, age group 75+)

Other people talked about the relief that they felt when they could leave decisions to the social worker.

> Interviewer: How was it decided what [the social worker] would do to help you?
>
> Service user: I think she just decided herself. And we just went along with it, because we were so relieved that we'd finally got help. Help that we'd been asking for, for the last year. We finally got it. (Service user in discussion group)

And the following service user went on to say that, for her, the main strength of specialist palliative care social work was that

> Somebody takes all responsibility away from you. They take charge, they just take charge of the person who is ill, is dying. And it's nice to have somebody else to share with... (Bereaved woman, white UK, age group 46–55)

Many people said that the social worker *just seemed to know* what was needed. They seemed comfortable with that as many of them said they had been feeling confused and overwhelmed by their situation and unable clearly to articulate their needs.

> She seemed to see what was needed. (Bereaved woman, white European, 76 years old)

> She just seemed to highlight or pinpoint what you needed, just sorted it out with you...in my eyes it was very, very good. She knew just what to do, what I needed and got on and did it. (Bereaved man, white UK, talking in a discussion group)

Assessment: Ongoing and supportive

Service users talked about assessment as a continuing and supportive process. They seemed very clear that the initial assessment had not been just a one-off procedure but part of an ongoing process with the expectation that circumstances would change. The knowledge that assessment went on this way was important to them:

> we just talked round things and we knew she would be here if we wanted her about anything, you know, and we had access to that... (Bereaved woman, white UK, 71 years old)

It was also clear that people did not see assessment as separate from support. They experienced support happening right from the word go.

> I think to start with it was just a big jumble and a lot of it perhaps the first few weeks it was all the anger about my husband dying, why has this happened to me? But after that, gradually bit by bit other things started to come out...but to start with there's no plan I don't think. I think you're just in such a muddle...it was just such a big help to me. (Bereaved woman, white UK, age group 46–55)

SPELLING OUT THE SOCIAL WORK ROLE

The majority of service users seemed very happy with the way that assessment happened. A small minority of service users, however, expressed concern that what the specialist palliative care social workers actually did had not been spelled out clearly as part of the assessment process. They felt that there was a need to make clear the nature and extent of the social worker's role and this did not always happen:

> They leave it up to the patient to tell them but it's just that I didn't know, I had no idea what I could ask them. (Man patient, white UK, age group 26–35)

> No, nothing was mentioned about benefits, nothing at all… No I mean I didn't need it, but obviously for a lot of people they do, I didn't, but you know it was never, ever suggested, offered. (Bereaved woman, white UK, age group 46–55)

SUMMARY

In this chapter, service users talk about how they get to see the specialist palliative care social worker, how social workers made contact with them and what they felt about this. The chapter highlights issues of choice, timing and referral.

Making contact: The process of referral

- Some social workers introduced themselves to all patients informally. Service users welcomed this and found it reassuring.

- Sometimes service users said they found it helpful 'not to be given too much choice' about being referred to the specialist palliative care social worker. This view seemed to be held more by men than women.

- Though many referrals came through other professionals there was evidence that some professionals were not always helpful or knowledgeable about referring people on to specialist palliative care social work.

- Social work support prior to people's death did not seem to be offered consistently or systematically. Some people felt they had slipped through the net.

- Social work support after bereavement seemed to be offered in a more proactive and systematic way.

- Many service users would have valued earlier contact with the specialist palliative care social worker, even from the time of diagnosis. Problems were not being picked up in other parts of the medical system.

- Service users appreciated it when support was offered again after bereavement, even where they had previously refused it.

- Service users valued leaflets and other information which let them know that social work was available. Sometimes people turned to these when they felt at their most desperate.

- There was strong evidence that many people valued social work support even when they seemed to have strong support from their family and friends.

The social work assessment

- Service users reported that palliative care social workers did not carry out assessments in a formalized way. No service users referred to forms or checklists.

- Instead an emphasis was placed on building the relationship between specialist palliative care social worker and service user.

- Service users reported feelings of being at ease with the specialist palliative care social worker from the beginning and thus being able to talk about issues that were important to them.

- They felt that the specialist palliative care social worker had really listened to them.

- Service users felt able to determine their own agenda and having feelings of control over what happened.

- They reported that the social worker was able quickly to pick up on cues as to what type of help was appropriate even when the service user was overwhelmed and not necessarily able to articulate what he or she wanted.

- In some situations the social worker took control and used his or her authority to determine the agenda and make decisions. Service users appreciated this authority and believed it had been used appropriately.

- Service users were aware of assessment as being a continual process, not a one-off procedure, and support was seen as being provided hand in hand with assessment.

- Some service users felt that specialist palliative care social workers had not spelled out their role sufficiently and that they had not initially realized the breadth of role and what they should have been able to expect.

WHAT DOES THE SOCIAL WORKER DO?

We have already seen that most people don't seem to know much about what social work is and what social workers actually do. We asked service users to tell us what their contact with the specialist palliative care social worker had involved. What did the social workers *do*? Service users' accounts were enormously diverse. In this chapter we have sought to capture both the variety and range of work reflecting service users' experience.

We have also looked in more detail at the experience of some specific service users. We have not done this because there is anything special or unique about them. Instead we have tried to illustrate service users' individual pathways through palliative care social work. We have preceded each of these accounts with a brief description to explain why that particular example was chosen. Although these examples tell individual stories, they all address one or more of the general themes that service users highlighted in relation to their experience of specialist palliative care social work practice. In this way we have tried to communicate some sense of the process and detail as well as the range of specialist palliative care social work practice.

THE BREADTH OF SOCIAL WORK SUPPORT

After the service users we interviewed had told us their accounts of their experience in their own words, we went through a checklist with them to see if the specialist palliative care social worker had helped them in any other ways in addition to those that they had mentioned. Table 4.1, which displays these findings, applies to the 72 service users who were interviewed individually.

The social work intervention which service users most often reported was individual counselling and support. But many also received practical and financial advice and support. The social worker could touch on almost any aspect of service users' lives.

Table 4.1: Range of social work interventions reported by service users

Nature of intervention	Number of service users reporting this (N = 72)
Counselling/individual support	65
Support for family/friends/loved ones	38
Financial/benefits advice	35
Representation/advocacy	29
Liaison/referral to other organizations	29
Practical help	22
Support through groupwork	20

As shown in Table 4.2, the range of issues in which specialist palliative care social workers might intervene to offer help was truly sweeping. This ranged from coping with anxiety and dealing with neighbour disputes, to homelessness and breakdowns in the welfare benefits system.

Table 4.2: Range and nature of issues identified by service users

Issue identified by service users	Range and nature of issue
Coping with change and loss	Relating to physical illness and impairments, mental distress, loss of mobility, loss of independence, disfigurement, isolation, loss of hope, multiple losses, impending death, bereavement, past bereavements, panic attacks, agoraphobia, loneliness, sadness, guilt, anger, fear, eating distress, desire to be dead, suicidal thoughts
Family support	Sharing information within the family, supporting children, liaising with schools, meeting children's present and future care needs, family breaking down
Personal relationships	Supporting people facing major changes in relationships within marriage and partnership, with families and friends and loss of friendships during illness and post-bereavement; supporting people who had experienced abusive relationships

Continued on next page

Table 4.2 cont.

Issue identified by service users	Range and nature of issue
Medical issues	Brokering role between hospital, medical personnel and patient/family. Treatment issues, need for information on illness/diagnosis/prognosis, coping with (side) effects, fear of treatment, whether to continue, whether to take up treatment, living wills, referral to complementary therapies
Support needs	Assessing personal and social care needs, liaising with other team members, financing and arranging liaison with social/care services, reviewing, meeting unmet need. 'Carer's assessment' and support
Welfare benefits	Assessing rights and entitlements; giving information and advice on applications, appeals, dealing with system and bureaucratic breakdowns
Employment	Loss of employment and return to employment, voluntary work, negotiating time off for sickness or caring
Financial and legal matters	Insurance claims, bills, debts, charity applications, paying for care, income tax, power of attorney, wills
Housing	Adaptations, re-housing, threatened homelessness, homelessness, rents and mortgages, move to sheltered or residential accommodation
Leisure	Relaxation, hobbies, holidays, recreational activities, respite
Linking service users together	Arranging day care; facilitating patient, children's and adult bereavement groups; encouraging service user led initiatives
'Other' practical issues	Getting family back from abroad when someone is dying; dealing with neighbour disputes, transport issues, funeral arrangements

FIVE KEY THEMES

Five key themes relating to social work practice and the support it offered emerged in service users' comments. These themes are:

1. that emotional and practical help are inextricable

2. the importance of the help social workers offered in negotiating systems

3. the importance of the help social workers offered with medical matters

4. supporting family and friends

5. bringing service users together.

Emotional and practical help are inextricable

Service users were frequently receiving support with both emotional and practical matters. They frequently did not make any clear distinction between emotional and practical issues, often seeing them as intertwined.

> One of the main things for me was losing my driving licence, it was very hard... I'd had it for 17 years... I'd had it taken away...it was hard to deal with physically and mentally... [The social worker] helped me speak to the DVLA, she had a word with some of the medical staff here, and that was quite useful to help me mentally, but also to prepare me for getting it back... (Woman patient, white UK, age group 26–35)

Some service users said they hadn't realized until later that they were being 'counselled' at the same time as being helped with practical issues:

> without our knowing she was sort of counselling us at the same time...it wasn't forced... (Wife of a patient, white UK, age group 46–55)

Help negotiating systems

A key role that social workers played for service users was helping them negotiate the complicated health and welfare systems upon which they were reliant. Specialist palliative care social workers were seen to be both knowledge-able about systems and to be effective advocates for service users having to deal with complexity and bureaucracy.

> She [the social worker] has various contacts with different organizations and different groups. That has been quite useful...[providing] representa-tion...adding power to my requirements, reinforcing what I needed. (Man patient, British Pakistani, age group 19–25)

Help with medical matters

Social workers played a very active part in supporting service users with the medical aspects of their illness. At times this included making contact with the hospital to seek clarification or to explain service users' confusion.

> Because [my wife] was still in active treatment as well as being an occasional patient at the hospice, and there are constant differences about drugs and things, 26 million – there must have been 200 different opinions, you know about medication and things. So often they were quite a good brokering agent between us and [the hospital]. So that was an unexpected help really. (Bereaved man, white UK, age group 46–55)

Supporting family and friends

Social workers did not only seem to see their role in terms of supporting people facing life-limiting illnesses and those who were bereaved. They also offered support for loved ones and family members while in contact with the patient.

> My son had quite a lot of days off work – [the social worker] wrote a letter for him to take to his boss…because my son didn't want to leave his dad, you know, and he didn't want to leave me…they weren't very good about him having time off…they were really awful. (Bereaved woman, black Caribbean, age group 46–55)

Bringing service users together

Over a quarter of the people we spoke to said that the specialist palliative care social worker had put them in touch with other service users. There was evidence that contacts made in this way were very important for service users and in some cases they maintained these links for many years.

> She's encouraged me – now they had an open day up at the hospice and they said 'Come' and I said 'No', and she said 'Oh come on, do you want me to take you?' And she did! Now it did me the world of good going. It was during a period of me not seeing anyone…and she came and picked me up and took me. And I was thinking about that for ages afterwards, because I met all sorts of people I knew and it was wonderful. (Woman patient, white UK, age group 75+)

EXAMPLES OF PEOPLE'S EXPERIENCE

We are now going to illustrate these themes of what happens in specialist palliative care social work and what practice offers, through some particular examples. These also demonstrate some of the varied contexts within which specialist palliative care social work takes place. As we have said, these were not chosen because they are special in any way, rather because they illustrate different approaches to the work. They also highlight some problematic areas, which will be explored more fully later in the discussion chapters. All the names (service users and social workers) have been changed to ensure anonymity and confidentiality.

Mike and Linda

This example relates to a patient who had a long and very distressing illness characterized by delays in diagnosis, and very late referral for social work support. Problems that clearly involved a 'social' component did not trigger referral, although this might reasonably have been expected. There were already strongly established problems by the time of referral and Mike and Linda both felt quite desperate. Their experience highlights the dual emphasis that the social worker can place on providing both practical support and emotional support for the service user and their wider family. The scale of Mike and Linda's practical difficulties was high, with repossession of their home a possibility.

Their experience also shows the social worker taking a very active role in helping Mike cope with his medical condition by enabling him to get clear information regarding diagnosis/prognosis when he felt this was being denied to him. The social worker used her authority to challenge both medical professionals and other family members when communication difficulties were becoming apparent. This example shows the social worker to have personal resilience in the face of setbacks and to be able to use her 'self' in a supportive way, for example in her use of humour. Two potentially problematic areas emerge, namely the delays in accessing the specialist palliative care social worker at the outset and the particular issues that can arise in working directly with teenagers.

MIKE AND LINDA'S STORY

Mike is a patient in the age group 46–55. He has cancer. His specialist palliative care social worker is based in an NHS hospital team. At his request, Mike was interviewed in his own home with his wife Linda. They have grown-up children and one son who is still at school. They both knew the social worker well at the time of the interview as she had been working with them for about a year. Mike was still receiving active treatment at the time of the interview but his health was poor. As he described it:

> I'm normally five days ill, six days ill and one day a good day, I mean I just don't know when I'm going to be good.

Mike spoke about the difficulties he had experienced in getting the support he needed in the first year of his illness. He believed he had initially been wrongly diagnosed and he was still clearly very distressed about this.

> [M]y doctor was treating me for nine months with a big infection of the prostate which it wasn't. And I kept going back week after week...saying no, this is wrong because it shouldn't be happening like that. I couldn't sit, I couldn't lay, I mean it was ridiculous...and basically I kept asking him to sign me off because I'm self-employed, and he kept saying to me we'll try these stronger pain killers and antibiotics.

Finally his cancer was diagnosed, but he described how the delays continued.

> I should have started it [chemotherapy] in January but I didn't start until May because there was apparently a mix-up, someone lost the files or whatever... I went back [into hospital] four times in that period and I was really ill at the time because obviously the thing was getting worse.

All this time Mike was not earning any money and his difficulties were mounting up.

> We was in a wreck to be honest with you...obviously it was affecting the family and as I say we was in financial problems.

We asked Mike if anyone at the hospital had ever suggested that he see one of the social workers. This was never suggested. Instead he told us:

> they said to me 'You need to see a Macmillan nurse'...but it never materialized...

Mike went on to tell us how his wife had felt so desperate that she attempted suicide:

> it's only lucky that one of my elder sons popped home on his lunchtime...he found her...

He described his desperation at that point:

> because of my wife doing what she did, you know and I was so frightened and you know specially being ill myself, I thought how can I leave her at any time and you know obviously I had to because I had to be in hospital...

Mike told a hospital doctor about Linda's suicide attempt and at that point he was told:

> [W]e'll get a social worker.

Even then things were not all plain sailing as the actual contact took four weeks to arrange. Mike and Linda were told repeatedly that the social worker wasn't available and they felt fobbed off.

> I felt I was being really let down.

They never really understood why that delay happened, but once contact was established both Mike and Linda felt they had received enormous support.

> [S]he's been absolutely brilliant for us, honestly I mean it...she actually listens to what we tell her...basically she helped us, like I say as a friend.

Mike identified a wide range of ways in which the social worker had supported them. She had given practical help. For example Mike said that he had feared that they were going to lose their home because of escalating mortgage arrears and the specialist palliative care social worker had helped them sort this out, in a very hands-on way.

> She come down, she had a meeting with one of the mortgage advisers...to be honest with you if it hadn't been for her I wouldn't have known what to do...

Similarly, she had guided them on benefit claims and had secured a grant from a charitable trust. They saw the social worker as being there for the whole family. Linda said she felt enormously supported:

> Yeah, I don't think I'm doing this on my own, I've got somebody else here to help me...

The social worker regularly saw their teenage son during her home visits, but she had also offered him one-to-one time with her, away from the home setting; an offer that, although it was refused, was very much appreciated by Mike and Linda. The specialist palliative care social worker had seen that the wider family were not pulling together and that tensions were building.

> [S]he come round one night to actually talk to the family about the boys helping and she stayed here till about eight o'clock and that's way past her time...

Mike and Linda did not know what was discussed as the confidentiality of the family members was respected, but they felt that tensions were eased and they appreciated the flexibility of the social worker in meeting at a time of day that helped the family actually get together to address issues that had been avoided before.

Mike and Linda referred to several other occasions when the social worker had helped them resolve strains within their own relationship; Mike referred to one occasion when the stress of the illness had led to a row:

> normally if I have a row with the wife I won't speak to her for a week or something, and next day she'd [the social worker] come round and she'd make sure we had a cuddle... I wouldn't have done that otherwise to be honest with you...

Linda adds:

> [S]he don't shout, she don't holler, she explains and she puts it in such a way as you think, well yeah, you're right.

They both appreciated the way the social worker used humour in these situations, lightening the atmosphere.

> [N]ow and again she'd come out with a joke and she makes us laugh and it eases yeah, you know.

But they also found that she could deal with their anger in a resilient and supportive way, when it directly spilled over on to their relationship with her. Linda recalled an occasion when in a particularly unhappy mood she told the social worker to 'piss off':

> she's not took offence or anything has she, she goes 'Okay, fine, phone you tomorrow...'

In a similar vein the social worker was not deterred when Linda, in a distressed state, told her not to visit one day. The social worker called at the house anyway.

> Yeah, out of her own bat because she was concerned, she was worried and she come up, knocked on the door, 'Are you going to let me in?' 'No!' 'Why not?'…'I just don't need to speak to you.' 'Okay, bye and I'll phone you tomorrow'…

Linda went on to say:

> I didn't feel irritated by it. I felt, not comforted, but reassured that someone was there that cared, that was spending the time to come down and make sure that I was okay.

Another prime role played by the specialist palliative care social worker was to enable Mike and Linda to find out information about the extent of Mike's illness. He had felt that at times he had not been told the truth and had been given false reassurances, which contradicted information given him by other consultants. He felt that his need to know what was happening to him was being ignored.

> She come up in a meeting with Dr —, myself, my wife, and his understudy, you know basically she was there to support us and to get things right… 'What is happening? Why do you keep saying to him yes you've got cancer, no you haven't got cancer?' …I mean basically she was there to get to the truth.

Linda added:

> It was nice to have her there because you felt you was on your own fighting against the system with no back-up and she knew the questions to ask, where we didn't, and she didn't push or she didn't probe, she listened and then she went, 'Well, don't you want to ask Dr — this?'…

Mike and Linda had never been asked for any formal evaluation of the specialist palliative care social work service. They hadn't been concerned about this as they had felt the experience had been very positive. We asked what, in the light of their own experiences, they felt would be helpful in training new social workers.

Linda felt:

> They've got to care about people…and knowing the family, you know getting to know the family not just…you're not a number, you're people you know…and obviously the first three, four, five visits to getting to know them, know what road to tread on and what way to go.

Fred

We chose Fred's example because it shows a specialist palliative care social worker working with a bereaved person using a completely different approach, where much of the actual support is provided by other service users with profes-sional back-up available should it be needed. The social worker's role here is more that of facilitator and enabler, bringing service users together and developing an environment and conditions so that they can interact. It also illustrates the social worker working collaboratively with other workers, including volunteers to provide a service. The emphasis here is on a 'hands-off' rather than the 'hands-on' approach seen in the first example. It is nevertheless clear that the social worker is perceived as being a very solid support.

Fred's example shows how he, in collaboration with other service users, has been enabled to rebuild a network of support for himself, a network that he could draw on into the future. It also demonstrates very clearly a positive outcome for this service user who has gone from deep distress, to very affirmative feelings about working in a voluntary role in the community supporting others, a role that clearly brings great satisfaction. But the example also highlights two potentially problematic areas for service users. These are the difficulties associated with moving on from a support group, and the daunting task of mustering the courage to join the group in the first place. Again, we see that referral for support happened only *after* bereavement.

FRED'S STORY

Fred is a widowed man in his late seventies. His wife died in a hospice in the north of England where she had been an inpatient for the ten days prior to her death from cancer. The couple had had some help prior to her death from a local day unit attached to a hospital, but the care seems to have been focused on his wife and Fred had not been much involved. Fred has one adult child and before his retirement he had worked in a managerial job.

After his wife's death Fred received a letter from the specialist palliative care social worker at the hospice inviting him to a fortnightly meeting with other bereaved people.

> I came down, but it took me about a month to come in…well I got to the door and I was, you know, I just couldn't push myself through the door, I suppose I was scared more than anything.

Fred did eventually take the plunge and began to attend regularly and found it very helpful.

> [F]rom there it got better and better and better until now I'm just with a circle of friends; most of the friends we had when my wife was alive seem frightened of me now.

Fred had known little about social workers prior to meeting the hospice social worker.

> [T]he view I had of social workers…they looked after children that had been abandoned and things like that, I didn't realize it extended to this type of treatment. I'd never been involved with them.

We asked Fred what his views were about the way he first had contact with the social worker. He told us about receiving the letter and that he knew he needed support from someone.

> I don't know what I should have done or where I should have been if it hadn't been for Marie and company because, well I'd gone to pieces you see entirely. And I suppose at the time, I was just clutching at straws, I didn't realize how strong the straws were.

We asked him how was it decided what Marie, the social worker, would do to help him. He said that there hadn't been any formal assessment.

> [T]here was nothing decided really, if I needed help it was up to me to ask... I thought it was the right thing to do, rather than them to be pushing at me all the time, let me go to them when I needed it you know...

The group met fortnightly and lasted for about two hours. As well as the social worker there were other 'helpers' there including a retired medical consultant. Fred would often talk to one of these people outside the group:

> that's what they come for, they're only too pleased to do it. We're pleased they are there.

He told us that it was also always possible to speak to Marie on a one-to-one basis if he wanted to after the group. After the meeting Fred told us that members of the group would go out for lunch:

> about eight to ten go out and we go to the pub across the road, we have a glass of beer in there and a jacket potato or something. That goes on from half past twelve till two o'clock...and we just sit talking.

> [S]everal of the ladies go out shopping together and go on holidays together.

Fred had been going to the fortnightly group for just over a year when we spoke to him and he knew that at some point he would be asked to move on to another group that met monthly. Fred acknowledged that people needed to move on:

> there are only so many spaces here in this group, the fortnightly group, and people dying every day of course you know people have got to come in.

But he admitted to anxiety over this move.

> It's a big break to try and go to another group and leave half of them behind. If you moved as a group it wouldn't hurt...

Fred was able to say that the new people joining:

> are like I was when I first came here. They need it, where we, while we think we need it, what we do need is the friendship, I think that sums it up.

We asked Fred what was the most helpful thing about his contact with Marie. He told us that it was:

knowing she was there.

And:

if I've asked any of them a question they've always answered it and they've answered it until I was satisfied with the answer you know.

Fred told us that he had never been asked to give feedback on the specialist palliative care social work service and he didn't particularly mind about this.

[T]he only thing I could say was how good they've been you know, that's all I could have said…if they asked me half a dozen times, that is all I could say…what she is doing is so good for me, I wouldn't like to criticize her.

At the end of the interview we asked Fred whether there was anything else he would like to say…anything that felt important to him. He said:

Well only that I've got this part-time job which I feel is very satisfying, because I'm helping unfortunate people and after my wife died I didn't feel there was any purpose in life. But since I've done this job I know there is, I feel the help I give other people is like the help Marie gives me, it's just you know a different person.

A structured bereavement group

We chose this example as it illustrates a very different kind of groupwork. One of the discussion groups that took part in our project was made up of five people: three men and two women who had originally met about three and a half years earlier at a bereavement group which had run for seven sessions. Nine members of the original bereavement group had continued to meet at each other's homes on a monthly basis. Taking part in our discussion group were Brian (age group 46–55), whose wife had died in the hospice aged 47 (Brian had also lost a young son some years previously); Martin (age group 49–55), whose wife had also died there and who had also lost a teenage daughter to cancer some years earlier; Maisie (age group 56–65), whose husband had died of motor neurone disease (MND); Beryl (age group 66–75), whose husband had died of cancer four years previously after 48 years of marriage; and Richard (age group 75+), whose wife had died of cancer. They had been married over 40 years.

We have included this example because it illustrates well the long-term impact a specialist palliative care social worker can have by bringing service users together and helping them get to know each other in a safe and supported way. Unlike the group Fred attended, which was open and unstructured, this group was a closed, time-limited group with a structured agenda led by a specialist palliative care social worker and a social work assistant. This example tells us something of what went on during the group sessions, but more than that demonstrates the continuing impact of the social work intervention long after the social worker had withdrawn from the group. It also highlights how individuals often have to grapple with multiple losses in their lives and the different levels of support they may receive in the face of these losses. Like Fred and many other people who talked about groupwork, we see how difficult it was for some of these service users to join the group in the first place. We also learn that one of the members of the original bereavement group had not found it so helpful. This person had lost a parent rather than a spouse like the others and had felt awkward in the group.

Our process notes record how satisfying it was to meet with this group of people and to witness the obvious affection, warmth and mutual support between them, particularly in the way they spoke about the two older men who were not there on the day of the discussion but who still met with them regularly. They laughed and joked together a great deal and it was easy to see the trust they had built up in each other. It was clear that from that initial bereavement group they had gone on to develop a network of friendships that were enduring and which had become, over time, immensely sustaining as the members faced new changes and transitions in their lives.

THE ONGOING STORY OF THE BEREAVEMENT GROUP

Interviewer: …[S]o when did you first meet with or talk to a specialist palliative care social worker?

Beryl: Not until we were invited here [to the bereavement group].

Maisie: …[I]t was about six months afterwards wasn't it?

Richard: Well in your case, I think in mine it was about seven months.

Brian: In my case it was sort of ten months after the event so I had quite a long time to get used to the idea.

Only Martin had had the opportunity to meet the social worker before the death of his loved one and then only briefly, although he had found it very helpful. Martin explained that his wife had refused to let their teenage children visit her in the hospice during her final illness and Martin found that extremely distressing and did not know how to handle the situation. He spoke at length to the social worker:

well I'd seen her probably three or four times in the afternoon and [my wife] died about one o'clock in the morning so she spoke to me for hours.

He described the social worker's support in those hours as being 'very important'. It also enabled him to make the decision to let the children see their mother before she died – a decision that he felt had been the right one for them all.

We asked the service users what they had felt when the letter arrived inviting them back to the hospice for the bereavement group. All had found this a difficult invitation and had felt uncertain about accepting it.

> Beryl: Well I know how I felt, I thought I couldn't...

> Maisie: Yes that's how I felt, in fact I asked my doctor, I said you know, should I or shouldn't I go – and the district nurse who had nursed my husband – and they said 'Yes, you should go'. It took about, oh, at least ten days for me to make up my mind...

> Beryl: My daughter...she persuaded me, she came up from the house and brought me here...it was so important.

> Richard: The first time I received that letter I didn't do anything about it, I didn't follow it up...

Some of the service users felt that the first meeting of the group was very difficult.

> Beryl: It was traumatic, the first meeting was...

But Brian, who had previously lost his young son, saw it in a different way:

> I thought I could probably contribute more because I'd coped with the worst thing you can possibly cope with you know... I couldn't sit down doing nothing could I?

Brian referred to the death of his son several times. Having got through that experience, without any professional support, he felt he had learned something about his own strengths and he felt able to offer support to others facing intense losses. Martin also remembered the lack of support he had experienced when his teenage daughter was ill and dying with cancer. This had been in the 1970s.

> Nothing offered at all...the wife was suicidal.

While people found that first meeting of 14 strangers very daunting, we were told that the specialist palliative care social worker and the assistant helped things along.

> Maisie: ...[T]hey were both very kind and I don't know, just put us at our ease and we were very tearful and very quiet to start with but...

> Richard: ...[H]er voice was one thing, she has a very kind and quietly spoken voice, now that impressed me and put me – it quietened me when I was very upset...but not like a condescending vicar, not an authoritarian sort of person...

> Beryl: She's got a very nice personality and that's very important I
>   think...

Richard appreciated the matter-of-fact way that the social worker had spoken to them.

> It's practical and unsentimental. I'd summarize it as what we needed and
> what we got from her... I was taking it for granted that she was sorry, you
> know that she was sorry but it wasn't made a lot of and the main thing was to
> get on to the next stage. And I think that's what you need at that stage, you
> need to progress.

Brian added:

> you see she's not frightened to talk about something, but a lot of people
> wouldn't talk about somebody that's died.

Not every member of the original group had been put at their ease. They recalled the difficulties faced by one woman, who had later withdrawn.

> Richard: [O]ne lady felt sort of ashamed that she was there because
>   her mother, her old mother, had died and she felt that we
>   had more reason and we tried to encourage her to keep on
>   coming but she eventually, she didn't come any more...

We asked what had actually happened during the group, what kinds of things had been discussed.

> Richard: I've got some notes that I made because I had to take notes
>   because my memory is so bad...she sort of went through
>   different aspects of bereavement: loneliness, being different
>   from others in the age group, and whether you ever laugh or
>   think it's unseemly to laugh; socially difficult to mix with
>   others; negative aspects of bereavement, of a new life;
>   practical jobs that have to be done that used to be done by
>   the other partner; how can I face 30 years like this and time
>   and waiting; other people who are around you...and so on.
>   ...and she covered a whole lot of things that are very
>   good to talk about...she discussed pain and displacement
>   activities, you know what you can do to sort of allay pain
>   and working through it, talking about it, what you feel and
>   the support you have from others. And then she asked and
>   discussed the Christian dimension for those that are
>   Christians, or have a religious aspect of it. And what phone
>   calls do for you whether you immediately get frightened
>   when the phone rings and you wonder what you are going
>   to have to face...physical and spiritual aspects, joining
>   causes...new activities or hobbies...all these things were
>   very well thought out I think... It's important to trigger off

aspects that we hadn't thought of discussing, and when she triggered them off we discussed them and learned something.

One thing she brought out...she very delicately explored whether we were on good terms with the person who had passed away...

Beryl: ...[S]he hasn't got a strict format as you say, but she guided us, she suggested things and guided us along in these discussions.

Richard: Yes, a very good chairwoman because she didn't dominate the proceedings...

Brian: I think in actual fact we probably are more experienced now and could probably help people in our situation...if there's another group started we could probably do more for that group now than anybody else because we've experienced it first-hand you see.

We asked members of the group whether they felt that it had been more helpful meeting as a group rather than if they had met the social worker individually. All agreed that it had been.

Beryl: Oh, I think so...yes because you've got the support of each other...

Brian: Well everybody's in the same boat virtually.

Martin had also seen the social worker individually after his wife's death and said it had been 'very helpful'.

The beginning of the group had been difficult and in a completely different way so was the ending.

Beryl: Well we didn't want to part up, we persuaded Elaine [the social worker] to have an extra session.

The group talked about the contact they had had with each other since that last meeting, how they organized it and how it had helped them.

Maisie: We do it once a month...yes, every month we swap houses... Richard orchestrates it...

Brian: I am the taxi driver...for this lot...

Maisie: Oh he takes us all over.

Two members of the group who were not present at the discussion but who still met regularly with the others had become partners.

Beryl: …[Y]es they palled up, bought a house together and live together…they were both working so they couldn't come today.

For the others the impact of the group had been less dramatic but nevertheless very important.

Richard: Well we look after each other, if someone's in a bit of trouble we help out and all that sort of thing.

Beryl: Brian comes over and does a lot in my garden for me.

Loneliness was mentioned as a real problem for some of the group members.

Maisie: I still do feel very lonely over a weekend…

Beryl: It's very lonely is the weekend – I still find it very lonely.

Brian talked about how he has tried to get Beryl out of the house and she agreed:

Beryl: You've got me out yes.

Maisie: Beryl's only just up around the corner and if I'm at a loose end I can give her a buzz and say 'Are you in, can I come in for a chat?'

Two older men also continued to meet with the group. They were both in their late eighties and one of them – Bill – was now living in a residential home.

The group talked about the support that Martin gave to the two men, shopping every week.

Beryl: Oh yes, we love our old men…very sorry but oh yes we love them dearly… [Martin] is always keeping in touch with Bill and going to visit him…

The group felt there was no reason why they would stop meeting in the future. They told us that they seldom talked about their bereavements any more though they knew they could if they wanted to. They were now more likely to talk about events and changes in their current lives. Maisie was soon to have her 60th birthday and would be facing retirement. She spoke of her apprehension about the changes her birthday would bring, but the group planned to meet in her house that day and she felt this would help.

Maisie: …[I]t's a friendship thing…

Doreen

FAMILY WORK

This example illustrates family work. We have also chosen it because it concerns a service user who lives with a long-term deteriorating condition and highlights some of the difficulties this raises. It shows the specialist palliative care social worker working with the whole family. It also demonstrates the appropriateness of the social worker's role continuing when the patient has been discharged from other parts of the palliative care service.

DOREEN'S STORY

Doreen is a white UK woman in the age group 36–45. She was referred to the hospice for pain management, but while she was on the inpatient unit of the hospice she had a relapse:

> I lost the use of my legs, there was a lot of emotional trauma for me.

She first met the specialist palliative care social worker when she was in the unit. She was referred by the ward nurses. She had never known any social workers before.

> I didn't know what I was getting into, but at the time I needed help with my emotions, it was just getting on top of me, I was feeling quite withdrawn... I didn't know who to turn to... I hadn't had any dealings with social workers before.

Doreen had found meeting the specialist palliative care social worker very easy.

> The approach was very gentle...she was very easy to talk to, very easy to talk to...she's like a best friend who you can tell all your problems to...a very approachable person to talk to... I don't have any recollections of uneasiness.

We asked Doreen how it was decided what the social worker would do.

> It was talked over one to one, what would I like, how would I like to proceed with this. It was more of a joint decision...everything has always been a negotiated decision.

Initially the social worker saw Doreen on a weekly basis on her own but after a little while she saw Doreen jointly with her husband and teenage daughter. At first they met in the family home, but it was felt that meetings might be more helpful in the larger space offered by the hospice. It was possible for the seating to be arranged more helpfully there.

> I feel Carol [the social worker] is managing to address an awful lot of my problems, making me deal with my problems, whereas before I would just shut them off and not really deal with them. She's making me more aware that I need to deal with my problems not just push them away to the back

because then they just eat away at my self-esteem. It has made me stronger in myself, and made me say things to my family that I would not normally have said.

Doreen was asked what she felt were the chief strengths of the social work she had received; what had been most valuable. This is what she said:

> She has made me a more stable person, she has made me a much stronger person, I feel at ease now saying what I feel... I am much more able to accept that my condition is not a punishment, whereas I did feel that it was a punishment and...I felt I put a lot of constraint on the family... It has made me realize it is not just my fault.
>
> I don't feel as if I'm running away now...

Doreen felt the biggest weakness in the service was the limited amount of time the social worker was able to spend with her.

> It was just an hour [each time] and we could have done with more...that was the only weakness... Now on reflection I can see that you can only deal with so much at one time...but at the time...

We asked whether Doreen had any ideas that might be helpful when training new palliative care social workers, and found she would have been happy to help in the training of students.

> I wouldn't have minded someone else coming in and listening, not taking part just listening...otherwise how does a social worker learn how to approach someone?

We asked whether the work the social worker had done with Doreen had ever been formally evaluated. Doreen said that she had never been asked to give feedback.

> Not about the social worker, no I haven't... I think an appraisal system...so that the social worker knows that she is achieving her goals [would be helpful]...because otherwise you don't know that the work has been effective.

She went on to say:

> I just think the service offered here is very good... I can ring Carol, whenever I've got a problem I know I can just ring and if she is not there, she will ring me back as soon as she can. It's been quite helpful, there have been various occasions when there have been problems with my daughter and she has always been there.
>
> I have been discharged from the rest of the hospice now; Carol is all I need.

SUMMARY

One of the most striking findings to emerge in this chapter from what service users said was the enormous range of issues that people took to their social worker and the apparent willingness of the social workers to listen to very varied concerns. Most people wanted help with both emotional and practical/financial matters and the two emerged as closely interlocked. The support from the social worker was frequently extended to family and friends as well as to the patient or bereaved person. Much of the work involved liaison with external agencies, and the social workers had extensive knowledge of other resources and groups. Advocacy was a central part of the work. It was also clear that social workers were able to use varied approaches, with individual, group and family work all evident.

Four particular examples were explored in more depth which highlight key approaches to practice referred to by service users. These individual examples also show up some problematical areas. These include late referral for specialist palliative care social work; supporting teenagers who may not be keen on one-to-one work; difficulties in helping service users join and leave groups in a way that feels positive and comfortable; and difficulties for service users who were in a minority position in a groupwork setting.

Some service users made it clear that they perceived support coming not just from the social worker and the broader palliative care team but also from each other. This support was particularly important for some, as it was not formally limited and 'boundaried' in the same way as the professional support. If service users chose it could, for example, go on into the future and, as the third example in this chapter demonstrated, it was sustaining to some service users even years later.

CHAPTER 5

WHAT SERVICE USERS VALUE MOST

We wanted to explore with service users what they found most helpful in the way that specialist palliative care social workers worked with them. As we have seen, social workers worked in many different ways and individual service users have particular preferences. However, as service users offered their accounts and ideas, some strong themes emerged about what they valued the most. These fell into three overall headings, which related to:

1. The quality of the relationship between service user and social worker.

2. The personal qualities of the social worker.

3. The nature and process of the work with service users.

Although for the sake of clarity we have organized what service users said under these separate headings, the headings need to be seen as interlinked and over-lapping in reality. The nature of the relationship with the specialist palliative care social worker was often closely allied to the way in which the service user perceived his or her personal qualities. Sometimes it was difficult to distinguish between what was a personal quality and what was a skill or a strategy being used in the process of intervention with the service user. These three facets or themes in the social work service that users described need to be seen as in complex relation with each other.

THE QUALITY OF THE RELATIONSHIP WITH THE SOCIAL WORKER

Service users described a number of distinct issues under this heading. All of these highlighted the central importance that the *relationship* with the social worker played in their experience of social work.

Prioritizing a positive relationship

Service users repeatedly spoke of how they valued a strong bond with the social worker:

> They may have the skill but they have to bond as well, there has to be that trust and that relationship... (Man patient, white UK, 50 years old)

At one of the steering groups the importance of relationship building was stressed as important and this was seen as lacking in the group members' current experience of dealing with non-specialist social workers:

> Just fill that form – you should be all right – bye-bye – signed and finished, back in the file. (Member of steering group)

The link with friendship

Friendship was seen as an important component of the relationship with the social worker. Service users repeatedly used the word *friend* when they were describing the specialist palliative care social worker. This was true across both sexes, and across all age groups. For example:

> I was looking forward to her coming as a friend, I felt I could talk to her about anything, I wouldn't need to watch my tongue... I had complete confidence in her, complete confidence. (Bereaved woman, white European, age group 75+)

> It was just like speaking with friends right from day one, and it just couldn't have been any better. (Woman patient, white UK, 67 years old)

> We are talking about a friend. We don't see her as a social worker. (Woman service user in discussion group)

Another woman in the same discussion group drew a similar distinction between friend and social worker:

> She's not just a social worker, she's like a friend, you know she hasn't got this habit of hop it, I'm a social worker, she's got something different about her you know. (Woman service user in discussion group)

This man spoke in very similar terms about his social worker:

> looking back now I don't class her as a social worker, I class her as a friend to be honest with you... Because like I say, she's been absolutely brilliant for us, honestly I mean it. (Man patient, white UK, age group 46–55)

His wife added:

> she's not dictating to you, she's there for you to ask her questions and she's giving you the answers. And in the meantime the friendliness is coming through, you know it is hard to explain, but yeah I feel very comfortable with her.

In slightly different vein, another bereaved person, a father of young children, told us:

> My children regard [the social worker] as being one of the family. That might not be an entirely professional way to regard her, but none the less that's the kind of impact it's had. (Bereaved man, white UK, age group 46–55)

The importance of reciprocity

Closely linked to the notion of friendship was the concept of *reciprocity*. This was important to some service users. We were frequently told that service users felt that they wanted the relationship with the social worker and the hospice to be a two-way process.

> I look upon her, to be perfectly honest, as a friend I can talk to. And when I was doing it, that's how I hoped they would look on me. (Woman patient, white UK, in her eighties)

Some people said that they liked to know a little bit about the social worker and their life. For example:

> it seemed unfair to tell [the specialist palliative care social worker] everything about me. I wanted to say well how are you today?…and you know I wanted to, she was much more of a friend, than, as time went on but also she was still my counsellor, you know she still kept the professional situation, yeah. (Woman patient, white UK, age group 26–35)

Or people felt that they wanted to give something back to the social worker or the hospice in return for what they had received. This man felt an enormous sense of gratitude to the social worker and the hospice; he felt they had helped save him from suicide.

> I said to [the specialist palliative care social worker] that I'd love to be able to pay something back in some kind of way that would be beneficial to the hospice to thank them for what they have done for me. So now…I help them out with the friendship group, which going by feedback that we are getting, seems to be working pretty well. But without the help of the hospice I know for a fact that I wouldn't be here. (Bereaved man, white UK, age group 46–55)

Flexible professional boundaries

Service users gave many examples of how their specialist palliative care social worker had 'gone that extra mile'. In some cases they seemed to be saying that the social worker had gone beyond their expectations of a person in a paid role and relationship. This had been much valued. It appeared that the social workers might be interpreting their professional boundaries in a flexible way to meet specific needs. Such flexibility was appreciated by service users. There were, for example, comments about social workers working out of their normal office hours.

> Sometimes she was going out at nine o'clock at night when she should have gone at six. (Widowed woman, white UK, 71 years old)

One man spoke about the time that the specialist palliative care social worker visited in the evening to see his young children, when one of the family cats had died, not long after the death of his wife:

and [the social worker] came and, you know, talked to the kids about it that evening…and when my dad died, and my older son was in a terrible state, she came that night as well, at nine o'clock. So pretty impressive support really. And I'm sure she would do that for everyone…that's the person she is. (Bereaved man, white UK, age group 46–55)

There were comments about social workers sharing their own feelings:

We've cried together, we've laughed together. (Bereaved woman, white UK, 71 years old)

Many people talked about the social worker laughing and joking with them and it was evident that this lighter side of the relationship was appreciated.

And then we would have had a good wee giggle and laugh. (Bereaved woman, white UK, age group 66–75)

Several service users mentioned being hugged by their social workers, the wife of a patient told us:

She'll give us a hug and that does for me, an awful lot.

Her husband went on to add:

She's genuine, honestly I think she genuinely cares about you. (Man patient, white UK, age group 46–55)

Another service user, a 70-year-old bereaved man, felt that touch was a vital part of the social worker's repertoire, in some situations more important than words.

If you go to someone and they are really down, if you just touch them, you see, you don't say much, you just touch them and say anything – it doesn't matter. They'll feel better, because you've made contact…you're not an official who's just coming with a board to write on, and that's it, you've actually touched them…it's really important, absolutely important, you see. (Bereaved man who had lost his wife, white UK, 70 years old)

This service user expressed a very similar view:

It's the approach…you need somebody to, say, give me a hug. Maybe that sounds very personal, but I think a hug is a very important aspect. (Bereaved woman, white UK, age group 75+)

No one mentioned finding hugging uncomfortable or inappropriate; in fact one woman told us that her social worker *doesn't do hugs* and she was sorry about this, as she would have appreciated a hug from the social worker whose support she prized highly.

I think with experience you can tell, you know, that it's not appropriate to give a hug and yet at other times it is appropriate…it can make such a big difference…one of the nurses there she gives you a big welcome and a big hug and it makes your day for the rest of the day. It doesn't matter how down you're feeling, it makes you feel really good. You're somebody…somebody wants to touch and hug you…because I've always felt…dirty and smelly…because of my stoma…somebody actually saying no you're not and able to give you a hug it means something. (Woman patient, white UK, age group 46–55)

THE PERSONAL QUALITIES OF THE SOCIAL WORKER

Many of the service users believed that the personal qualities of the specialist palliative care social worker had been a decisive factor in determining the success of the social work intervention with them. This comment summed up many more comments:

I can't speak any [more] highly of her because she's just fantastic really, probably the person but also the role, mainly the person. (Woman patient, white UK, age group 26–35)

Service users raised two related issues in their comments about the personal qualities of specialist palliative care social workers. They stressed the kind of qualities they valued and how they saw these relating to the 'kind of person' the social worker was. Service users emphasized human qualities of kindness, warmth, compassion, caring, sensitivity, empathy and thoughtfulness. These were frequently mentioned as vital qualities in the social workers who had worked with them. The following comments were typical:

It's her caring and understanding. That's what most people need. And her kindness and putting herself out to help. (Woman patient, white UK, age group 56–65)

I felt right from the word go that she cared. (Woman patient, white UK, in her eighties)

She's extremely sensitive and extremely open to people's circumstances, very sensitive… (Woman patient, white UK, age group 46–55)

Sometimes service users described their specialist palliative care social worker as demonstrating a caring nature but in fact what they experienced could also have been interpreted as helpful strategies or skills.

[My husband] died the last year in May and the day before I got a lovely card from [the social worker] to say 'I know this is a difficult time for you but if you want me you know you have just have to give me a call and I'll be there'. Is that not nice? I was so touched I had that card on the mantelpiece for about a fortnight, it was so thoughtful. (Bereaved woman, white European, age group 75+)

> [A]nd when I was in hospital and had a big operation [the social worker] turns up when I was feeling low with me bunch of flowers and visited me. (Woman service user in group discussion)

Another woman in the same discussion group added:

> And if you are ill she don't forget about you, she'll even come to your house, comes to your house, she's just got that kind of personality.

This man, talking in a discussion group with other bereaved people, recalled how he had felt the social worker's manner had put him at ease:

> [H]er voice was one thing. She's a very kind and quietly spoken voice, now that impressed me and put me – it quietened me – when I was very upset.

He went on to add that she was *practical and unsentimental*.

Many of the service users told us that they did not see the personal qualities of the specialist palliative care social worker as being something that could be learned. They thought that the person had a nature and personality that suited the work they were doing. Thus they thought that such valued social worker qualities were part of the person, rather than something that they had gained from training.

> I just felt she was a nice person. (Widowed woman, white European, age group 75+)

THE NATURE AND PROCESS OF THE WORK WITH SERVICE USERS

There was great consistency among service users in what they valued about the nature and process of the social work that they experienced. This was the case across different categories of service user. It also seemed to be true regardless of the particular service setting involved or the social work method or approach employed. Taken together service users' comments suggest that they valued a sensitive, participative and responsive model of social work practice. This was reflected in a range of issues that they highlighted.

Being able to determine their own agenda and work in partnership

Working in partnership with the specialist palliative care social worker and having a sense of control over the whole process emerged as very important to many service users. Both those service users who had seen the social worker on a one-to-one basis and those who had taken part in groups felt they had had a real say in the process. These comments were typical of many others:

> First service user: She hasn't got a strict format...but she guided us, she suggested things and guided us along in these discussions.

> Second service user: Yeah, a very good chairwoman because she didn't dominate the proceedings…(Man and woman in group discussion of people who were bereaved)

> She always asks you what do you hope to gain today in our meeting…so that you can have the chance to say… You're making a decision of where we are going and that's what I like… (Woman patient, white UK, age group 46–55)

> She doesn't take a particular course of action or whatever, without first talking about it, and then she asks me if that is what I want to do… [I am] consulted and there is communication… (Man patient, UK Asian, age group 19–25)

> [S]he always said it's what you want, I'm only guiding you, but it's what you want…it's what we think, or what pleases us, or what we feel we should have. (Woman patient, white UK, 84 years old)

> That's what's nice, it's being part of it, not sort of dragged along. (Man patient, white UK, age group 36–45)

> We discussed everything from my childhood to everything and she never even turned round and told me what to do, but she always managed to point me in the right direction, so that I could find the answer myself – if you can understand. (Man patient, white UK, age group 46–55)

> If I don't want to go down a line, they don't go down that line. It's as simple as that, it's what I want. (Man patient, white UK, age group 46–55)

> The thing about any medical intervention…is it's something [that] is done to you… If you are going through a process of counselling it's done with you…that's the difference. (Woman patient, Jewish, age group 56–65)

Some patients made it clear that not being directed by the social worker was not the same as being left directionless.

> She does direct kind of thing, otherwise I'd just witter for hours… If I had an issue…if you can imagine it like a big kind of ball of string – excuse the metaphor – and she just slowly kind of untangles it and divides a bit off, bits off, so that I talk about little bits, and it all kind of comes together. It's kind of like that. So it is kind of directed, but it's not in a forceful way. (Bereaved woman, white UK, 18 years old)

Someone to listen

The role of the social worker as a listener was crucial for many service users. This capacity to listen was valued in its own right. It was also important that the social worker took what the service user said as a starting point for what they did in their contact with them. For instance:

The strengths were that there was somebody there to listen to you and to help you, yeah listen, not advise you. (Bereaved man, white UK, in discussion group)

[J]ust listen to you, whatever you know , your problems are or how you feel, she'll be at your side...but they just sit and listen. And that helped me, having somebody offering to listen to me. (Bereaved service user commenting in discussion group)

She was just prepared to listen, she listened basically and where she felt that she needed to give some counselling, advice, whatever, she would offer it to me but she wouldn't force it on me. (Woman patient, black UK, age group 26–35)

Having an accepting, non-judgemental attitude

Service users found it extremely helpful to be able to express their feelings and for these to be validated, without the specialist palliative care social worker adopting a judgemental attitude.

[S]he made it okay for me to have the feelings that I was having. When I felt frustrated she made it acceptable that I was frustrated; when I was disappointed or upset or tearful, she made it acceptable. (Woman patient, white UK, age group 26–35)

She just never judged me for anything you know. I told her some horrible things, that you do in your life and there just wasn't the judgement there and there wasn't the 'oh you poor lad or you naughty lad'...you felt you were talking to someone that wasn't forming an opinion good or bad about you, it was just straightforward. (Man patient, white UK, age group 46–55)

Being treated respectfully

Respect is a word that service users frequently use, sometimes because, in their relations with health and welfare services, it can be in short supply. Respect was seen as one of the real strengths of service users' contact with specialist palliative care social workers. For example:

Well, esteem, pure esteem that's the feeling we had, that she cared about us you know. (Man, age group 66–75, in a discussion group of bereaved people)

Being given time

Service users frequently referred to the positive sense that social workers communicated to them that they had *time* for them.

Time is such an important word with everything. She just seems to have the time that the rest of them – rat race – doesn't.

I can't emphasize the time scale of things, there's no rush, you don't feel as though you are being a burden or that you know you are wasting their

> time somehow. You know she's always got the time that you need. (Two comments from a widowed mother of three young children, age group 26–35)

Being given time emerged as being absolutely central to service users' conception about what was most valuable in specialist palliative care social work. Like the woman quoted above, service users repeatedly said that they felt the social worker had *time* for them. Many felt this had been rare in their experience of health care. But rather than the actual amount of time spent with a service user, it was more the 'quality' of that time. Comments like these were typical:

> [F]rom the minute [the social worker] walked in you feel you are the only person she's got to look after and see to, which makes you feel comfortable. (Woman patient, white UK, age group 66–75)

> You can tell, you know each time you made an appointment, how busy she was but that would never come across…she was totally relaxed and she was so into you, she was so relaxed, interested… (Bereaved woman who was also a patient, white UK, age group 46–55)

Like those women, several other service users commented that they knew that the social worker was very busy but that this did not detract from the time they had with him or her. They felt that they received the social worker's full attention.

> That's my time and I know she's there for me, but I know from chatting to her, either before or after, how busy she is. But it doesn't make any difference to my hour…and she's really with me the whole time. (Woman patient, white UK, age group 66–75)

> She'd say a few words, and then she'd let me carry on and…voice my feelings. And then she would listen…and to see a person sitting there looking at you and listening to what you are saying, there's not many people will do that. And I mean…[the social worker] she's got so many other things she's got to be doing. But then she'll sit down and she'll talk to you as if you are the only person there that she is involved with. (Bereaved woman, white UK, age group 56–65)

Being available and accessible

Closely linked to the feeling of 'having time' was the idea that the social worker was available and accessible to the service user. Service users commented time and time again on how highly they valued this accessibility – the sense that if they needed to, they could see the social worker.

> It was only a case of asking one of the nurses could I speak to [the social worker] and she was available. And if she couldn't give you a full interview or whatever she always made time for a quick word and then made

arrangements to have further conversation the next week or when she could. (Man patient, white UK, age group 46–55)

We knew she would be here if we wanted her about anything, you know, and we had access to that and if she wasn't here they would bleep her for me...in fact I think I could say I saw her every day I was here even if it was only 'Hello, how are you?' ...she was certainly very much hands on, she wasn't one for sitting in her office. (Bereaved woman, white UK, 71 years old)

First service user: It's always there if you need it [social work support], it's always there.

Second service user: If you ever need her she is there. You've just got to ring up. If she's not here, the message gets to her that you need to speak to her and she rings you back. (Two bereaved service users in a group discussion)

[W]hen I used to phone them up and say I've got a form to fill in and they'd say, 'No problem'. Nothing was too much trouble. They'd say 'All right we'll make an appointment, you come so and so day' and that's what really was helpful; some social workers will say, 'No I ain't got time' but they could always fit in a place for me. (Bereaved woman, white UK, age group 36–45)

I do believe honestly that she'll always have time for me, you know all the time when she was busy she'd say 'I'll come back to you', she'd phone me back when she was out of the meeting or whatever and it wasn't out of sight out of mind, so that made me feel good. (Man patient, white UK, age group 56–65)

One woman who was bereaved acknowledged that at times she had felt quite desperate and suicidal and she appreciated that the social worker was able to provide a service that actually matched her level of need. She said:

She gave the time and actually could fit me in not just once a week, if it needed to be two or three times, she would do it, whatever. And that meant such a lot because you can't stick to a plan when you've got those sorts of [problems].

We probed to find out whether this degree of accessibility opened the 'floodgates' and whether it left social workers overwhelmed with calls for help. We got the impression that service users found the idea of being able to access support extremely sustaining, part of their coping strategy, but they did not necessarily call on it. It was the sense that it was there, if need be, that was what was important. This woman was typical:

Service user: I knew that she was at the end of the phone and it was arranged, that if I needed, I could ring up and say, 'Look I need you now'.

Interviewer: Did you ever do that?

Service user: No! ...my husband and I have a scale of one to ten
                     and the lowest I ever got was down to about two or
                     three. I knew I could cope, but if it got any worse...
                     (Woman patient, white UK, age group 66–75)

One of the steering groups made us aware of the change in levels of accessibility
between having a specialist social worker on site (a service which they had previously had but which had been cut) and having to rely on a generalist service:

You call to get an appointment and it's two, three, four weeks – it's like come
on, I'm having the crisis now... (Member of steering group)

Providing continuity of support

Closely linked to being given time and being accessible was the broader notion
of *continuity* in social work support. Service users told us how valuable they
found the continuity that the social worker could offer.

I felt that because she knew me right more or less from the beginning, that it
was very easy to talk to her about it all...you build up quite a bond. (Woman,
white UK, age group 46–55, who was both bereaved and a patient)

Most of the service users we spoke with had known one specific specialist palliative care social worker throughout, and this was often cited as an important
aspect of the relationship with them. It was also often strongly contrasted to the
type of relationship they had with medical personnel in the acute setting.

And you don't always want to see a different doctor all the time or a locum;
you want to feel safe, familiar with somebody, somebody that knows all
about [the patient] and you don't have to keep going through it with
somebody new all the time...so many different doctors, so many different
nurses wouldn't know what was going on with him and you could scream.
Well I did scream, I did cry you know... (Bereaved woman, white UK, age
group 26–35)

This father, whose wife had died, stressed the importance of continuity of care
for his children and for himself:

The thing that I've experienced...is the long-term nature of – particularly
with the children – the long-term nature of losing someone...having the
availability of long-term support if needed – I don't want to make people
dependent, but like when we had tragedies in our family, they have always
been available... Things crop up when you least expect them, but just
knowing that that service is there, that you might not see them for two or
three years, but then suddenly you may need to see them for a couple of
sessions and I think that has been very valuable and I would stress – I would
like to stress that. (Bereaved man, white UK, age group 46–55)

One of the steering groups raised the issue of continuity of care as something which we needed to be particularly aware of and make clear. They felt that constant changes of personnel were extremely detrimental and difficult to cope with; at the very least they made people feel very exposed and intruded upon.

> [With continuity] you don't have to sit there and explain to a complete stranger your life history... (Member of steering group)

Being reliable and delivering

> Husband:　　She is the one person I would call on...
>
> Wife:　　　　Because you know that she comes up with the goods. (Man patient, white UK, age group 46–55, talking with his wife in their joint interview)

> The most important thing is if she says she is going to do it, she'll do it, which you find a lot of other professionals won't do. They say oh yeah they'll do it and six months later you are still in the same position. (Woman patient, white UK, age group 26–35)

Being responsive to everyone's needs

Service users highlighted that they valued the social worker's recognition not only of their own needs, but also the needs of the whole family or group of people linked with them.

> My mum up till then had been my family carer, and basically my body carer. I was quite a lot of pressure on my mum, so she didn't have time for my brother and sister and other things. So when [the social worker] realized that, she managed to get funding to employ [a] carer. (Man patient, Asian UK, 24 years old)

Having a good level of knowledge and expertise

This was a common concern of service users and summed up in one joint interview:

> She not only understands the patient, and the partner of the patient, she understands the systems as well... It's obvious to us that she knows her job inside out. And just by the way she comes back at you with an answer and what she's saying, you know she knows what she's talking about and that she knows her job and what is available. And if she's not sure, she'll tell you, but she will find out. (The husband of a white UK woman patient, age group 56–65, talking in a joint interview)

Making home visits

Most of the specialist palliative care social workers undertook 'home visits' – that is to say, they visited people in their own homes as well as seeing them in the hospice or health service setting. For some of the service users this was very important. For a few it felt like the only appropriate location, in view of their limited strength and energy.

> I was very ill, I mean I had hardly any energy and what is usually offered is places for patients to go. If you can't even get up the stairs…and if you don't want to be seen…at that point I was wearing a wig…it was the last thing I wanted, to go out… And it was ages before I went for a check-up because I wouldn't go back to the hospital…for somebody to come here, this is where I feel safe, and talk to me. (Woman patient, Jewish UK, age group 56–65)

Others said that they felt less apprehensive and more in control about receiving social work support when they were in their own home.

> The first time she came over here [her home], which was quite nice because it was sort of on my own ground. I know it seems a bit strange, but I think I would have felt more nervous than I already did if I'd had to go over there to see her, because it would have been a whole new situation. It was quite nice to just sit in here, have a drink, a cup of tea or something. (Bereaved woman, white UK, 18 years old)

> I just found it more comfortable to have the meeting at home you know, sort of here quite comfy and I feel more relaxed…before I was ill… I was very much a quiet person and I didn't like discussing my problems…so to start with I was a bit worried about that and I felt more relaxed being at home and I felt I could talk more. (Man patient, white UK, age group 36–45)

Some service users felt unable to face the emotional upheaval of going back to the hospice for bereavement support as it stirred up too many distressing memories:

> You could see him deteriorating every day, every night, every day and obviously then I couldn't go back to [the hospice] so [the social worker] said she would come to the house which I was very grateful for. (Woman whose son had died, white UK, age group 56–65)

Others preferred home visits because it meant that the social worker got to know other family members who might be missed if contact was restricted to the palliative care setting.

> Because my husband was ill at home as well, so she needed to speak to him as well. (Woman patient, white UK, 67 years old)

Some service users lived in remote rural areas and distances meant it was impractical for them to get to the hospice, especially if they did not have their own transport, or if their health was poor. Others had young children which made travelling to see the social worker more difficult.

A different viewpoint on home visits

Not all service users, however, valued home visits. While most did find them invaluable, there was some evidence that this wasn't always so. It was clear that there needed to be proper discussion with the service user to check that this was their preferred setting. One man said his deceased partner had found it very difficult seeing the social worker at home because he believed that she had less privacy from family there and needed to get away from the house to be enabled to speak as freely as she wanted to. Thus:

> It was that kind of contamination to her home space and then these rather entangled relations with her family in this home space...which [the social worker] was coming in to actually talk to her about, which she used to get very anxious about. (Bereaved man, white UK, age group 26–35)

Some others found that going to see the social worker at the hospice simply provided a welcome break from home.

THE SCOPE OF SPECIALIST PALLIATIVE CARE SOCIAL WORK

Many of the people to whom we spoke said that they appreciated having the support of a professional who could help with a broad range of issues that they felt were important to them.

> There's none of this business of that's not my job. (Husband of a patient, white UK, age group 56–65, talking during their joint interview)

Sometimes service users wanted to bring up issues that were not directly related to their illness or their loved one's death, but were unresolved matters from earlier life they wanted to explore.

> That was the reason I went there [to see the social worker]...to discuss – well things that were floating through my mind, about past things which you don't think about when you are living a normal life... Everything seemed to come to the surface probably because I was so low. (Woman patient, white UK, age group 56–65)

It was easy to see how valuable having a 'one-stop' service was for patients and bereaved people who were completely overwhelmed by their emotional and practical needs.

> In the first few months after my husband died, I would say she was the person I would turn to all the time for absolutely everything, whether it was something simple like having an argument with a friend, to having problems with the kids, money worries... (Widowed mother, white UK, age group 26–35)

It was clear that service users felt supported by knowing that there was professional help available that was wide ranging and that would encompass any issue. Anxiety was in effect contained by this knowledge.

> I know that if there is anything that is worrying me or I need to know or ask, I can ask her, and if she doesn't know she will know who to ask. (Man patient, white UK, age group 26–35)

> Basically she catered for what came along really. (Woman patient, white UK, age group 46–55)

Using a wide repertoire of social work approaches

It was apparent that individual service users sometimes favoured one social work approach over another and it was appreciated when the social worker worked in a way that met individual preferences. It became evident that specialist palliative care social workers were skilful in matching the approaches they used to specific service users.

This is illustrated by these comments from two patients. The first is from a woman who reported that she had specifically told the social worker that she did not want a counselling-based relationship; the second person said she wanted only a very focused counselling approach from the social worker.

> We would chat in a friendly manner…about everyday life… (Woman patient, white UK, in her eighties)

> There is nothing worse than counsellors coming – it's all right to say, 'Oh yes it's windy out there' – that's fine – 'Oh yes it's cold' – that's okay, but to go on talking about other things that are not significant, it seems to be a waste of time, really. (Woman patient, white UK, 45 years old)

These two women had actually seen the same specialist palliative care social worker who had adapted her approach to suit each of them. Both felt that she had offered the right type of support and had met their needs.

The first woman we just quoted was not the only person to say she did not feel comfortable with a formal counselling approach. For example:

> I saw a counsellor…but everything was stage-managed, you went in and the chair was there and the box there with the tissues in…she was very nice don't get me wrong but I wasn't comfortable. (Wife of a patient, age group 46–55, who was present at the interview with him)

The same woman went on to contrast the social worker's approach:

> Yeah, whereas with [the social worker] I could make her a cup of tea, she would sit here and chat with us but in between that chat she's counselling without us knowing and it's comfortable…and also the way she talks to you, she talks to you as if you're one of her you know.

SUMMARY

This chapter focuses on what service users see as the most positive aspects of social work. There was strong agreement among service users about what they valued most in specialist palliative care social work. This was true of different groups of service users and in all settings. They particularly valued:

- the quality of the relationship between service user and social worker
- the personal qualities of the social worker
- the nature and process of the work with the social worker.

The quality of the relationship between service user and social worker

- Service users valued a genuine relationship with the specialist palliative care social worker.
- Friendship was seen as an important part of the relationship with some service users valuing reciprocity.
- Service users appreciated it when specialist palliative care social workers had professional boundaries which were flexible.

The personal qualities of the social worker

- The importance of appropriate personal qualities was stressed repeatedly as being vital. Service users highlighted a range of qualities they saw as essential for good practice, including kindness, warmth, respect, compassion, caring, sensitivity, empathy and thoughtfulness.
- Many service users saw these qualities as being inherent in the person rather than learned skills.

The nature and process of the work with the social worker

Service users also identified a number of skills which they saw as key for user-centred social work.

- Being able to determine their own agenda and work in partnership with the specialist palliative care social worker.
- Being listened to with a non-judgemental and respectful attitude.
- The social workers giving them time and being accessible and available, ensuring continuity of support.
- The social worker being reliable and delivering promised action.
- The social worker being available for both the service user and those close to him or her and being willing to offer home visits (and offering choice over this).
- The social worker having a good level of expertise and willingness to learn.

- The social worker being available to talk about any issue of importance to the service user. This made people feel that their anxieties could be contained.
- The social worker offering a wide range of social work approaches that suited individual preferences.

CHAPTER 6

WORKING WITH DIFFERENCE

We want to focus on difference in this chapter and consider how it is addressed in specialist palliative care social work. In our project, we wanted to see whether people's journey through specialist palliative care social work had varied because of their personal, social or cultural characteristics and circumstances. We explored our data to see if we could identify any variation in needs, service delivery or levels of satisfaction between different groups of service users. We considered age, gender, employment background, ethnicity, religion and location, as well as type of illness and impairment/disability. We have set out in Appendix 1 why we think we gained little information in relation to people's sexuality, although we know that issues of sexuality and sexual orientation have important implications for palliative care provision and practice and one of our steering groups included a number of gay men living with HIV/AIDS (Cox 2004; Lemieux *et al.* 2004; Rice 2000).

By far the most striking finding was the degree of consistency across all these groups in relation to the level of overall satisfaction with the specialist palliative care social work support that service users had received. From what they told us, we could not detect any major differences between groups. It was almost impossible to pick out any clear-cut differences in relation to satisfaction with the nature of the social work contact. Particularly noticeable was the absolute consistency with which each service user said he or she had felt the social worker had valued him or her as a person. This appreciation of the service user as an individual provides a helpful starting point for considering the experience of service users in relation to specialist palliative care social work and difference.

SEEING THE PERSON AS AN INDIVIDUAL

Being treated as an individual was undoubtedly very important to the service users and this was emphasized to us time and time again. One woman stressed how, in her experience, everyone was treated with the same respect for his or her individuality, but this did not mean treating them all the same. In practice it meant offering a different service according to individual needs and preferences:

> I think you are treated as an individual in every single way. And I am sure that everybody who comes in is all treated differently, because they get to know what each person is like, and what each person's different needs are. (Bereaved woman, white UK, age group 26–35)

It was also clear that 'individuality' meant different things to different people. For this man it meant being seen as a whole person rather than just a sick person:

> One thing I had trouble with in hospitals is that they treat you just like this faceless person sometimes, and I used to feel just like a broken down television set. But at [the hospice, with the social worker] they make you feel like you were an individual again...whereas the hospital they just take all that away from you. (Man patient, white UK, age group 36–45)

Some service users felt that the social worker had respected their individual needs in terms of tuning in to the specific way that they wanted to deal with the illness facing them.

> We wanted to know what was going on, you know, we wanted to keep on top of it as much as possible by knowing the likely time scale and outcomes...some people probably don't want to know, and they probably would tune into that. But we did... They work with you and adapt to the way that you're feeling. (Bereaved man, white UK, age group 46–55)

Some service users commented on the fact that the social worker was able to recognize them as an individual, but also showed an awareness of how their individual identity had been challenged by their situation.

> [The social worker] definitely saw me as a person and saw, I think, probably that I was not the person I used to be. (Service user in group discussion)

Several service users contrasted the respect they had felt from the social worker to the way they had been treated by some doctors:

> ...We were being fobbed off, basically fobbed off and Mr — spoke to you as if you wasn't a person, you know he talked down to you, he actually talked down to you. (Man patient, white UK, age group 46–55)

While there were no discernible differences in levels of satisfaction expressed by service users about specialist palliative care services, there were some other differences between groups that are worth noting.

AGE

Seventy-one per cent of the patients we interviewed were aged 65 or under compared to 35 per cent of all palliative care patients in the UK (minimum data set figure for 2000/2001). While we cannot claim that our respondents by any means constitute a representative sample of all users of specialist palliative care, this figure might suggest that the younger patients are disproportionately high users of specialist palliative care social work resources. This would be consistent with the increased chance that patients in younger age groups are dealing with untimely death and leaving younger families, both of which may be seen to represent a heightened need for social work involvement. It would appear that the social workers were aware of this level of potential need and were responding to it. It could equally indicate that, while there might be high levels of need among older patients, these were not being recognized or met.

Children and young people

Although we did not interview children or young people directly, the picture that emerged from the accounts of their parents was not consistent. There was evidence that some social workers were doing intensive individual and/or group work with children and young people which was very highly valued, at least by the parents. However, there was also evidence of children and young people who had little or no direct contact with the social worker, despite the illness or death of a close family member.

One service user who felt she had received enormous support from the specialist palliative care social worker suggested that there could be more on offer for children. She said:

> The only thing I did suggest to them was the fact that they didn't involve children more, and they did actually do a children's day not so long back – the social workers and some volunteers... I thought that was good, because sometimes the kids do tend to be overlooked. People speak to the adults, because they think, if the adults are all right, the kids are going to be all right.
> (Bereaved woman, white UK, age group 46–55)

We were sometimes told that a child had refused contact because of shyness, but sometimes parents did not seem to be aware of whether such contact was possible. We further reflect on this finding in Part Three of the book where we discuss the findings from the project.

Older service users

A number of older people emphasized that it had been important for them that the social worker had seen beyond ageist stereotypes and responded to them as individuals, addressing their particular needs. One older woman patient, for example, recounted how the specialist palliative care social worker had supported another patient in the next bed, who was almost 90 years old, with a move from the hospice to a nursing home. She had witnessed the way the social worker had persisted in her hunt for a nursing home that truly met the individual needs of the person. She had found this very reassuring:

> [S]he found her a lovely nursing home and it wasn't the first or the second time she took her to see one, something that would suit her, you know something that she would be happy in…she took her to see these places till she found her a place that she was going to settle and be happy in…she would have found me a place where I would be happy to stay in, not just any place but a place where you'd be happy in. (Woman patient, white UK, age group 75+)

Another woman patient in her eighties also spoke about being treated as an individual by the social worker:

> [M]y needs were queried and I wasn't treated en masse like a lot of over eighties who are put on the scrap heap – 'they're just useless' – but I was treated as though I had a brain and they respected my wishes. And no, I've no complaints, I was treated as an individual. (Woman patient, white UK, age group 75+)

This was a view echoed by this service user:

> She has this gift, I think, of getting to the elderly, being able to speak to them as human beings, you know and not just old fogies, or whatever you want to call them. I think a social worker has to have that gift, to like people. (Bereaved woman, white UK, age group 75+)

These positive views of older people being treated with respect by the specialist palliative care social worker stood in very sharp contrast to the way some service users described treatment of older people by medical services. One woman talked about how she felt her father's medical care had been poor, and symptoms had gone unexplained and untreated for a long time:

> We felt if somebody took more interest in him…he was 83, doctors don't seem to have much time: there's no time for the elderly people. And we've got the same problem with [her mother-in-law]. They go, 'Oh no, she's mad'. She's got dementia, but she's not mad. She just can't say what she wants to say. She knows what she wants to say, but when she opens her mouth, it doesn't come out… But if you take the trouble to sit down and relax with her, you can find out what she wants. But doctors haven't got this time…the nurses didn't really have time either. (Bereaved woman, white UK, age group 46–55)

Another striking feature of the interviews and discussions with older service users was the particular importance many of them attached to being able to offload worrying paperwork onto the social worker. It was clear that some had felt completely overwhelmed and unable to deal with things like benefit claim forms, letters telling them they had been overpaid benefit or letters about rent arrears. These issues were frequently mentioned by older people as causing them particular anxiety and were emphasized over the other needs that they had discussed with the social worker. This group of service users especially appreciated practical, hands-on support (for example, advice, advocacy and liaison with other services) from the specialist palliative care social worker. This was support which was given without limiting or damaging autonomy. For example:

> I would have felt very much that I wasn't in control of my life if I didn't have help filling these forms in. There are so many frustrations of things that you can't do…but when someone helps you fill it in, instead of taking control of it altogether, they're doing it for you but you're telling them what to put down…you still feel in control and it does make a difference. (Woman patient, white UK, age group 66–75)

It is difficult to state categorically that this need related to age itself. It may also have been related to other factors, such as class background, level of income, wider attitudes among older people to debt and poverty and whether or not people lived alone.

GENDER

We found nothing to suggest that there was any difference in levels of satisfaction with the specialist palliative care social work service between men and women. But there did seem to be other differences between men and women in relation to specialist palliative care social work. For example, as we have already mentioned, there could be different needs for information about the service, such as being told clearly what services a specialist palliative care social worker might be expected to provide in the first place.

Another aspect that was noticeable was that frequently women service users mentioned that their male family members did not want to talk, and would not seek professional support; this potentially left the women service users feeling total responsibility for providing the emotional support for the men. We did not seem to find any male service users expressing similar concerns about supporting the women in their lives.

As has previously been mentioned, we could not say whether it was statistically significant, but in terms of our impressions our process notes record how positively men in particular viewed their experiences of groupwork. Their enthusiasm seemed infectious and they rated their experiences of groups very highly.

Another issue mentioned by one male service user was that he believed oncology and support services in hospitals were more focused on women:

> at the hospital where I had the radiotherapy…they had clubs and that but it was all women, women, women, breast cancer this and breast cancer that and there was nothing for men. And they had a club; a room where you could go and get a sauna, hair treatment, relaxation and it just wasn't for men. And many of us, well two or three of us spoke…we said well if that was all for men

> there'd be a kick up because it wouldn't be for women…and there was just nothing, there were things for women but there just weren't for men. (Man patient, white UK, age group 46–55)

It is worth noting that some of the woman patients also commented that hospital-based support services were geared towards breast cancer and if you had a different kind of cancer there was less help available. Whilst none of the service users directly made the same criticism of hospice or specialist palliative care services, several service users did talk about their attendance at hospice groups for women with breast cancer, but no one mentioned groups for people with other specific cancers.

ETHNICITY

The number of people we spoke to from minority ethnic groups was small in absolute terms, although a significant minority of participants in our study. It is difficult therefore to make anything more than very tentative suggestions for areas of difference in needs, or service delivery. There is further discussion of issues of ethnicity in Chapter 9.

It did seem to us, however, that this group of service users more frequently mentioned issues relating to poverty or poor housing. Our process notes, for example, told us how one service user from an ethnic minority group was living in very inadequate conditions, in a freezing cold and poorly furnished house. She told us that the specialist palliative care social worker had rapidly begun to tackle these issues.

> She was the one who did many things that make them realize that they are short-paying me… (Woman patient, black African, age group 36–45)

This indication of a higher incidence of poverty is not surprising, as these service users came, in the main, from the large urban centres where these issues are common and faced disproportionately by minority ethnic communities. Service users from these communities generally raised a broader range of issues than the general sample, but again this was consistent with other service users from urban areas and may have been related to this rather than ethnicity itself. As with other service users, general indications were that specialist palliative care social workers were able to encompass the broader range of service users' issues and concerns within their role.

RELIGION

Although we did not specifically ask questions about religion the importance of religious beliefs emerged in some of the interviews.

> She knew from the beginning that, as a family, we were Christians and had a certain outlook on life and death and anything she did, didn't conflict with

that. You know because she obviously took into her view, what our view was. (Bereaved woman, white UK, age group 66–75)

Another service user with strong Christian beliefs raised an issue that was of importance to her:

when it comes to palliative care…they should be prepared for that person to get healed… (Woman patient, black UK, age group 26–35)

Whilst she did not make clear whether or not the specialist palliative care social worker had 'accepted' this or not, the service user said this about the counselling provided by the specialist palliative care social worker:

yeah, I think it has done a really good deal, a great deal of good, I think it has given me a chance, you know, to talk about issues that have been inside…

EMPLOYMENT BACKGROUND

Again it was very difficult to discern real differences in terms of satisfaction with specialist palliative care social work between people who clearly came from very different economic backgrounds. What was apparent was that the specialist palliative care social workers were seeing people from very wide-ranging social and class backgrounds. It was also the case that some people from managerial and professional employment backgrounds, at this stage in their life, required advice and information about welfare benefits and help in negotiating benefit systems, which they might never have expected to need before.

Another finding emerged more from our observations in process notes than from what service users told us. We found, when we interviewed people in discussion groups which were based on existing patient or bereavement support groups, that participants often came from markedly different employment and class backgrounds. Yet it was apparent that they were immensely supportive of each other. Sometimes we were told that this contact and support had been sustained for years.

TYPE OF ILLNESS OR CONDITION

There was a clear difference between those service users who had been diagnosed with cancer and those who had other illnesses and conditions. This had much less to do with the particular illness involved, than with the health service responses to it. Several service users with a non-cancer diagnosis told us that they felt that their need for information and support was not always being met; that palliative care services were more generally geared to working with people with the more prevalent types of cancer. It should be said that some service users who had very rare cancers also shared this view. For example:

You know everything's sort of – I feel anyway – that it's sort of geared to cancer and that, but people really often don't understand what people suffer with MS…with a 22-year illness, you know, they're fed up of hearing about it really. (Bereaved woman, white UK, age group 56–65)

This woman also stressed how important it had been to her that the specialist palliative care social worker had been prepared to learn about the illness:

[He] said it had been a learning curve for him, because he'd learnt so much about it.

Another service user said that she felt her specialist palliative care social worker did not know a lot about mesothelioma (asbestos-related cancer), but had sought out the answers.

[S]he was dealing with people that had normal cancers…[but] she put me on the right track really you know about some things that I needed to do…some social workers are just not aware enough of some diseases that are there… (Bereaved woman, black Caribbean, age group 46–55)

SUMMARY

- We sought to explore difference in people's experience of specialist palliative care social work. While some differences did seem to emerge between some groups, there were no discernible differences between groups in terms of their view of the quality of specialist palliative care social work. Most striking was the extremely high level of consistency across all groups in terms of their satisfaction with the specialist palliative care social work service.

- Being treated as an individual was emphasized as being of fundamental importance and without exception every service user said that he or she had felt valued as an individual. This meant different things to different people and the specialist palliative care social workers had been responsive to this.

- Older people particularly stressed their need for help with practical matters, such as form filling, and the value of advocacy. Several older people commented on the respect that they had experienced from the social worker who, they felt, looked beyond ageist stereotypes.

- A mixed picture emerged in relation to children and young people. Some service users stressed the excellent direct work done with them, but others said that they felt more should be available. Some said they did not know whether direct support was available for children. Several parents said that their children were too shy to accept direct help, but felt the children's needs had been addressed as an important part of their own support.

- Gender did not seem significant in terms of variation in satisfaction with the service provided by the specialist palliative care social worker, but there were indications that men may want different things from the social worker. For example, they seem to have different information needs; they may particularly value groupwork; and men and women may have different experiences in relation to supporting family members of the opposite sex. Women may experience this as an added responsibility. There were some indications that services may not be equally accessible to men and that patients with some types of cancer, specifically breast cancer, are better supported than others with other conditions.

- Service users from black and ethnic minority backgrounds seemed to highlight issues of poverty and inadequate housing as being important to them. Specialist palliative care social workers seemed to be very responsive to these types of issues.

- The importance of respecting religious beliefs was stressed by a small number of Christian service users and this included respecting the view that healing through their faith was possible.

- The employment background of service users was diverse. People from professional and managerial work backgrounds, like other service users, brought needs for advice on welfare benefit issues and for help in negotiating benefit systems to specialist palliative care social workers. The importance of social workers' skill in negotiating benefits systems regardless of people's employment background becomes clear. There was good evidence of service users from diverse backgrounds offering each other support.

- There was evidence that people with a non-cancer diagnosis or with diagnosis of a rare cancer felt their needs were not always recognized by palliative care services, including the specialist palliative care social worker. There was, however, also evidence that the social workers sought to remedy this deficit in their knowledge, and this was appreciated by service users.

CHAPTER 7

EXPLORING OUTCOMES: EVALUATING SPECIALIST PALLIATIVE CARE SOCIAL WORK

In this chapter we explore three key issues which we heard about from service users:

1. Adverse criticisms that service users made of specialist palliative care social work.

2. The outcomes they saw such social work offering them.

3. Their views about the evaluation of specialist palliative care social work.

We look at each of these in turn.

A LESS SMOOTH JOURNEY: ADVERSE CRITICISMS OF SPECIALIST PALLIATIVE CARE SOCIAL WORK

Most people's journey through specialist palliative care went very smoothly and we heard remarkably few criticisms or complaints about the social workers or the service that they provided. However, for just a small number of people, the journey was not so easy. Two people told us they were unhappy about the service they had received on an individual basis and a very small number of other people had some critical comments to make, although they stressed that, overall, they were very satisfied with the specialist palliative care social work service.

We were particularly anxious to look carefully at these more negative comments, not least because they were relatively uncommon. We explored these examples in some detail to see if there were any characteristics that united them and to try and determine the lessons that might be drawn from them. It also seems important to say that other service users spoke in very glowing terms about the same social workers who were involved in these cases.

On the basis of such small numbers, it is probably not appropriate to talk about the issues emerging as distinct themes. But there did seem to be some striking similarities in these examples and the particular issues involved might have had an impact on the social work done with the service user. It also seemed to us that these issues, although we have put them under different headings were, in reality, undeniably intertwined.

We have deliberately avoided providing the usual demographic information about these service users to ensure that they could not be identified. One of the regular concerns of service users who take part in research and evaluation is that criticisms they make of provision may have negative repercussions. While we do not expect that to be so in this case, we still think it is helpful to mantain this principle to safeguard people's confidentiality and anonymity.

Where relationships with patients may be unclear

In some of the cases involved, the service user (all people who had been bereaved) and the patient were not 'close' relatives or married partners. For example, they might have been step-relatives, half-brothers or half-sisters, in-laws or non-cohabiting partners. The fact that the service user's relationship with the patient may have seemed unclear to the social worker could unfortunately create difficulties. It seemed to influence the service received from the specialist palliative care social worker in several ways.

For example, one of the service users indicated that, although she was very involved in the care of her relative, she had not seen herself as an important part of the picture – although she clearly was. When, for instance, we asked whether she felt she had had a chance to talk to the social worker about the things that had worried her, she said:

> Well no, not really. I never thought it was important for them to cotton on to me, I thought they were there for [the patient] and that was it... I don't think I'm important at all.

We asked whether it was explained to her what the social workers could offer her:

> No...it seemed to me, they came to see [the patient] and when they came I could just sit and listen...

It seemed to us that this woman was to a degree quite uncertain and ambivalent and may have been very reticent about spelling out her own needs to the specialist palliative care social worker. This was not picked up on and as a result she may have been somewhat excluded. Her interpretation was:

> that was my fault for not pushing it, not expecting it.

Second, some people could miss out on offers of support because they were not perceived as being as close to the patient as some other family members. One man, a close friend of the patient, told us:

> her mother had some counselling support...her father, her brother, her sister were offered support... I was out of that loop.

Perhaps in some cases the real intensity and importance of the relationship was not fully appreciated by the specialist palliative care social worker or there were complexities to the relationship that were hidden. One service user told us of a long period of estrangement between herself and the family member she looked after:

> [She] didn't really want to be in touch with me, she hadn't been here for ten years...

Another woman spoke of her family background:

> Look, I've not seen this woman [the patient] for 15 years...my mother died when I was five, she came to look after me when I was little... I feel very guilty, half of me is saying I'm doing this [looking after the patient now] through guilt, half of it's through love. I don't know what I'm doing you know.

As well as having these ambivalent feelings, this service user also told us about some extremely painful family history that she had only learned about as she had cared for the patient. She felt this had been very significant for her but she had not had the time or opportunity to talk about it in depth with the specialist palliative care social worker. When we asked what she saw as important for training new palliative care social workers she said:

> Oh I think to go into the background more. I'm sure it's not just me where there was a complicated family issue. There must be other families in the same situation. Even straightforward relationships in a family, I think...it would help if they could try and understand – if they had time to listen.

A young male patient also made a similar point to us, not directly as a criticism of his social worker, but more as an observation about training needs. He said that relationships within his family had become fractured during his illness, largely because of his anger and changed personality. This family breakdown had clearly caused him a great deal of distress. He admitted that he had been reluctant to deal with the problems and had not directly asked the social worker for support with this aspect of his illness. He felt that she had concentrated on practical issues, which, he acknowledged, were also desperately important for him. He asked for more direct questioning by specialist palliative care social workers about how relationships actually are between family members. He seemed to feel certain that, had the social worker become involved, she would have been able to sort something out. He suggested that trainee social workers be taught of the impact of illness on the family:

> just to be aware that...you are not yourself, you are a different person. And just to try and keep those relationships...[to ask] how do you get on with your stepmother? Or just be aware that there may be weak relationships that are going to break down because of this.

Practicalities squeezing out other key issues

Sometimes tensions emerged between dealing with practicalities and addressing other important issues. In some cases practical issues could dominate and squeeze out other issues that were really important. As we have seen, practical matters can be so overwhelming that they seem to absorb all the energies and focus of both the social worker and the service user, allowing other issues to go unaddressed. This can happen because both service users and social workers become preoccupied with them. This seemed to have been a factor in those instances where people were unhappy with the specialist palliative care social work they experienced.

One service user said that when she was asked whether she wanted to talk about her complex family situation, she had; but she then went on to spell out all the day-to-day pressures she had faced on top of her normal job, and these had then taken priority.

> It was quite difficult because…I have the children, but we got a bed-settee and myself and my partner slept downstairs and [the patient] had the bedroom.
>
> [A]s well as running a family and the shopping and the cleaning, the cooking, the washing and the ironing…I'd never been involved in anything relating to death before, I didn't have a clue… [M]ore than anything…being involved with the different departments…you need someone to help you coordinate all this bumph.

The breakdown of teamwork

Evidence also emerged of where teamwork had broken down both within the palliative care unit and with colleagues working in the community. It was striking in the two cases where there was direct negative criticism of the specialist palliative care social work service that there had been a much wider breakdown of services, both within the dedicated palliative care service and in community services more generally.

One woman was very unhappy about her relative being discharged from the palliative care unit in the first place as she believed she was not well enough to cope with the realities of being at home. Then, to make matters worse, the community support organized by the specialist palliative care social worker did not materialize.

> She was in and out of there [the palliative care unit] all the time…but whenever she went back, the first thing they did, was talking about sending her back home again. And they did this even at Christmas time… Nobody turned up to see [her], to wash her or dress her wound…nobody gave her any food.

This wasn't her first experience of a breakdown in services following a discharge from the unit. It had already happened once before:

> The carer was coming in to wash her then and I came in on the Saturday and she said, 'Oh sorry I'm still in my nightdress but you have to excuse me because the carer hasn't been in to wash me yet.' And nobody came and nobody came on the Sunday either so from the Friday till the Monday nobody had been to see her. And the girl who came then said, 'Oh yes this happens sometimes, a carer decides she's not going to do any work on a weekend and she just don't come in.'

It was clear that this service user felt very strongly that her relative had been badly let down by the doctors at the palliative care unit who had a set agenda regarding discharge and she felt that the specialist palliative care social workers had gone along with this.

> [They] tried to do what the palliative care unit wanted them to do…it's the medical side which has let [the patient] down, it's not the social services I don't think.

But she felt that the social workers in the palliative care unit had already decided what was to happen when the patient was discharged, before speaking either to her or the patient. When we asked whether she felt she had had a real say in the social work process she said:

> No, no, definitely not. They came with the whole sheet and said, 'Now this is what is going to happen.'

The other person who was very critical of specialist palliative care social work had also experienced a lack of team working. She felt she had relied heavily on the social worker to play a coordinating role but it seemed as if the social worker may not have had the necessary level of back up from other members of the multidisciplinary team:

> the Macmillan nurse…she was a bit of a non-event because I only saw her three or four times… As I say the Macmillan nurse was neither use nor ornament, she came once or twice and talked to both me and [the patient] and more or less said, 'Well if the Good Lord takes you, you'll be in a better place'…which left us all feeling far more down…and it wasn't what I expected from a Macmillan nurse. I expected her, I suppose, to be able to fill in, between me and [the specialist palliative care social worker] the gaps that were left.

This service user went on to tell us how angry she had felt.

> I was very angry with [the social worker] a lot of the time, I just felt I was being deserted, but it wasn't [her] fault, but you don't realize that until after-wards. You just need that contact even every couple of days… I just needed someone to let me know that something was happening.

A lack of good medical support seemed to be an ongoing feature of this service user's experience. Her relative had gone into a nursing home and she found that there, too, her relative did not get the care required.

> One Sunday morning I had a phone call from her... 'I don't know what to do...they've got no morphine for me and I can't have any until the doctor comes tomorrow...' I rang the [social worker] on the Monday and said, 'Look this is getting ridiculous, she's not even getting the drugs she needs now.' But perhaps it wasn't [the social worker's] problem but I didn't get any real support and I had nowhere else to go.

This service user described how she felt she had to assume more and more responsibility:

> Because I couldn't get any help, anyone to mediate between me and the nursing home, I ended up taking charge of all her drugs and all her money and trying to sort everything out. I was going to the nursing home twice a day to give her her drugs. I was telling the nursing home when she needed repeat prescriptions and I was dealing with all her finances, which was just too much and I couldn't get my problems across to the nursing home at all. At that time my dealings with [the specialist palliative care social worker] tended to tail off because it was making me more upset than it was helping.

She mentioned how her attempts to involve the Macmillan nurse had come to nothing.

> Oh I phoned and left messages many, many times and I was never contacted... It used to be an answering machine and I used to leave messages, but no one ever got back to me.

The other service user who was unhappy with her specialist palliative care social worker also told us that she had felt isolated from medical support at the hospice:

> The top people, the medical people, I fairly seldom met at all.

Bereavement follow-up had been minimal. We don't know what support was offered, but in both cases the service users had felt there had been little follow-up after the death of their relative, and one service user felt that she had been left holding on to angry and painful feelings:

> I hated everybody there, I really did. I mean, I got cards, condolence cards and so on and I just hated them, I didn't want to know.

In both cases we felt that these service users had many feelings about their experiences, which remained unresolved at the time of their interviews.

OUTCOMES OF SPECIALIST PALLIATIVE CARE SOCIAL WORK

In this section we focus on the impact or 'outcomes' that specialist palliative care social work resulted in for service users. Any policy or provision may have many outcomes. It may have economic, social, political, cultural or employment outcomes, for example. Our concern was solely the outcomes for service users as they experienced them. Did they feel specialist palliative care social work had affected them? If so, how had it changed things? Was it helpful or unhelpful? How important has it been to them? In other words, what real difference, if any, had the journey through specialist palliative care social work made to the lives of service users? Of course, it is always difficult to untangle any one influence in people's lives. Different factors interact with each other and can sometimes be difficult to distinguish. We have simply relied on what service users told us.

We did not ask one specific question to seek people's views on this subject. Instead we looked at their comments in response to all the questions that were asked and noted any that indicated a change in someone's life related to the social worker's intervention. Where a substantial number of service users identified the same changes, we categorized these into themes. We have illustrated these themes with comments from service users. It became clear that specialist palliative care social work had had significant effects on many service users' lives. These particularly related to:

- supporting service users' personal capacity
- reducing social isolation
- increasing support for loved ones
- reducing anxieties about practical problems
- providing support with medical issues

Supporting service users' personal capacity

Specialist palliative care social work comes to people at very difficult times in their lives. The challenges they face cannot be overstated. Yet service users specifically identified social work as having made a real difference in how they experienced their situation. What became clear from what people said was that specialist palliative care social work could make a difference in their subjective and objective situations. This is a point that is sometimes perhaps not made clearly enough in relation to 'helping' services. Account has to be taken of both the issues facing people and how they understand and are able to deal with them. If we start with the subjective situation, it was clear that the social work interventions enhanced service users' ability to cope and increased their feelings of control and safety. Strong evidence emerged that it helped them find belief in their own ability to handle anxiety and distress. It had helped them to find ways of managing their difficult thought processes, which previously threatened to overwhelm them. Thus, for example, people said:

> I think it's been the single most useful part of helping me deal with my loss by a long, long chalk. (Man who had lost his partner, white UK, age group 26–35)

> It has helped me to deal with bereavement more easily. Although the pain is still there, it is a big help when I have a talk with him [the palliative care social worker]… (British man of Asian origin, age group 56–65)

> We talked about…how to actually cope with the emotional things such as fear and anxiety, because that is more traumatizing than the cancer itself. You know it seems to be. (Woman patient, white UK, 45 years old)

> I was in the middle of the wilderness and I just hadn't a clue which way to go… [The social worker] helped me so much to find value again; confidence, which way to take a career, she just helped steer me, prompt me…she didn't tell me what to do, she just helped me make my own decisions. (Woman recovering from a brain tumour, white UK, age group 26–35)

> The doctor operated on my [body] and removed all the disease and all that but he didn't take the disease out of my head and you know [the social worker] done that you know. (Man patient, white UK, 50 years old)

> I think that is one of the things I found so difficult, why I couldn't cope with it, and it was [the social worker] constantly saying to me, this is quite normal to feel like this, because you sometimes feel as though you aren't normal and she was constantly reassuring me, you know, you are normal, this is a normal thing, you will feel like this…and as she was saying it, I felt, that's me so I must be all right, I must be a normal person somewhere, because it can be quite frightening, because you are not in control at all – well I wasn't. (Bereaved woman, white UK, age group 26–35)

SUPPORT TO KEEP GOING

Several people told us that the social worker had made a crucial contribution to their life. They had increased their self-esteem, morale and reduced suicidal feelings and ideas. Some of these service users thought that they had reached the very lowest point. They were feeling utter despair when the social worker began working with them.

> I was just stuck at the lowest ebb and it completely like changed my life, meeting [the social worker], because I could talk to her about anything and she's there to listen to you and she offers so much help and now…I don't really know what I would do without her. (Woman patient who has MS, white UK, age group 46–55)

Another woman had said she had thought about ending her life:

> she [the social worker] made me realize I did have a life to get on with. (Bereaved woman, white UK, age group 36–45)

This man thought the social worker had offered him crucial support:

> I really struggled and to the extent where I twice tried to commit suicide... I got to speak to [the specialist palliative care social worker]... And that's why I'm still here...she got me back to think sensibly and got me back trying to do things... (Bereaved man who had lost his wife, white UK, 52 years old)

Another man talked about how the social worker had kept him going and renewed his belief in himself and living:

> She's made me value my own life, value the importance of my life and made me feel important as an individual which was lacking and which was very important to me – very, very important...
>
> I don't think I would be here, I tell you now; well I know I wouldn't be here... I would have done something, I couldn't live like I was, I couldn't live with this, how I was doing; I felt of no value at all. I don't think I would be here without [the social worker]... So I cannot put a price on what she does. (Comments from a man patient, white UK, 50 years old)

Reducing social isolation

For many people, the outcomes they talked about did not directly stem from the social work process but from increased contact with other service users, which had often been initiated by the social worker. Social workers had been able to reduce people's sense of social isolation and exclusion by offering them more opportunities to gain mutual solidarity and support from other service users. These women, for example, talking in a discussion group, explained that through their attendance at a bereavement group they had met new people:

> First service user: We've met each other and we've become close friends and as you go through life you make many acquaintances, but you don't make many friends.
>
> Second service user: No that's right and that's what I've found particularly in my case...these are true friends.

Frequently the social work support had revolved around bringing the service users together in group settings and facilitating those meetings. The majority of service users told us that they had found meeting with other people in a similar position very helpful:

> when you know there's other people suffering like you are – so you're not abnormal, because you've strange thoughts and he says, 'No it's quite normal', so that makes you feel better. (Bereaved woman, white UK, age group 56–65)

One service user told us how the specialist palliative care social worker had asked him to run another group as a follow-up resource for other service users when the bereavement group run by the social worker ended:

> it's called a friendship group because everybody is friendly and everybody that we speak to is finding it's doing them the world of good. And I just think it's a brilliant thing. (Bereaved man, white UK, age group 56–65)

Increasing support for loved ones

Service users highlighted the importance of the support that social workers offered loved ones and family members, including children. Some service users reported that this had helped their children cope better with their grief:

> she helped him talk about the thing that he most needed to – his dad – and helped him come to terms with things…he so enjoyed it, he lightened up, he was, you know, he was a loving, pleasurable little boy again. He wasn't so cross with everything, he wasn't cross with his dad, he could talk to his dad, talk about his dad… (Bereaved mother, white UK, age group 36–45, talking about her five-year-old son)

> The quality of life that I think my children have is very, very significantly different to what it might have been had we not had all the help that we've had. It has made a fairly crucial difference… (Bereaved father, white UK, age group 46–55)

> Just talking to me. Talking to my husband, she very quickly realized she had to do something, or we were going to disintegrate as a family. (Bereaved woman, white, age group 46–55)

Even when the social worker did no direct work with family members, service users said the support had reached the wider family:

> I can pass on what I learn from him to my daughters and my son… (Bereaved British man of Asian origin, age 56–65)

Patients also reported increased peace of mind knowing that their family had the social worker to turn to:

> I know that if and when or whenever something happens to me now I know my wife will be able to phone here and get help for my daughter. And if it's just a case of a blether or whatever to help the stress…or financial help they're needing, I know she'd be there for them…and it's just knowing that, relieves your mind. (Man patient, white UK, age group 46–55)

Reducing anxieties about practical problems

Reducing service users' anxieties about practical matters and increasing their access to services through information, liaison and advocacy was an enormously important outcome for many people.

I was having a lot of pressure with tax forms and all this and that. So when I seen [the social worker] she took all that worry off me by filling in the forms... The worries go off your shoulders. (Comment in discussion group between patients)

I've never had anybody close to me die. I didn't even understand about funeral arrangements or death certificates, about benefits and all that. [The social worker] took care of it. She made appointments if I couldn't do it, or I felt unable to do it, she arranged it all. She spoke to people from the council for me, because we live in a council property...to get it put into my name. She rang the schools up for me, because I felt unable to do that, to explain to the schools what had happened. [My son] was just moving up to secondary school, so she rang them up and explained that his dad had just died...in the beginning she really just sorted everything, which I know makes me sound totally useless, but at that time that's what I was. It took me all the time just for me to get through the day. (Bereaved woman, white UK, age group 26–35)

IMPROVING PEOPLE'S FINANCIAL SECURITY

While death, dying and loss tend to be framed primarily as emotional issues, for many people they create difficult and harsh financial problems. Here is where specialist palliative care social workers are perhaps able to make the most obvious impact on the objective difficulties that people may be facing. Indirectly through their work with other agencies, they can often address people's urgent and immediate financial difficulties. Service users reported how their social workers improved their quality of life through improving their financial security. This was extremely important for many people and for service users from disadvantaged communities it had added meaning. For example:

she's given me a lot of dignity because I've been able to have enough money to cope... (Woman patient, white UK, age group 56–65)

Providing support with medical issues

While the role of the specialist palliative care social worker is not a medical one, they can play an important part in supporting people to cope with their medical situation. This was vitally important for some service users who found they did not get the information and support they needed from the medical teams that they had contact with. Social workers were able to help them to cope with medical aspects of their illness. For example:

the opportunity to talk to somebody who understands your concerns about cancer. I really think that was its biggest strength...you can't talk when you go to the hospital, you get two seconds with the person, once a year...I could be dead before I go for my next check-up. (Woman patient, white UK, age group 56–65)

EVALUATING PALLIATIVE CARE SOCIAL WORK

Given the broad interest currently in consumer or user involvement and feedback in health and social care, we wanted to find out whether, as far as service users knew, there was any formal evaluation of the service that they received from palliative care social work. We also wanted to explore their attitudes towards the level of their involvement in such evaluation. We were interested in whether either the agencies involved or the specialist palliative care social workers themselves undertook any such formal evaluation. In the event, an overwhelming majority of service users told us that they had never been asked to give any kind of formal feedback or evaluation of the social work support that they had received. Thus if there was such evaluation, it generally did not seem to include the views of service users.

It was clear that most service users had been asked, informally, by the social worker whether they felt they were receiving appropriate support. This was part of their practice and their ongoing review of the service user's situation. But in contrast, service users had not been offered any way of formally evaluating the input of the specialist palliative care social worker, either by the organization itself or passed on by their social worker. This meant that in effect there had been no formal feedback about the social worker or social work service to the broader palliative care service and to the management team. From what service users said generally, this had not been sought by services, regardless of whether they were in the statutory or non-statutory sector. As some of these service users were still actively receiving support it might have been the case that evaluation was planned for the end of the involvement. However, such attempts at evaluation had not happened in any of those cases where work with the service user had been completed. Given the current emphasis on quality and choice agendas in health and social care, this was a surprising omission and an unexpected finding.

We asked service users whether they would have liked to have had opportunities to provide more formal feedback. There wasn't a consistently held view on this issue.

Evaluation or complaint?

Many service users said that not having a formal opportunity to offer evaluation and feedback was not something that they particularly felt concerned about. They made up a sizeable minority of service users. They said they were not really bothered. Significantly, they said that they felt they would have been able to say if they were unhappy about any aspect of the service. However, an important issue emerged here. It seemed that many people clearly linked the words 'feedback' and 'evaluation' with 'complaining'. This assumption affected their attitude to evaluation. Most people were not of a mind to complain. But understandings of evaluation were mainly framed in these terms. This man's comment was typical:

> I mean if I had a dodgy social worker, then yes. But because she's been so positive and she's helped so much…then I didn't really question it. (Man patient, white UK, age group 26–35)

This group also included a smaller minority of service users who did not wish to be asked for formal feedback. A few people, both patients and bereaved, felt very strongly that they did not want to be asked for feedback, because they felt that this would have been an additional burden.

> I think if I had not been happy I would have let them know. And I was happy, and it would have been one more thing to do, along with a million and one other things that you have to do when you are on your own with two kids. So I wouldn't have been happy actually. (Bereaved man, white UK, age group 46–55)

One patient indicated that giving formal feedback might be burdensome for people who feel they are not conventionally articulate or who are very ill:

> Well if she had asked me I'd have had a go at answering it like, you know, but I'm not very good at things like that. See [my wife]…she does everything like that…I can't even write now. I can just write my own name can't I? It is a scrawl. (Man patient, white UK, age group 66–75)

One man had very forceful views that evaluation, and indeed involvement of the service user in decision-making processes generally, should be done very carefully and sensitively and not in a 'managerial' way that could be oppressive in itself. He told us that:

> The present whole managerial culture is about throwing the ball back in the person's – who is being helped – court and so the patient now becomes a customer and so on at its very worst and I feel there is a social violence implied in this… Sometimes the patient just has to be taken care of. (Man patient, white UK, age group 56–65)

The value of feedback

In contrast, a sizeable proportion of service users said that they would definitely have liked the chance to provide formal feedback on their experience of specialist palliative care social work.

> I think somebody should have come out and said 'What do you think of [the social worker]?' (Bereaved woman, white UK, age group 56–65)

There were several strands to this desire to give feedback. First, an appreciable minority of service users wanted to be able to say how positive they felt about the service. For example:

> And as my husband said to me we should write. And I must admit I have been very neglectful...we felt that she [the social worker] was just a lifeline. She was a lifeline, no doubt about it, for my family. (Bereaved woman, white UK, age group 75+)

Others felt it was the only way that weak areas could be identified and improvements made to the service. For instance:

> I don't have any negative things to say...but at the same time I feel it's good that you do these sort of surveys because, especially since they are confidential, if there are things happening at least you find out and [can] rectify them. Whereas if you never did anything like this it would just go on and on, you know. (Bereaved woman, white European, 76 years old)

One person, who had two small criticisms although he had been extremely happy with the overall service, stressed the importance of being able to keep feedback anonymous.

> If there was an anonymous way of actually communicating the two critiques that I've had...that's a way of actually improving [the service]... I wouldn't have wanted to actually say it to the individual concerned so it would have remained unspoken... (Bereaved man service user)

Some people expressed an idea of contributing to the future care of others. From the authors' experience, this desire to make some kind of bequest to help others for the future is not unusual among palliative care service users. Thus:

> I think it would be nice if they did ask people just so that perhaps people who came along afterwards benefit from that, you know from other people's experiences...tiny things can help a lot because it is so hard. (Bereaved woman, white UK, age group 19–25)

Other service users wanted to give something back to the service, because they had valued it themselves.

> I am quite happy to do this [the interview] because I feel as though I am giving something back, because I seem to be taking quite a lot, because I don't know if I give anything back...like money or anything. I don't pay her and so I think it's only fair to do that, to give something back. (Bereaved woman, white UK, age group 15–18)

It is interesting that many people said that this study was the *first* chance that they had been given to give feedback on the service that they had received. Indeed one of the reasons they had agreed to take part in our study was because it was a way for them to express their positive feelings about the social work received and they definitely welcomed this opportunity.

SUMMARY

This chapter examines three interrelated issues: first, adverse criticisms service users made of specialist palliative care social work; second, the outcomes they saw such social work offering them; and finally their views about the evaluation of specialist palliative care social work.

A less smooth journey: Adverse criticisms of specialist palliative care social work

- A very small number of service users expressed dissatisfaction with the specialist palliative care social work service.
- These cases shared some common characteristics.
- The service users who expressed dissatisfaction tended to be more distant relatives of the person who had been the patient (for example step-relatives, half-siblings, in-laws).
- The relationships between service user and patient were complex and earlier estrangement had sometimes been a feature.
- Practical tasks seemed to have absorbed much of the time of both social worker and service user, sometimes to the exclusion of other issues.
- There tended not to have been in-depth discussions about the complexity and meaning of these relationships between social worker and service user.
- There appeared to be critical breakdowns in the support being offered by the wider team, both within the palliative care service and the community. The social workers were not seen as actively dealing with this.
- Bereavement follow-up was not seen as being readily available and there still seemed to be unresolved feelings about this among service users at the time of interviewing them.

Outcomes of specialist palliative care social work

Palliative care social work had a significant positive impact on the lives of many service users. Service users identified a range of positive outcomes which it had for them, both improving their own capacity to deal with the difficult situations they might be facing and supporting them with material problems they might face. Thus specialist palliative care social workers:

- enhanced service users' ability to cope and increased their feelings of control and safety
- increased service users' self-esteem, morale and helped reduce suicidal feelings

- reduced people's social isolation and exclusion and increased opportunities for mutual solidarity and support between service users

- increased support for family members and other loved ones, including children

- reduced people's anxieties about practical matters and increased their access to services through liaison and advocacy

- improved service users' quality of life through improving their financial security

- increased service users' ability to cope with medical aspects of illness by providing support, counselling and information.

Evaluating palliative care social work

Feedback and evaluation from service users are increasingly identified as important components of health and social care. However, neither seemed to be sought in relation to specialist palliative care social work.

- There was very little evidence of there being routine and regular formal evaluation of the work of specialist palliative care social workers seeking the views of service users. It was clear though that informal evaluation and review by social workers themselves took place as part of their practice.

- There was no consensus in the responses of service users to the question of whether they would have liked to provide such feedback.

- A significant minority of service users said that this was not important to them. They equated feedback with complaint and said that they would have felt able to complain if there was anything wrong.

- A small minority of service users had strong feelings that providing formal feedback could be burdensome at a difficult time in people's lives and on top of other concerns that they might have.

- A substantial proportion of service users, however, felt they would have liked the opportunity to give feedback, because they wanted to say how good the social work service had been.

- Some people expressed the view that while they personally had no criticisms of the service, they saw that routine evaluation was an important way of identifying issues of concern and putting them right.

- Confidentiality or anonymity of feedback was stressed as important for service users giving feedback.

Part Three
Developing the Discussion

So far we have tried to present the key issues about specialist palliative care social work identified by service users. We have sought to prioritize their comments and their experiences as they go through their palliative care journey. We have sought to organize this material according to the themes and issues which service users themselves highlight. This final part of the book develops critical discussion of specialist palliative care social work, building on what service users have to say about it and exploring their views. It relates their comments to wider discussions and developments. We look at some of the key issues that we think emerge from what service users say. What is therefore distinct about this part of the book is that here we are offering our own comments and interpretations drawing on service users' views and ideas. Here we try to develop our own discussion of and commentary on the findings from the study that we have undertaken.

This includes exploring the implications of social work's broader image for specialist palliative care social work and problems of referral relating to specialist palliative care social work. We discuss the nature, strengths and weaknesses of practice and the relationship between theory and practice. Finally we consider some of the broader problems which may be inhibiting the contribution that specialist palliative care social work can make to inclusive and holistic palliative care policy and practice and the implications of the study on which this book is based for the future.

CHAPTER 8

ACCESSING SPECIALIST PALLIATIVE CARE SOCIAL WORK: A BROADER IMAGE PROBLEM?

Our focus in this chapter is how service users come to access specialist palliative care social work. More accurately, our concern is with why they may *not* access such social work. Two key elements seem to be at work here: one relates to service users themselves, the other to the palliative care system. Taking service users' comments as our starting point, what we want to consider is how service users' and the palliative care system's understandings of social work may inhibit access to what our study indicates is a highly valued service. We shall look at each of these elements in turn, starting with service users' perceptions of social work.

SERVICE USERS' PERCEPTIONS OF SOCIAL WORK

The project on which this book is based highlighted the very poor images of social work that many service users carried and how this might impact on their expectations of, contact and involvement with specialist palliative care social workers. We suggest that it is imperative for specialist palliative care social workers actively to address some of these beliefs about social work so that their potential for further damage is limited.

Positive feelings about specialist palliative care social work

The overwhelming message from the service users to whom we spoke was that specialist palliative care social work had played a crucial part in the way that they had coped with illness, impending death and bereavement. Our experience was that, despite pressing interviewees as much as possible for the more negative aspects of their experience of specialist palliative care social work, those interviewed genuinely seemed unable, or were unwilling, to report adverse criticisms beyond the most minor. On the contrary, most of the service users we spoke to were very keen to tell us how important the social worker had been to them and their families. Over and over again, service users told us that they wanted to take part in the study so that they could tell someone how excellent the social worker had been. People's willingness to take part in the study was demonstrated to us very vividly on the occasion when one of the team was very late for some interviews because of a broken-down train. The service users chose to wait for over two hours, saying that it was very important to them to have the opportunity to share their positive experiences of specialist palliative care social work.

It is important to acknowledge, however, that we only interviewed people who had reached the palliative care service and who had then also gone on to see the specialist palliative care social worker. Given that most service users told us that their initial view of both of these services (for different reasons) had been very negative – and that many admitted resistance to referral – we have to question just how many individuals are completely lost because of this resistance, first, to specialist palliative care and, second, to specialist palliative care social work. Conservatively, we have to expect that many service users may not access what is widely seen by those who do as a beneficial service.

The negative context of social work

It was not really surprising to hear that service users had resisted palliative care, as people's fears and lack of knowledge of hospices are well recognized. What was reassuring was the extremely rapid change of mind, in most cases, when individuals were actually brought face to face with the service. Other studies report similar findings (Cohen *et al.* 2001). Nor were we surprised to find that service users came into specialist palliative care with negative views of social workers, but we were perhaps surprised both by the strength of these views and by how consistently these views were held across a broad spectrum of people – both with and without direct experience of social work.

Prior to their experience of specialist palliative care social work, very few service users had a positive picture of social work, though many did acknowledge the structural and resource issues that they thought might sometimes be hindering successful social work practice. It is important that social work takes account of such negative attitudes. There has long been a strong view in social work that its negative stereotyping is crucially related to reactionary and hostile politicians and media, but this is clearly not sufficient explanation.

The steering group discussions focused several times on service users telling us that, as researchers, we had to understand that the things that were being said about specialist palliative care social work had to be distinguished from their experiences of social work in other contexts. Social workers generally were seen as failing not just on one but on many fronts, and in particular were linked with insensitive and inappropriate handling of child protection issues. One set of process notes record that one man grew tearful when the discussion centred on this aspect of social work. Feelings ran high among service users and there was evidence that in some cases these negative feelings were based not just on hearsay or press reports but on personal experiences of involvement with social services' children and family teams.

Some of the parents, especially the lone parents involved, talked quite openly about the fear they had that if they agreed to see the specialist palliative care social worker, they risked their own child being taken into care. One person told us that he would definitely have been too anxious to let his teenage daughter, whose mother had died, see the hospice social worker, whom he clearly held in high regard, because of his previous disturbing experiences of social work. He was unclear whether there were any links between the hospice social worker and the local authority social work team. These types of anxiety become more understandable when we remember that there was also a widespread lack of clarity about what social workers in palliative care actually do.

It might be tempting to dismiss such parental anxiety as ignorance or as just ensuing from media misrepresentation of social work but, all too often historically, social work has let parents and children down (Packman and Hall 1998).

Spelling out the social work role clearly

This raises questions about how many other people may actually shy away from specialist palliative care social work because of such fears. Do specialist palliative care social workers need to spell out their supportive role for children more clearly and directly address service users' anxieties about potentially losing their children? While some service users told us they had found the specialist palliative care social worker absolutely crucial in supporting their children in the face of enormous loss, there were other parents whose children had not seen the social worker. We were told several times that this was because the children themselves had chosen not to see the social worker, perhaps because of shyness. While it should not simply be assumed that all children would benefit from seeing the social worker, again we have to ask whether some of these parents might be blocking this opportunity for their children to receive support because of unallayed fears and unanswered questions about the nature and role of social work in palliative care. This would be a logical and understandable response, given the concerns and feelings many service users expressed.

Social work and the loss of independence

A second aspect of service users' pre-existing concerns about social workers was their readiness to link social work to loss of independence rather than to efforts to sustain independence. Many service users saw social workers as bossy and controlling rather than empowering. They had pictured the people who need social workers as either not wanting independence or being incapable of it. As loss of independence and loss of control are often cited by people living with life-threatening illness as one of their greatest problems (Anderson et al. 2001), it should not be surprising that relatively few of the service users had referred themselves to the specialist palliative care social workers.

Social work was still inextricably linked in some people's minds with marginalization, stigma and degradation. Again it might be expected that there was often initial ambivalence about seeing the specialist palliative care social worker, especially given people's general ignorance about what specialist palliative care social workers actually do.

RELIANCE ON OTHER PROFESSIONALS FOR REFERRALS

We have seen that there were very few self-referrals to specialist palliative care social work. We look at referrals in more detail later in Chapter 9, but there is a relevant point to make here. If referrals are not going to be made at the request of the service users themselves, then specialist palliative care social workers will need to either rely on other professionals for referral or take a very proactive approach themselves to seeing service users.

There was little evidence that any of the service users had been referred to the hospice or specialist palliative care service specifically for social work support. However, there was evidence in many people's accounts of service users who had been very distressed by their situation and who seemed to have been entirely appropriate referrals for specialist palliative care social work *not* being referred until very late in the day. We need to ask whether medical and nursing colleagues, both in acute services and in primary care, are aware of the potential support that is available to patients through specialist palliative care social work. Some service users told us that, from their experience, they did not believe other professionals knew about social work.

Consideration also needs to be given to the bigger issue of whether these professionals could also have themselves internalized the negative images of social work which are so pervasive. The study did not set out to explore the attitudes of other professionals towards specialist palliative care social work. There was only the one instance of a social worker being openly belittled by other professionals to a service user. But in view of the gatekeeping role played by other professionals in palliative care, it is essential that specialist palliative care social workers are themselves clear about the importance of what they have to offer service users and are prepared to make clear to other professionals, not just the breadth and scope of the role, but also the value and centrality of their work for service users.

OWNING THE PROFESSION

This problem of service users not necessarily being clear about the nature and purpose of specialist palliative care social work also seemed in some cases to be compounded by social workers themselves. We were struck by the number of service users who were unclear that the person they had seen was indeed a social worker (although they all were, as this was a basic criterion for selection). Two factors seemed to be operating here:

1. Social work was being called by other names, such as 'family support'.

2. The social workers had simply never introduced themselves explicitly as social workers, leaving at least one individual to believe the social worker was, in fact, a nurse (sometimes they had introduced themselves as counsellors rather than social workers).

It was clear from discussions in one of the steering groups that many service users did not realize that social workers using other titles were in fact social workers at all. Although the picture was by no means clear, there were some worrying indicators that specialist palliative care social workers did not always *themselves* see social work in a positive light and sought to distance themselves from its more negative connotations. Their hesitant and apologetic approach to the title 'social worker' can be seen as an expression of this.

While it is easy to understand why departures from using the term 'social worker' might have come about, this raises further questions about whether the social workers could unwittingly be further undermining the image and credibility of social work. Here were some outstanding examples of social work functioning well and being seen in very positive terms by people who did not actually realize that they were witnessing social work at all.

It would also be interesting to find out more about whether service users see someone calling himself or herself a 'counsellor' as able to offer as holistic a service as someone using the title of 'social worker', or whether single people feel that a 'family support worker' has relevance to them. Whilst it was beyond the remit of this study to explore such questions further, there did seem sufficient evidence to suggest that there is some reluctance amongst specialist palliative care social workers to 'own' their own profession, a finding corroborated in Currer (2001). How might this impact upon the ability of specialist palliative care social workers to persuade other professional groups of the value, legitimacy and importance of the social work service?

Finally the question needs to be raised that if there is a pervasive negativity about social work in general, together with a lack of clarity about specialist palliative care social work in particular, then can those responsible for funding and staffing palliative care services be expected to have an informed view about the importance to be attached to specialist palliative care social work? We may doubt it. It is easy to imagine that when staffing is being considered for new or expanding teams, decisions are made to look for professionals from disciplines such as psychology that have arguably enjoyed a better press than social work. It is important that such decisions are taken for appropriate reasons, based on meeting need, rather than for the wrong reasons, such as having a negative and inaccurate view of what social work has to offer users of specialist palliative care. There are still hospices and palliative care teams who do not employ any specialist palliative care social workers and many more where the social worker works single handed. In the light of what the service users we spoke to told us about the crucial importance of social work, for them, in helping them cope with life-threatening illnesses, family crises, death and bereavement, this omission would appear to be very serious indeed.

SUMMARY

In this chapter we considered some of the negative ways in which social work in general is viewed by potential service users and looked at the way that this may impact on the take-up of specialist social work within palliative care.

There seems to be particular anxiety among parents about the motives and intentions of social workers (relating to perceptions of child protection social work) and a lack of clarity about the social work role within palliative care. This may have particular implications for the support of children and young people in specialist palliative care social work. Social work also appears to be linked in people's minds with lack of independence. Social workers tended to be viewed as bossy and controlling. Such views are likely to deter self-referral.

It is not only service users who may be influenced by such negative images of social work, but also health care and other professionals – as well as some social workers themselves. This is a factor which may restrict access to specialist palliative care social work. There appears to be a reluctance to embrace the title 'social worker' among some specialist palliative care social workers. While this may be understandable, its possible consequences in terms of further weakening the role and identity of the profession need to be explored further.

CHAPTER 9

THE PROBLEM OF REFERRAL

The issue of referrals is a fundamental one for specialist palliative care social workers. As we have seen, few people were referred to a hospice or palliative care service specifically for social work support and yet many service users told us that they wished they had met their social worker much earlier. Some even said they would have valued this type of specialist social work support right from the point of diagnosis. It was clear that many service users and their loved ones were reaching the specialist palliative care setting without ever having been offered support other than that provided by the medical professionals with whom they came in contact. Service users were clear that, however good this support might have been – and many spoke extremely well of it – it was fundamentally different from the type of help they were able to get when they finally met the social worker.

The question of how people get to see the specialist palliative care social worker therefore takes on a new urgency, especially in the light of the evidence confirming that many service users began with very negative views of social work and were therefore unlikely to seek to refer themselves to a social work service. The findings from our study are also reinforced by other work high-lighting the lack of social work involvement in palliative care. For example, in 2005 Clausen and others reported on the experiences of 40 people with lung cancer and advanced cardiac failure. They found that:

> social workers were conspicuous by their absence from the lives of these forty vulnerable adults, who were living and dying in the community with many unmet needs which, potentially, could be met by social-work input. The study highlights six areas of concern in which social-work assessment and intervention could have impacted on dying patients' quality of life and that of their carers: loss and dependency, family-centred issues, carers' needs, practical tasks, emotional and spiritual struggles, and finally, support needs of staff. (Clausen *et al.* 2005, p.277)

MEDICALLY ORIENTATED REFERRAL

Our findings raise an immediate issue about referral. Given that many service users said they wanted early referral to the specialist palliative care social worker, why were so few patients referred to specialist palliative care specifically for this kind of support? Almost all service users stated that their referral to specialist palliative care had come about for symptom control or another medical reason. Our findings are corroborated by a study looking at the reasons for referral to specialist palliative care by general practitioners (Shipman *et al.* 2002), where there is certainly no direct mention of social work services. We do not know whether funding arrangements determine the priorities of referral or whether psychosocial issues simply do not lead to the same urgent concern as medical issues among those professionals responsible for the bulk of referrals to specialist palliative care. Eagle and De Vries (2005) offer some additional insight. In a qualitative study looking at admission to hospices, they found that admissions for purely psychosocial reasons (even in crisis) were reluctantly agreed even when there were beds available.

> Of the total admission requests (n=42) two were for psychosocial care. The limited data relating to such requests is significant by its absence... It appeared that a psychosocial admission was deemed appropriate only as a last resort. (p.588)

Gott, Ahmedzai and Wood (2001) found that doctors and nurses in an acute hospital setting had very different views about which patients had palliative care needs. There was agreement in only a small percentage of cases. They found that nurses were more likely than doctors to pick up on psychosocial issues and on the needs of non-cancer patients. It would also be interesting to see how assessment by a social worker might have differed. They concluded that:

> within research and audit, it has been seen that relying on the perceptions of one staff group is not adequate when assessing levels of palliative care need within hospital settings. (p.459)

It could be that the specialist palliative care units themselves give out a strong message that medical needs will receive priority in bed or other resource allocation – we don't yet know.

What does seem important is that social workers working in specialist palliative care play their part in actively challenging the view that medical need should always come first. One of the basic definitions of palliative care is that it 'integrates the psychological and spiritual aspects of patient care' (WHO 2002). It has traditionally been associated with a holistic approach to care and support. Yet it was evident from many of the service users' accounts that psychological need had not led to referral. It seemed as if referral only happened once the severity of physical symptoms had caught up with the severity of emotional distress. Still less was there evidence that social problems, for example housing or financial difficulties, had played any part in bringing about a referral. Yet service users told us that these were sometimes the very issues that had caused them the most difficulty and suffering and made their illness particularly hard to deal with.

When other professionals play a gatekeeping role, it is important that they are provided with relevant, up-to-date and clear information about the scope and potential of specialist palliative care social work and of its importance to service users – who do not necessarily put their medical concerns at the top of their own personal hierarchy of need. There is evidence that the social work role is not well understood by other professionals (Bliss 1998; Bliss, Cowley and While 2000; Davies and Connolly 1995; McLeod, Bywaters and Cooke 2003). It is important that the message gets through to referring bodies that the specialist social worker can be accessed without the patient necessarily needing other specialist medical input. If specialist palliative care social work is not available in this way in all settings, then questions need to be asked about why it isn't and why priorities have been set in such a way.

The findings from this project are mirrored elsewhere in social work. Bywaters (1991) found that referrals to social workers in acute general hospitals were left to 'whim and chance'. Another study looked at referrals to social workers in an acute elderly unit of a district general hospital (McLeod 1995). It found that self-referral was rare; no direct approach was made by the social workers to service users and knowledge of the social work presence on site was limited. Some older people were not referred to the social workers despite having serious problems. The fact that these were not being dealt with 'presaged the collapse of independent living and further deterioration in health' (p.342). McLeod concluded:

> An interprofessional referral system which excluded older patients' participation on an equal footing – depriving them of information about social workers and direct access to them – posed substantial problems for patients' well being (1995, p.343)

SEEING THE SOCIAL WORKER IN SPECIALIST PALLIATIVE CARE

Once referral to the specialist palliative care unit has been made there is still the question of how the service user gets to see the social worker. This study suggests that this is an issue which has not yet been systematically addressed.

Preferences for proactive and informal approaches

Our findings showed that service users liked it when specialist palliative care social workers were proactive about getting in touch with them. They especially liked informal approaches made by the social worker in person. These seemed to make people feel cared for and safe. It was apparent that the specialist palliative care social workers had a high level of interpersonal skills that quickly enabled people to feel at ease, immediately countering preconceived, negative feelings about social workers in general. They gave social work a human face. We were often told that 'she didn't seem like a social worker'.

Some of the men we spoke to liked the fact that they had not been given too much choice about being referred to social work and that the social workers concerned had just turned up uninvited. Had these men been asked if they wanted to see a social worker, they agreed that they would probably have said 'no thank you', thereby isolating themselves from the very support which they found so crucial. The importance of this cannot be emphasized too strongly because among these service users were individuals who felt certain that, had they not seen the specialist palliative care social worker, they would have gone on to attempt suicide.

We know from conversations we have had with social workers that some do not work in this proactive and informal way and indeed would worry that what we are suggesting would represent a reduction in patient choice over whether or not to see a social worker. There is clearly a tension here. There was certainly no evidence from any of the service users we spoke to that they had felt obliged to go on seeing any social worker who had made informal contact. On the contrary, we were left with the strong impression that, by their very nature, the informal contacts had gone a long way in countering some of the most negative views service users held about social workers.

Inconsistent patterns of referral

Other themes that raise concern emerge from people's accounts. There seems to be little consistency in how referrals to the specialist palliative care social workers are made. In some settings, as we have indicated, the social workers clearly had a policy of introducing themselves to all new patients and yet in other settings we found that the patient had only been referred quite late in the day. It appeared in some cases almost fortuitous that they had been seen at all. Some service users felt other people might easily slip through the net.

When we spoke to *bereaved* service users, however, the picture of referrals was different and clearer. Many of these people said they had been contacted as part of the 'system' of bereavement support. Patients had certainly not mentioned systems to us. The structure of support for bereaved people seemed more transparent and included leaflets handed out on bereavement, and letters inviting them back to the specialist palliative care unit for either individual or group support. Bereaved service users were aware that others had received similar letters and some referred to telephone calls made by the social worker 'out of the blue' enquiring whether they needed support.

The general impression that we formed was that referral systems for patients and those close to them were inconsistent and in some cases far from watertight. Structured systems for bereavement support were more apparent, both to us and to service users themselves. Some of the people who had been bereaved told us how distressed they had been when they were looking after the person who had died. Sometimes the experiences had been harrowing both for them and for their loved one. Given this, it remains unclear why some of them had only been seen for the first time after bereavement. Service users' fears that people could slip through the net seemed to have some justification. Many of the people who were bereaved said that they wished they had met the specialist social worker earlier – *before* their loved one died.

POSSIBLE EXPLANATIONS FOR INCONSISTENCIES

It is important to ask why there might be a lack of clear referral policies for patients and their families. At present we can only speculate. There are a number of possibilities. For example, are some specialist palliative care social workers afraid of being overwhelmed by the number of patients and their families who potentially could profit from social work support and for that reason have not developed effective referral systems? Are they rationing support through operating what is in effect an inconsistently applied and unstructured referral policy? Given the fact that many specialist palliative care social workers operate in small teams or work single handed, it would not be surprising to find that they were, consciously or unconsciously, acting in ways to limit demands made on them.

A second possibility is that some of the social workers are not clear about the role they have with patients. Are they confident that the kind of help that they can offer is fundamentally different to that already being provided by other members of the multi-professional team? It wasn't possible to answer this question with the data we had, but it is worth pursuing. In particular we wonder whether some social workers may be uncertain about their own counselling skills in the absence of a formal counselling qualification. There was certainly a hint of this in two cases where individuals were referred by their social workers to counsellors, though the service users in each case felt that, in fact, the social workers' greatest strength had been their counselling skills! It may be that sometimes social workers are not confident of their level of knowledge and skills and are therefore underestimating the particular contribution they can make to the patient and those close to them. Yet service users seem to think that they do have a particular professional contribution to make and value it.

THE ROLE OF OTHER PROFESSIONALS

This brings us back to the role of other professionals in referring service users to specialist palliative care social work. If social workers are seldom the first specialist palliative care professional to be involved with a patient, just how big a task is it to persuade others, who are already seeing the patient, that the social worker needs to be involved? What impact may other professionals have acting as gatekeepers? As long as there is no policy of seeing all new patients automatically, it is important to think about the context and process within which the specialist palliative care social workers might 'pick up' new referrals.

Multidisciplinary teams within hospices and other palliative care teams often have meetings where the patient's 'case' is presented by the key worker, who is frequently a named nurse, and comment is then invited from other members of the broader team. The medical model of care generally predominates in these situations. We would suggest that it is easy for the perspectives of the nurse and the doctor who 'clerked' the patient into the unit to take precedence, even in teams that truly value multidisciplinary working and emphasize holistic care. Heaven and Maguire (1997) reported on research which showed that hospice nurses failed to pick up on a range of concerns that were of importance to patients and in particular they failed to identify emotional concerns. If nurses are not consistently picking up such concerns, then they cannot be shared with the broader team in multidisciplinary meetings. In such circumstances, it wouldn't be surprising if sometimes it appeared that there was no role for the social worker. Even when such issues are picked up and documented, other research suggests that action is not always taken (Anderson et al. 2001). That study found that patients in palliative care and heart failure clinics disclosed their most troublesome concerns and these were documented in medical or nursing notes, but action on their concerns was less likely to be taken if these were social or psychological rather than physical. Thus:

> between 24% and 31% of social/functional problems were not addressed by staff, suggesting the need for more information about local services and referral pathways, or that social worker input is required. (Anderson et al. 2001, p.286)

It was apparent from some of the service users that we spoke to that they had only shared the depth of their distress once they had learned to trust the quality of the relationship with the social worker, so the level of unmet need may be greater than studies suggest.

Given the fact that so many service users said that they would have liked earlier involvement from the specialist palliative care social worker, it does not seem unreasonable to question how appropriate it is to leave judgements on when social work is relevant to team members from other disciplines, especially if they do not include social workers in the decision-making process. At the same time, there is the danger that a stretched social worker managing single handed in a busy unit may be only too glad of this extra layer of filtering.

We have sometimes sensed, undertaking this study and meeting specialist palliative care social workers, that there can be some embarrassment about 'pushing' social work support within palliative care. We have not detected the same reticence on the part of the other services, such as physiotherapy, occupational therapy or complementary therapies, that are on offer. It seems important once again to ask just how damaging negative perceptions of social work generally may be, how much they are internalized by social workers themselves, what their effects are for specialist palliative care social work and how far reaching the implications may be for service users.

WHY THE DIFFERENT PICTURE FOR BEREAVED SERVICE USERS?

We also need to consider why the picture of referrals is different in the context of bereavement. Again there are a number of possibilities. For example, it may be that specialist palliative care social workers have a greater confidence in their role, their knowledge and their skills in the area of bereavement. Do they see it as being more 'rightfully' their area? It certainly is a field that is less controlled by other professionals. There are fewer gatekeepers operating there.

There also appears to be a stronger tradition of social work debate in this area. For example, there seem to be more professional journals addressing research and practice issues in relation to social work with bereaved people than to social work with people with life-limiting conditions. Bereavement seems to be an area that specialist palliative care social workers themselves feel confident enough to write about and share practice readily. Our impression is that there is far less written by specialist palliative care social workers about practice with patients and their loved ones. Bereavement work is also an area where specialist palliative care social workers work closely with volunteers, often trained and managed by social workers themselves. This may make social workers feel less threatened by a potential 'flood' of referrals. It may offer them a stronger sense of having help at hand. We also wonder whether managing volunteers boosts social workers' feelings of professional competence and control. In essence it looks as though bereavement support may be an area of specialist palliative care that has been largely seen as the preserve of the specialist palliative care social worker and one where they have been able to develop their expertise, professional skills and indeed their professional confidence more fully.

Other restrictions on access to social work

Not all hospices, however, see a role for specialist palliative care social workers in their bereavement support programme. Sometimes they opt instead to employ counsellors in this role who are not always qualified social workers. This raises the question of whether bereaved people then receive as broad and flexible a service as they might. Many of the bereaved people we spoke to had complex problems relating to housing, finances and legal issues. They told us how important it had been to them and how relieved they were that the specialist palliative care social worker had been able to take on these worrying practical and social issues, as well as helping them and their family members cope with the emotional aspects of their loss.

This also has ramifications for the groupwork undertaken with service users. Counsellors tend to work on an individual basis with service users. Can we expect counsellors to bring service users together in groups as readily as specialist palliative care social workers do? Service users were very positive about the value of supporting and getting support from other service users. The wide repertoire of social work approaches, using individual, family and group work, emerged as an important strength of palliative care social work. It is important to know whether this aspect of specialist palliative care social work is diminished or lost, to the potential detriment of patients and their families, in those palliative care units that have chosen to structure their teams without a social worker in the bereavement service. Further research is likely to be needed here.

REFERRAL AND EQUALITY ISSUES

We now want to turn to another aspect of referral that demands further investigation. Earlier in the book, in Chapter 6, we explored issues of difference in relation to users of specialist palliative care social work. We wanted to see if there were any significant differences for people in terms of age, 'race', gender, sexuality, religion, class and so on. As we reported, what was most striking was the high level of consistency across all groups. In terms of satisfaction with the specialist palliative care social work service there were no discernible differences between groups. We were aware, however, from the literature of some differences in access to palliative care (Oliviere and Monroe 2004). A further issue emerges from our findings in relation to access to specialist palliative care social work. It does appear that there are specific groups which may be slipping through the net more readily than others because of the way in which referral processes currently work in palliative care. We were led to this view because we found we had to put much more effort in to recruit some service users to the project than others. This suggested to us that there may be some further inequalities in who gets seen by a specialist palliative care service worker. Certainly fewer members of some groups seem to reach them. We next discuss these issues in relation to some specific groups of service users where they particularly seemed to apply:

- men
- children and young people
- Black and minority ethnic service users
- people with different diagnoses.

As we have already said, we gained little information in relation to people's sexuality, so that there may also be additional exclusions relating to gay men, lesbians and bisexuals, but we do not have data relating to it. Also we did not interview anyone identified as having learning difficulties, although we know that people with learning difficulties face particular issues and barriers in the palliative care system (Hogg, Northfield and Turnbull 2001; McEnhill 2004; Wijne 2003). Macmillan Cancer Relief jointly with the National Network for Palliative Care of People with Learning Disabilities recently set up an information and support service for people with learning difficulties, service workers and carers.

Men and referral

We found it particularly difficult to access men in our project. Data published for 2000–2001 (Hospice Information Service 2002b) show that men and women are overall fairly equally represented as users of specialist palliative care services, though there were more women (55%) represented in the older age groups of patients, and more women (56%) were users of day-care services. It seems important to audit whether specialist palliative care social workers are seeing fairly equal numbers of men and women or whether they see significantly more women as our recruitment difficulties might suggest. If, as we suspect, many more women are seen, what does this mean? We have to consider how the predominance of women workers within specialist care social work may impact upon the gender profile of the people who use their services. Do men feel uncomfortable about seeking help generally or would the patterns of uptake be any different if there were more male social workers? Some commentators argue that men find it easier to express emotion in front of a woman counsellor or group facilitator (Crossland 1998), but the picture remains unclear.

There is also the issue of whether, because of their more active coping styles, men are perceived as being less in need of support than women, and so are less likely to be referred. This is a possibility put forward by some researchers (Barbarin and Chesler 1986, cited in Thompson 1997). Do some men fear that social workers will focus exclusively on their emotions and worry that they will be trapped with feelings of discomfort and awkwardness?

Certainly we were told on a number of occasions by female service users that their husbands, brothers, fathers, sons, did not want to talk to any professional about the illness or loss they were facing. These women tried to offer these men support themselves, but sometimes found this very difficult. For these women, this was an added burden as they struggled to cope with their overall situation. Others have written about this difficult role many women play (Brody 1978, cited in Bright 1996; Kayser and Sormanti 2002).

Our study revealed that men who did access the services of the specialist palliative care social worker spoke about the support they received in just as positive terms as the women. As we have already indicated, some of these men told us that they were glad the social worker had been quite forceful about seeing them. But what might be done to support the men who, while resisting referral, are not necessarily coping well?

One service user felt that it would be helpful to produce leaflets which were written by the specialist palliative care social workers and specifically aimed at men. For instance, she believed that a leaflet about breast cancer written specifically for men would have been helpful, and she felt that her husband would have read such a leaflet even though he found it difficult to talk to her and refused to speak to the social worker directly. Leaflets have typically been produced which are aimed at either adults or children and young people. Leaflets produced for men have usually been about male cancers. Perhaps additional thought should be given to whether men and women have different information needs and if so what these might be.

Certainly our study does seem to indicate that men, particularly younger men, liked to have the social work role spelled out very clearly to them. This did not always happen and was a source of concern for some people. If men do find it more difficult to talk about their situation, initial assessment based on a more informal approach, where the emphasis is on the service user telling their story, may prove inappropriate and rather difficult for some men. A more proactive approach from the social worker may be needed. We are not suggesting here an approach which is controlling, but one which is more structured where, in spelling out their role, the social worker gives more cues to men around which to offer their account.

Alternatively there might be a place for written 'checklists' or self-assessment forms. These would not be to replace, but to supplement, the informal assessment. The evidence is that when such forms are used to gather evidence for research there is a high level of willingness to disclose troublesome issues (Anderson *et al.* 2001). It may be that practice could be enhanced by the use of some of these same forms for assessment purposes. All these questions and issues seem well worth pursuing.

We were also struck by the very positive way in which many of the men described their experiences of groupwork, especially when it gave them the opportunity to meet other men in similar situations to themselves. Some men also spoke positively about the help that they had been able to provide for other service users, and this seemed to have played a significant part in the maintenance of their self-esteem. It seems possible that groupwork might, for some men at least, offer a more easily accepted way of accessing the support they need and value. A few men commented that they felt that women had groups specifically aimed at them (usually for women with breast cancer) and they clearly would have liked something similar. Certainly this seems to be a profitable area for further thought and discussion. We became aware that not all social workers offered groupwork and, where it was offered, it seemed more generally aimed at bereaved people rather than patients or those offering them support. This could be seen as a gap, which we would venture might particularly impact on men. Clearly there are resource implications. It was all too apparent that there were very real limits on what small teams or individual social workers could realistically be expected to offer.

In addition specialist palliative care social workers might also need to think further about how they can sustain women in the work that they do supporting the men in their lives. While this was clearly happening a great deal, fresh thinking may still be needed about how best social workers can offer such arm's length support.

Children, young people and referral

Our original intention in this study had been to include bereaved children and young people under the age of 19 among those we interviewed. Ethical approval was granted for this aspect of the study. However, in practice, it proved difficult to access children and a decision was reluctantly made to limit the study to adults and to flag up the continuing need for such research (although one 18-year-old was included).

Our findings suggest that although the specialist palliative care social workers were seeing parents, including parents of young children, only a small proportion of these social workers seem to have worked directly with the children of the family. This was something of a surprise as, within specialist palliative care, social workers have been active in developing services for children (Monroe 1998; Oliviere, Hargreaves and Monroe 1998). We are not assuming that all children will need professional support (Worden 1996). As suggested in the findings, it may be, though, that some parents act in ways to restrict or block social work contact with children, because of their wider concerns about social work. In addition, young people themselves often resist offers of support. Research shows that the great majority of bereaved adolescents do not feel the need for professional contact (Harrison and Harrington 2001).

However, a small number of parents did express the view that there was more scope for work with children and it appeared that these parents had not only not blocked the referral of their children, but would actually have welcomed it. But they did not know whether direct support for children and young people might be available. Again this raises questions about whether all specialist palliative care social workers feel they have the skills and experience to offer a suitable service to children. If not, have they worked out strategies for ensuring that children and young people are supported? This seems particularly important in view of the mounting evidence that many children and young people carry huge, but often hidden, responsibilities as 'carers' for sick and disabled parents and if left unsupported are likely to suffer both educationally and in terms of isolation from social and other opportunities (Dearden and Becker 1997, 2000; Walker 1996).

The indications in this project are that where direct work was taking place with children either individually or in groups, it was valued highly both by parents and the children themselves. Literature can also sometimes help bridge the gap where there is no direct contact. Many specialist palliative care teams have produced literature for children and young people about aspects of loss, death and bereavement. But this raises a question. Is it sufficient to meet their needs in the absence of direct work or are some children and young people losing out on support that they might value at such critical times in their lives? There has been a move to provide information and support for bereaved young people through the use of the internet. An example is the website www.rd4u.org.uk, which is part of Cruse Bereavement Care's Youth Involvement Project. It gives young people the chance to share their experiences directly with one another through their message board system. Private messages can also be left for the team and can be responded to if an email address is given. Many young people appear to find this approach helpful and the site is well used (though there are comments that fewer boys are writing to the message board).

It would seem that new technology may offer specialist palliative social workers new tools that may prove helpful in making the service accessible to young people who do not respond to more traditional approaches. It may also be that social workers are reluctant to take on more work with children and that this is again related to their inadequate resources. If so this needs to be flagged. It raises a more general point. If social work within specialist palliative care is under-resourced there is likely to be little scope for the development of innovative and creative work.

Black and minority ethnic service users and referral

In our study we had intended to talk to service users from as many different ethnic backgrounds as possible. This did not prove easy. Although the number of people from minority ethnic groups in the study was proportionally more than those who use specialist palliative care services, the actual numbers were still small. There is ongoing and well-documented concern about equality of access to specialist palliative care and whether services are meeting the specific needs of different minority ethnic groups (Hill and Penso 1995; Koffman and Higginson 2001; Smaje and Field 1997). Our study could throw no extra light on this issue, but in view of the very small numbers of people from minority ethnic groups that we were able to involve in the study we would venture that, at the very least, specialist palliative care social workers should be auditing their own referrals to ensure that, once in the specialist palliative care system, people from minority ethnic backgrounds do not meet further barriers in accessing the full range of services, including specialist palliative care social work. Social workers may also be able to play an active part in outreach work. This seems to be essential to ensure that people from minority ethnic groups know about specialist palliative care services (Karim, Bailey and Tunna 2000).

Our study does not reveal any significant differences in what people from minority ethnic groups want from specialist palliative care social work, nor in their experience of it, compared with other groups. However, as we have reported, there does seem to be some evidence that major issues relating to poverty and poor housing were highlighted by more people from minority ethnic backgrounds than others. The numbers were too small to say that this was a statistically significant finding, but it would certainly be in line with findings from elsewhere, which indicate that these are issues disproportionately affecting black and minority ethnic communities.

Specialist palliative care social workers have much to offer towards helping with the specific kinds of welfare rights issues associated with such structural problems. It is vital that the breadth of their role is made clear to all service users. However, as we have indicated, this was not always done. It is also another reason why it is essential that the holistic nature of the social work role is recognized and maintained in specialist palliative care services if the needs of all communities are to be met. We would also raise the question of whether specialist palliative care social workers could themselves do more to ensure that specialist palliative care services are being accessed by people from all sections of the community. It is also likely to be helpful to monitor the ethnic composition of the workforce.

Diagnostic category and referral

Specialist palliative care is open to criticism for its failure to meet the needs of people with diagnoses other than cancer. Independent hospices originated as a cancer service and some still restrict access along these lines. Yet there are now pressures from government policy, progressive practitioners and service users for specialist palliative care services to be much more inclusive. Certainly our sample included a greater proportion of service users with a non-cancer diagnosis than the national norm for palliative care services, which is estimated at 4.8 per cent (minimum data sets – National Survey 1999–2000: Hospice Information Service 2003). There is consistent evidence that people with diagnoses other than cancer are not reaching palliative care (Elkington et al. 2004; Gore, Brophy and Greenstone 2000; Ingleton, Skilbeck and Clark 2001). Specialist palliative care social workers cannot themselves resolve this problem, but they should do everything possible to ensure that the services they offer are relevant and will meet the needs of those people with a non-cancer diagnosis who do engage with the service overall. There was evidence in the study that service users with other conditions did not feel the social workers were well prepared. They mentioned lack of knowledge about their specific condition; lack of knowledge of relevant services; and lack of knowledge about legal implications of some industrial diseases. All perceived the social workers as willing to seek information and to learn from the service users themselves, but did highlight that there were training needs to be addressed.

THE IMPORTANCE OF AUDITING REFERRAL

The focus of our project was specialist palliative care social work *practice*. It was not intended to explore in depth the process whereby service users do or, more to the point, do not access that practice. However, the study has highlighted problems of access and referral and the part that referral may place in reinforcing inequalities in access to specialist palliative care social work. Practice has to be considered in this context. This is an important finding from the project. It does seem important to ask whether specialist palliative care social workers know enough about the profile of their caseload and patterns of referrals. Extraneous and discriminatory factors at work on these need to be identified and addressed. They need to know whether there are holes in their systems and, if so, which groups of service users are most likely to be slipping through. Ultimately this is likely to have significant funding implications. If gaps in service provision are to be plugged, if referrals are to be increased, made at the right time and equity ensured, we can expect the demand for specialist palliative care social work to increase. This will require an expansion in numbers of specialist palliative care social workers as well as the addressing of organizational and management issues. There needs to be a systematic audit of referral to specialist palliative care social work to gain a clearer picture of the nature and scale of need and to provide an evidenced basis for seeking to respond to that need.

SUMMARY

This chapter examines the problems relating to referral which are denying people a valued source of social support from specialist palliative care social work. Service users place particular value on specialist palliative care social work. Yet few seem to be referred to palliative care services specifically to access such social work support. Many do not receive it at all and some say they would have liked to receive it earlier. There is a low rate of self-referral to specialist palliative care social work and service users repeatedly mention late referral by other professionals. The problem seemed to be greater for patients than bereaved people.

The chapter explores issues of:

- inconsistent referral
- late referral
- the role of other professionals and a medical model in referral
- differences in relation to referral emerging between patients and people experiencing bereavement.

It also explores other possible restrictions on access to specialist palliative care social work. In addition, it examines equality issues in relation to referral. Some groups of people seem to be less likely to be referred to specialist palliative care social work than others. This seems to include:

- children and young people
- men
- black and minority ethnic service users
- people with different diagnoses (particularly non-cancer diagnoses).

The authors examine issues that may be operating in relation to each of these groups to limit their access to specialist palliative care social work. They highlight the importance of auditing referral and access to specialist palliative care social work as a way of overcoming for the future the difficulties identified in this study.

CHAPTER 10

THE NATURE, STRENGTHS AND WEAKNESSES OF PRACTICE

As we highlighted in the last chapter, a key concern about specialist palliative care social work is the barriers in the way of service users accessing it. Those service users who did access specialist palliative care social work generally found it very helpful. In the next two chapters we want to develop this discussion by exploring in more depth some of the strengths (and perhaps weaknesses) of specialist palliative care social work practice. To do this, we consider more closely in this chapter two of the areas which service users identify as being important to them. The first of these is the nature of the relationship between service users and social workers. In particular we examine the concept of 'friendship', which service users frequently highlighted as an integral part of this relationship. We then discuss the social work process, looking at different approaches and at the meaning and importance of 'holistic' care and support. In Chapter 11 we review some of the theoretical work relating to loss and bereavement and make links between these, specialist palliative care social work practice and the experiences of the service users we spoke with.

As we have reported, almost all the service users we spoke with were very positive about their experiences of specialist palliative care social work. The characteristics of the social work support, which were emphasized as being of most importance, were consistently highlighted across all groups of service users. It was difficult and sometimes almost impossible to pick out differences – in levels of satisfaction – between men and women, between patients and people who had been bereaved, between younger and older service users and between people from different class or ethnic backgrounds. We would suggest that this is because these service users were receiving a service that was essentially led by the needs expressed by service users, tailored to the needs of individual service users, and that this meant in practice that it felt appropriate for all. What though were the characteristics that were valued most consistently?

THE IMPORTANCE OF THE RELATIONSHIP

One of the first issues to become apparent as we interviewed service users was the importance that they attached to the quality of the relationship they had developed with the specialist palliative care social worker. For example:

in the end it's really got to be a one-to-one thing between the people, you know, providing that a certain professionalism is preserved. (Man patient, white UK, age group 56–65)

Coupled with this was the sense they expressed of working with an ally. Another patient told us:

I'm more confident and I feel that I've got somebody on my side…that's the main thing for me is that I'm not on my own. (Man patient, white UK, age group 56–65)

Service users' emphasis on the relationship in social work should not come as a surprise (Ryan *et al.* 1999; Sudbery 2002). Its importance for successful social work practice has long been stressed. Biestek in 1961 writes of the centrality of the interpersonal relationship to the practice of social casework:

In surgery, dentistry and law for example, a good interpersonal relationship is desirable for the perfection of the service but it is not necessary for the essence of the service… A good relationship is necessary not only for the perfection, but also for the essence, of the casework service in every setting… (1961, p.19)

But more and more this aspect of practice has been negated, with the increasing trend for social work within statutory services to be reduced to a time-limited, check-box exercise where practical needs are scrutinized, but where the relationship between social worker and service user is very much a secondary consideration. Pressures towards this approach can be traced to the community care reforms of the early 1990s and the introduction of a managerially led model of 'care management' (Payne *et al.* 2005). But since then the role of social worker as organizer and referral agent or 'navigator' has continued to be stressed and less attention has been paid to intrinsic activities of social work practice or of being a social worker. With teams increasingly working on separate elements of the role, and especially with assessment and intervention split, there is every opportunity for relationship building to fall by the wayside and for what Harlow (2003) has termed 'managerial-techniques' practice to dominate. Within this formula, emotional needs run a high risk of being overlooked, as Howe (1996) puts it:

Relationships between social workers and clients change their character from interpersonal to economic, from therapeutic to transactional, from nurturing and supportive to contractual and service oriented. Welfare service become commodities to be traded… (p.93)

One of the strongest points to be made at the steering groups held as part of this project was that the members drew a sharp distinction between specialist palliative care social work and the way social work was being practised in other settings where they felt the emphasis was more on business than relationship building, as these two comments by members of the steering groups illustrate:

> Everything is conducted in a very business-like mentality, you know, and they are forgetting why they are there in the first place.

> They've got a job to do and they do their job and that's it. The caring aspect is not there. You are just a number. 'I've got to go and see number 1, number 2, number 3' – at the end of the day he goes home and he's finished.

As we indicated in Chapter 5, what service users seemed to value highly was the way in which the specialist palliative care social worker was someone who was prepared to stay alongside them in their passage, however harrowing, through illness or bereavement, almost as a 'friend', while demonstrating all the skills and knowledge traditionally associated with effective professional social work. It was as if they recognized and appreciated the expertise of the social worker without perceiving him or her as an expert who was remote from them and their lives. On the contrary, repeatedly we were told that service users viewed their social worker as a *friend*.

The attributes of friendship

We wonder whether 'friend' is a word that is shied away from in social work discussions and literature. Being viewed as a friend by the service user might after all imply a worrisome blurring of boundaries, a threat to professional identity and competence. Moreover some service users may not want this type of relationship, preferring something more formal. Being a friend to someone might well be viewed as something 'easy' to do and not requiring any particular skills. Most of us feel we are capable of friendship whereas the kind of friendship that seemed to be meant here, we would argue, was one requiring high levels of skill and expertise.

Because the service users to whom we spoke so consistently used this word and set it so resolutely against the notion of a professional, we think it is worth thinking more about what they might have meant by it and just what calling someone a friend implies about the nature of the relationship between service user and specialist palliative care social worker. Complex issues are raised here about the nature of social work, what people value from it and its identity as a 'profession' which we would suggest cannot be ducked.

More like a real friend?

It did not seem to us that service users were simply referring to the social worker as someone who was 'friendly', but rather that they perceived the social worker as having the attributes of a 'real' friend. Nor were we convinced that they were talking about being 'befriended', a role that has been seen in nursing research as more functional and with more boundaries than being a friend (Turner 1999, pp.153–60), though not all would agree with this; for example: 'The request to befriend can be very seductive; but it is important to resist it, since it blurs professional boundaries' (Faulkner and Maguire 1994, p.105).

Friendship literature makes it clear that although it is difficult to define friendship, there are some consistent core features of friendship that characterize the relationship, including bonds of affection, reciprocity and equality (Blieszner and Adams 1992; Duck 1991). Allan (1996) wrote:

> Within friendship there is little sense of social hierarchy or status difference...whatever the social differences outside the tie, at the core of friendship is the notion that friends regard and treat one another as equals within it. (p.89)

This certainly seemed to be how service users characterized their relationship with their specialist palliative care social worker, as can be seen by many of their comments (in Chapters 3 and 4). Service users did not appear to feel the relationship in any way diminished them or made them feel inferior because of their dependence on the social worker. This stands in really stark contrast to the way in which they had talked about their prior perceptions of social work, which had mostly been seen in negative terms as disempowering and built on strongly hierarchical and dependency-related relationships.

Balancing power and reciprocity

Power is generally seen as being more equally shared in relationships between friends than it is in relationships between 'clients' and 'professionals'. Given the powers and role of conventional statutory social workers, for example, this seems justified rather than surprising. And yet, with these service users, there was a real sense that they saw the power as shared. This was important to many service users as it made them feel free to say and do what was important to them. A number said that they felt able to talk to the social worker without feeling intimidated or as if they were using up the social worker's valuable time inappropriately. We were told constantly that they felt really listened to. A small number contrasted this with how they felt about their relationship with their medical consultant. Some expressed feelings of dissatisfaction with that relationship where the power was perceived as being almost entirely in the doctor's hands.

Reciprocity can also be seen as a key component of friendship and this ensures that, within friendship, the balance of power sits more equally between parties and the relationship is not exhausted by excessive demands from or upon either party (Allan 1996). Reciprocity was important for some service users. A number of people said they wanted to give something back to the social worker, in effect to keep the relationship balanced. Knowing a little about the social worker's life allowed people to show interest, concern and kindness; in other words, to engage in an ordinary balanced two-way human relationship. A number of service users said they valued chatting as much as, or in some cases more than, being 'counselled' and possibly chatting is an important part of keeping the relationship balanced, of keeping the 'expert' part of the relationship within bounds. While it could be said in many cases that the relationship was not 'balanced', since the service user at a very difficult time clearly needed more from it, this is not how it felt to them.

Some indicated that they 'gave back' to the social worker and the team by supporting fundraising initiatives of the hospice. Several indicated that they saw taking part in our study as a way of giving back to the social worker, which certainly presented us with some methodological issues to disentangle. But it also suggests that this feeling of wanting to give something back has implications for the potential of user involvement. It could also be seen as having regressive potential, leaving service users feeling indebted when this should not be the case.

Warmth and affection

Bonds of affection, a core element of friendship, were very apparent in service users' comments. Several service users reported acts of kindness and caring from their social workers and many times we were told that the social worker 'went beyond the call of duty'. We were told about being driven to hospital in the social worker's 'own time', about bunches of flowers and messages of support at anniversaries. We do not know whether or not the social workers themselves saw these acts as simply part of their professional repertoire, but they were interpreted as more than this. In service users' eyes they represented feelings of warmth, caring and affection on the part of the social worker. Carl Rogers (1961) writes of an important attainment in the counselling relationship:

> It is a real achievement when we can learn even in certain relationships, or at certain times in those relationships, that it is safe to care, that it is safe to relate to the other as a person for whom we have positive feelings... (p.52)

Many people told us that the social worker was 'genuine'; that he or she was not just 'doing a job'. Firmness and the ability to 'talk straight' were also mentioned as positive aspects of the relationship. Several people felt the social worker could, like a good friend, be honest with them and tell them if he or she thought they might be wrong about something.

Being known as a real person

But as well as these core characteristics, the notion of friendship appears to have other levels of meaning that relate to issues of identity and being known for what you are really like. With real friends pretences can be dropped and some see friendship playing an important role in helping individuals develop and maintain their sense of identity at times of transition and change (Jerome 1981; Norris and Tindale 1994). It was fundamentally important to the service users who participated in the project we carried out that they were seen as a 'real person' and not simply as a 'client' or a 'patient'. Friendship seems to suggest the idea of an ongoing relationship with a degree of continuity, which allows for this type of knowing. Again many of the people we spoke to had built their relationship with the social worker over a long period, sometimes years, and this continuity had enabled them to become known 'warts and all'. In turn this seems to relate to the building of trust so vital when someone is disclosing innermost thoughts and feelings. Other studies have also highlighted the importance service users attach to continuity (Beresford *et al.* 2005a; Harding and Beresford 1996).

Some of the service users told us how vitally important it was that the social worker really *knew* them so that decisions about such things as choices of nursing homes might in the future be made sensitively and in harmony with the service user's own personality – if they became too ill to play a big part in decision making. Currer (2001) talks about the concept of social death in relation to older people and admission to residential care. 'The experience of being treated as dead before you are... Residents themselves, relatives, or staff may view entry to residential care as a form of social burial' (pp.25–6).

For some service users, their feelings of vulnerability in the face of illness or imminent death were made easier to cope with because they had built up trust and confidence that the specialist palliative care social worker had really listened to them and would be able to advocate for them effectively should the need arise. This ability to advocate depended on the patient or bereaved person being known as a *real* person – for who he or she was. The importance of this cannot really be exaggerated: many authors show the impact of life-threatening illness on people's sense of self (Bailey and Corner 2003; Kayser and Sormanti 2002; Shapiro, Angus and Davis 1997). The service users to whom we spoke frequently felt that their identity was threatened by their illness or loss and yet they believed that the social worker somehow helped preserve the notion of the person they actually were.

The recognition of boundaries

We were struck by the importance of this theme of friendship and recognized that to emphasize it might lead to some critical questioning over whether professional boundaries and even the whole notion of 'being a professional' or 'acting professionally' were being put at risk. We certainly did not detect any suggestion from service users of a lack of professional good sense with relation to boundaries, but we felt that it was a profitable subject to explore more fully with a steering group, the members of which were all service users themselves. This was very helpful. These service users all said very clearly that they *did* see their social worker as a friend and that this was a very important aspect of the relationship for them. They told us that they *did* like to know something about him or her and his or her day-to-day life; they did not want a one-way relationship. But they were absolutely clear that they also understood that it was a friendship that had limits. They realized where these lay and they did not feel any need to overstep them. In fact part of the reciprocity within the relationship lay in not demanding too much from the social worker. Service users showed that they were concerned about this.

> I think sometimes I feel as though I've worn [the social worker] down with this family. (Woman patient, white UK, age group 46–55)

Throughout the study several service users picked up this theme of not taking too much from the relationship.

Friendship: An everyday kind of word

Another reason why service users placed so much emphasis on the concept of friendship might be because they wanted to convey the everyday nature of the relationship with the social worker; that is, it didn't feel to them like a professional relationship as it is conventionally understood. So often we were told 'she isn't like a social worker' and 'she is just an ordinary person'. This led us on to think about professionalism and the language of social work. Two recent studies have explored the language used by social workers in their day-to-day work with each other. Hawkins, Fook and Ryan (2001) found that rather than talking about 'empowering', 'advocating for' or 'collaborating with' service users, social workers were more likely to talk about 'interviewing', 'assessing', 'treating' or 'intervening with' their service users. They wrote: 'Social workers' language use appears to be quite incongruent with our stated mission of social justice' (pp.1–13).

Expanding on this theme, Becket (2003) looked at the preponderance of military terms in the everyday language used by social workers. He mentioned as examples 'duty', 'field' and 'intervention', as well as 'going in', writing:

> I believe that when we speak of a social worker 'going in' there is, on the edge of our minds, an implication that he or she is carrying out a potentially dangerous operation in hostile territory. (pp.635–6)

What these writers are highlighting of course is the code for 'doing to' and not for 'doing with'. The words we speak and the jargon we use are one of the powerful ways in which we identify not only our professional image, but also our value system. The service users involved in this project seemed to us to be saying that they preferred it if their social workers did not come too closely wrapped up in such expressions of status.

Simply good counselling?

It could also well be argued that what service users were describing as 'friendship' was simply an effective counselling relationship built around a good range of counselling skills and values. They didn't use these words, but our participants certainly highlighted accurate empathy, genuineness and unconditional positive regard as central to the relationship (Egan 2002; Rogers 1961). However, it seemed to us that perhaps by their dogged use of the term 'friend' they were trying to convey that something else was equally important to them. We suggest that it was something akin to the ordinariness of the relationship that was crucial to them. Friends are essentially people 'like us' and above all else they are people with whom we feel comfortable. It seemed that perhaps we were being given a very powerful message that what mattered to many service users was that they could remain themselves within the relationship and that, moreover, the social workers could remain themselves, leaving (at least some of) the 'trappings' of the professional outside the relationship.

No one told us that they found the social worker over-friendly or too informal and the very small number of people who had indicated that they had wanted a more formal counselling relationship with the social worker seemed to have experienced just that and all were very happy with the nature of their relationship with them.

It seems to us that it is important not to allow anxiety about professionalism to get in the way of proper exploration of concepts such as friendship within the professional relationship, exploration that can reveal key concerns for the service user. Equally, we learned from the steering group discussion that it is important not to underestimate the sophistication and good sense of the majority of service users who appeared to us to be well aware of all the benefits, for both parties, of maintaining appropriate but flexible boundaries.

Having said all this about the relationship between service users and specialist palliative care social workers, we must add that while service users were keen to tell us that this relationship was fundamentally important, it was not sufficient in itself. Specialist palliative care social work needed to and did offer much more. It is that we want to turn to next.

A HOLISTIC APPROACH

Throughout the study service users kept us constantly aware of the principles that underlie palliative care and in particular of the idea that palliative care embraces the total care and support of the patient. This closely coincides with traditional definitions of palliative care as being 'holistic' in approach. The World Health Organization definition of palliative care (1990, cited in Hospice Information Service 2002a) sees the 'control of pain, of other symptoms, and of psychological, social and spiritual problems [as] paramount' (p.ix). Certainly specialist palliative care social work exemplified this 'holistic' approach. Service users' comments demonstrated that this was more than a paper definition.

Assessment skills

However, the essential starting point for offering such a holistic approach to support is the process of assessment. Before someone can offer the kind of holistic service with which palliative care has been associated, they need to be able to find out the real concerns of service users. As we indicated earlier in the findings of the project, in Chapter 3, assessment appears to have been carried out by specialist palliative care social workers in most cases in a very informal manner. But this should not obscure the considerable assessment skills that were demonstrated, judging by service users' accounts of what happened.

Despite the informality of the approach, it was apparent that service users felt that their real concerns had been heard. They had felt in control of the process and had felt supported throughout the assessment. They had felt that they were really being understood. Authors have commented on the risk that social workers may introduce their own prejudices and stereotypes at the assessment stage (Milner and O'Byrne 2002; Thompson 2002). The service users to whom we spoke seemed to have been encouraged to give their own accounts, to have been understood on their terms within their own realities, and they seem to have valued this highly. Milner and O'Byrne (2002) wrote:

> This involves entering much more into dialogue with service users, adopting a stance of uncertainty, and a willingness to listen to their accounts and co-construct more helpful accounts with them. (p.2)

Many service users said that being encouraged to offer their own accounts in this process – to 'tell their stories' – gave them immediate comfort. This is not unexpected (Fairbairn 2002; Gilbert 2002; McAdams 1993); as Gilbert (2002, p.224) observed:

> Our personal narratives are not merely a way of describing our lives. They are the means by which we bring order, that is we organize our experiences and the information we encounter. This then provides structure to that which we experience, creating order in disorder and establishing meaning in what can seem a meaningless situation.

What is clear is that there was no separation in service users' minds between being assessed and being supported. Assessment was far from being a one-off discrete event, but rather was an unfolding process throughout the period of contact and was closely intertwined with support. It was carried out in a supportive way. This contrasts strongly with the character of assessment in much latter-day social work practice, where there is pressure from a system of one-off assessments, time limits and crucially where there is separation of assessor and supporter (Harlow 2003; Regan 2001). Gostick and others (1997, p.63, cited by Stanley 1999, p.427) studied quantitative and qualitative methods of obtaining information in community care assessments and noted the difficulty of combining the two. They found that 'the informal traditional approaches to assessment may often be the only sensitive and appropriate method'.

It seemed that in the majority of cases where someone was too ill or distressed to make his or her needs known (and there were several examples of this), the social workers had the necessary skills to determine a sensitive and appropriate course of action. Several times service users told us that they felt safe when the social workers had used their authority in this way.

Despite most people's clear satisfaction with the way assessment was carried out, it is important, as we have already indicated, to sound a cautionary note. This concerns the question of whether social workers always spelt out the nature and breadth of their role as fully as they might have done. While this issue only cropped up in a very small number of cases, it is important not to lose sight of it. Notwithstanding this reservation, it was apparent that, despite any lack of formality, explicit frameworks or paperwork in the assessment process, service users were generally satisfied with outcomes. Ironically, this appears to be the opposite of what has happened in statutory services where despite increasing formal procedures and growing mountains of forms, service users frequently report patchy and unreliable services and low levels of satisfaction (Addington-Hall and McCarthy 1995; Rhodes and Shaw 1999).

Members of our steering groups told us that they were all too aware of the pressures on social workers in statutory settings and the impact of this on their practice.

> I think they are overwhelmed by the numbers. They have so many cases to deal with...there is no capacity to cry because they don't have time. (Member of steering group)

The conflicting pressures on statutory social workers that constrain their assessments should not be underestimated. Parry-Jones and Soulsby (2001), in a study into needs-led practice spanning five years, found that social workers, while welcoming the needs-led philosophy underpinning community care assessments, found it increasingly difficult if not impossible to put into practice. 'The main constraints were a lack of resources (financial, service provision, and staffing) and the conceptual difficulty of separating "need" from the "need for a particular service"' (2001, p.414).

This study found that social worker's assessments were not validated:

> The introduction of resource panels, requiring social workers to submit their assessments and recommendations for care to gain a decision over funding, appeared to undermine both the needs-led approach and the professional autonomy of social workers. (Parry-Jones and Soulsby 2001, p.414)

It seems as though in some ways service users risk getting the worst of all worlds when being assessed for community care. Not only are the assessments likely to be resource- rather than needs-driven, but the whole experience of assessment is coloured by constraints that prevent social workers using their professional knowledge and skills to effect (Postle 2002). Richards (2000), who has carried out an ethnographic study of community care assessments for older people in two social service departments, found that assessments carried out in this way are not necessarily even cost effective:

> By marginalizing the older person's insights, the risk of unwelcome or inappropriate interventions may increase. A user-centred approach by contrast requires information gathering and provision that is meaningful to the older person and sensitive to their efforts to analyse and manage their situation. These efforts are often revealed in narrative form as the person tells their story, which in an agency-centred assessment is easily overlooked or ignored. (Richards 2000, p.37)

It should be said though that not all studies have found formalized assessment frameworks to be incompatible with good practice. Corby, Millar and Pope (2002), looking at the children-in-need assessment framework, found that:

> Used with skill and sensitivity, the framework helped create conditions in which some parents changed their attitudes to social workers, as well as to their own strengths and difficulties as carers. (p.13)

What seems to have been critical here is that the social workers were actually allowed to practise with *skill and sensitivity*, whereas so many other types of assessment frameworks seem to deny them that opportunity. As Postle highlights in her study of care management, what is then lost is the very essence of social work (Postle 2001).

The range of social work support

Repeatedly service users told us that the specialist palliative care social workers were able to address in a very 'hands-on' way a huge range of issues, both practical and emotional, and that this was vitally important to them. We will now explore some of these issues.

PRACTICAL ISSUES

Practical concerns dominated many service users' accounts and included debt, inadequate housing and homelessness, problems with employers, benefit and financial issues and lack of access to or problems with other services. Sometimes these were of critical importance to service users – perhaps the difference between having a roof over their head or not, having money to eat or not. A number of service users – and particularly older people, lone parents and people from black and minority ethnic groups – made it abundantly clear that their need for help with day-to-day poverty was paramount. It was interesting to note from some of the transcriptions just how much of the interview time was taken up by service users telling us about their difficulties with meeting the basic necessities of life. One set of interview process notes highlighted that a service user's home was freezing cold. In her interview she spoke barely at all about her illness, but at considerable length about her struggles with poverty and the effort the social worker had made to get her income increased.

This of course should come as no surprise. As Jones reminds us, 'social work in Britain and elsewhere is immersed in poverty' (2002, p.7). Yet palliative care and palliative care social work tend not to be seen like this, perhaps because, unlike other areas of practice, they are seen as more universal services and are not associated particularly with 'the deprived' or 'undeserving'. McLeod and Bywaters (1999) highlight the inequalities faced in ill health and particularly how the extra disadvantage faced by some marginalized groups carries through and is magnified in ill health. Certainly we found that some of the service users from minority ethnic groups lived in very low-grade housing, which was having a serious negative impact on their well-being and any sense of well-being. Others have focused on the inequalities after death when families face funeral costs (Drakeford 1998). Social workers can play an important part in countering these types of disadvantage. This can operate at an individual level, for example:

> Through social work people can gain assistance in securing more of the conditions needed for better health: increased income, improved material resources such as safe, appropriate accommodation; practical, interpersonal and social support; information, advocacy and brokerage with professionals... (McLeod and Bywaters 1999, p.553)

It can also significantly operate at a structural level. The Association of Palliative Care Social Workers has campaigned successfully against many issues of disadvantage affecting its service users; for instance, against inequitable benefits for widowed fathers and against rules for disability living allowance that in effect stopped many dying people from ever accessing this valuable benefit.

It is important to note that although many of the service users we spoke with had already had long involvement with primary care, acute services and in some cases with social services, many welfare issues and other concerns did not appear to have been addressed earlier by these. This finding is backed up by other recent studies. Soothill and others (2003) explored the unmet needs of cancer patients and their carers in three health authorities in north-west England. They first asked both groups which issues they rated as important and then asked whether they felt they had any unmet need in those areas. Of those who rated help with financial matters of importance to them, 40 per cent of the patients and 33 per cent of the 'carers' reported unmet need in this area. Twenty-eight per cent of patients who had said help with filling in forms was important to them had unmet need in this area, as did 33 per cent of carers. Soothill and his colleagues found: 'Needs of a more broadly social character – emotional, identity and practical needs – were more likely to be unmet among both patients and carers, but particularly carers' (2003, p.11).

Lidstone and others (2003) found a similar pattern in their survey of the needs of cancer patients attending hospital outpatients' clinics. Using the 'Symptoms and Concerns Checklist' with 480 patients, they found that patients identified an average of ten items of concern to them during the previous week. The researchers found that, of the six items reported by more than 50 per cent of the sample, four were psychosocial in nature. The researchers felt these could have justified attention by a palliative care specialist.

Given the constraints on care managers within social services and this evidence of the unmet needs of hospital patients, it should come as no surprise that the service users in our project reported that many distressing issues were longstanding and entrenched, and they needed very active support to tackle them.

ACTION AS WELL AS ADVICE

The 'hands-on' aspect of social work support is important to service users. Many pointed out that the social workers did far more than just give advice or information. Time and again we were told that the social worker had taken on a task that the service user had simply no energy left to deal with. They actively involved themselves: researching and sharing information, advocating for the service user, writing letters, filling forms, drafting appeals, liaising with others, challenging decisions, chasing up responses and much more. In other words, an important part of their support lay in the fact that they saw a matter through all its stages, right through to resolution. This ability to deliver seemed to generate a great deal of appreciation and satisfaction amongst service users. This is perhaps not surprising as it contrasts starkly with so much of service users' experience of dealing with other services when it was common to be passed 'from pillar to post'. Many service users, for instance, said that this was their experience when dealing with local councils, the Benefits Agency and the Inland Revenue. It was also sadly the experience of some when dealing with statutory social services.

One of the members of the steering groups commented on the frustrations of being referred on by social workers in local authority teams:

> I think they should be there to help people not to refer them on somewhere else.

Given the enthusiasm, since the establishment of 'care management' in the UK in the 1990s, for the role of social worker as planner, manager and referrer rather than direct provider of support, this message needs to be taken very seriously by social work thinkers and policy-makers. This is especially so, given the renewed support for such ideas contained in the 2005 Green Paper on adult social care, *Independence, Well-Being and Choice: Our Vision for the Future of Social Care for Adults in England* (and the subsequent White Paper, Department of Health 2006), which identifies the social worker as a 'navigator' helping people to negotiate the service system, rather than someone with their own specific professional role and capacity to offer support (Department of Health 2005).

Several service users told us that their specialist palliative care social worker had used their power and authority to challenge poor or discriminatory services. It seemed to us that generally the social workers were well versed in welfare rights or at least had access to sound advice in those areas and were prepared to use their knowledge to tackle inequality and injustice. The picture wasn't entirely positive however. We were alerted to the fact that in one or two settings in affluent areas, service users had never been asked whether they needed this type of welfare support.

> No, nothing was mentioned about benefits, no nothing at all. (Bereaved woman, white UK, age group 46–55)

This could suggest that some social workers were making assumptions about need based on the general prosperity of their area and did not routinely explain to service users that financial help and advice was available. Conversely it was clear that other social workers in similarly affluent areas were being very proactive in telling *all* their service users about the range of help available, making no presumptions about circumstances. This may explain why in those areas the service users we spoke to did raise a far broader range of issues with the social worker. We realized from their accounts how disadvantaged they would have been if this type of support had not been readily available. McLeod and Bywaters (2002, p.46) suggest that social work can sometimes compound inequalities in health: 'Frequently even assisting in maximising benefit take-up is considered not to be core business.'

It was difficult to gauge from our study just how often issues of poverty or financial distress were ignored. No one specifically complained about this, but there certainly were one or two cases where our own concerns were raised and noted in interviewers' process notes. Though these instances were very small in number, for the individuals concerned the implications may have been serious. MacDonald (1991), writing in an American context, sums up the dangers of taking a narrow social work approach:

> Many [US] social workers today think of themselves as therapists or coun-
> sellors and tend to eschew other modalities of practice. But in hospices,

> many of the most serious challenges – involving underserved populations, inadequate or inequitable resource allocation, and fundamental problems of social policy – transcend agency boundaries. (p.279)

Specialist palliative care social work currently operates relatively free from the constraints that have so ground down social workers and care managers in statutory services. Jones (2002) talks about research carried out with state social workers in the north of England:

> My interviews have revealed starkly the changed character of state social work and the manner in which its caring and supportive aspects have been supplanted by a more bureaucratic and regulatory approach to the plight of clients… I was regaled with tales of bureaucratic hurdles, forms and reports, meetings of panels of managers who had to be persuaded to release even the smallest of resources. It became evident that many of these controls had an interrelated focus of managing inadequate budgets and controlling the activities of social workers. (pp.14–15)

It would be cause for concern if even a very small minority of specialist palliative care social workers were voluntarily limiting their role in supporting service users experiencing problems of poverty. Most do not hold budgets and cannot directly tackle low levels of pensions and benefits, but service users told us repeatedly of ways they had been able to help address these types of issues. Addressing issues of income maintenance and social security clearly needs to be seen as part of the routine role of specialist palliative care social workers. It is apparent though that at present this is not always the case. Some social workers do not see this as an intrinsic part of their responsibility, yet it can be of great importance to service users.

Emotional support

Although we have put 'emotional support' under a separate heading, this is a somewhat false distinction. We have only done this in order to enable fuller discussion of the issue, rather than to suggest that it represents a separate sphere of activity. Service users did not compartmentalize the practical support that they received from the social worker from the emotional support they offered. It was much more typical for service users to see the two as interwoven and interdependent. This is an important point because, as we have seen, there is an increasing trend for emotional needs to be overlooked in statutory social work as it is currently being practised in many settings (Howe 1996; Weinberg *et al.* 2003).

The service users we spoke to made it clear that their emotional needs had been met. There was considerable evidence of social workers working with intense emotional pain. Sometimes nurses are viewed as being interchangeable with social workers when it comes to providing emotional care. Julys and Davis

(1987, cited by Reese and Brown 1997), for instance, found that hospice directors felt that nurses were just as qualified as social workers to provide psychosocial care. There has been little research in this country into this belief. Reese and Brown (1997), in a study into 'home hospices' in America, looked at the range of issues discussed between patients and their respective nurses, social workers and clergy. They found that, while there was certainly overlap, nurses, clergy and social workers did consistently focus on different issues, all of importance to patients. Social workers in particular were more likely to discuss what they term 'death anxiety' than either nurses or clergy (this term included thoughts of losing control over their mind, worries about leaving loved ones behind, worries about painful death and worries about prolonged illness).

People in our study had talked about most of these issues with the specialist palliative care social worker and told us that they had been helped to cope with feelings of despair, anger, helplessness, fear, sadness and guilt. They did not generally mention having had the same discussions with other members of the team. Several of the service users we interviewed talked to us about suicidal feelings and suicide attempts, which they had been counselled through by the specialist palliative care social worker. Those people specifically identified the specialist palliative care social worker as the professional who had been most helpful to them. This support had really mattered. Some stressed to us that they believed that they literally owed their lives to the skilled help they had received.

Multiple losses, multiple problems

We were told – again on several occasions – how the social workers had helped service users deal not just with one loss, but with multiple losses. In particular, it was striking how many service users told us that they had lost a child earlier in their lives. Several said they had received little support at the time of that death. A number of service users told us that they had brought to the specialist palliative care social worker complex and entrenched problems that they had been experiencing for many years, and for the first time they felt able to tackle these problems and cope better despite their illness or bereavement. This suggests that the social workers' resources were being effectively targeted on those who had complex issues and difficult past experiences to deal with. It also suggests that the relationship was one based on trust, so that service users felt safe enough to raise some of these past issues afresh. It also highlighted a real willingness, on the part of the specialist palliative care social worker, to support people with the issues they were actually grappling with and not just the ones that appeared most current or most pertinent.

The issues that really matter

In Chapter 5 we reported that many service users said that they had felt able to go to the social worker with any issue that they faced and that this was perhaps one of the ways in which the principle of holistic or total care was most firmly upheld by the social workers. Service users felt that no limits were set by the specialist palliative care social workers, in regard to what they could or could not ask, and because of this they felt able to address the issues that really mattered to them. The specialist palliative care social workers clearly had the ability to think on their feet and were able to come up with suggestions and ways forward for problems that could not easily be solved.

It might be argued that service users were simply dragging up a whole gamut of irrelevant problems, perhaps to avoid talking or thinking about the reality of their current illness or loss. If so, we certainly got no sense of this and there was no evidence to substantiate it.

So many people stressed the fact that they could talk to, or ask, the social worker about *anything* and identified this as one of the chief strengths of specialist palliative care social work that we began to feel that this might be a very significant element of service users maintaining or rebuilding control in their lives. Several people told us of their exhaustion at having to negotiate and renegotiate their dealings with hospital and social service departments because of ever-changing doctors, nurses and home carers. Harlow (2003, p.35) talks about 'conveyor belt care' and 'speedy throughput' as being typical of much current social work practice. Smith, Nicol and Devereux (1999), in a study which looked at the numbers of doctors encountered by a group of 50 patients during their cancer care (median time period of two years and one month), found that the median number was 32 (within a range of 13–97). Our service users stressed a similar lack of continuity as a very real burden. It was sometimes portrayed as one of the most difficult and wearisome aspects of coping with their illness.

In contrast, many of the service users had known the same specialist palliative care social worker throughout their illness or bereavement and sometimes they had remained in contact over years. This clearly had a bearing on the value they placed on the relationship with the social workers. Possibly this continuity coupled with the feeling that they could take almost any problem to the specialist palliative care social worker lent service users a sense of safety in an otherwise very uncertain and unfamiliar world. It promoted a real belief that, regardless of what cropped up in the future, there was someone and somewhere to take it. This was particularly important for some patients approaching death who felt they were leaving their family with that kind of all-encompassing support.

Several service users told us that in the depths of their despair they had been referred to psychiatric services and in some cases they had been hospitalized. All of these people expressed the view that the holistic support they had received from the specialist palliative care social worker had been as important to them as that received through psychiatric services and sometimes had seemed more important simply because it didn't narrow its focus and it tackled – in a way that felt very comfortable – the full range of their problems as they arose. It is well evidenced that the psychiatric system frequently does not feel comfortable in the same way (Coppick and Hopton 2000; Newnes, Holmes and Dunn 2001). There is a growing body of literature regarding the role of palliative care services in screening patients for depression and other mental health problems (Goy, Schultz and Ganzini 2003; Meyer, Sinnott and Seed 2003). It is right that individuals should be offered the full range of support available to meet their needs, but it is interesting that seldom is any consideration given in this literature to the role social workers might play in supporting people with mental distress. Our findings would support the view that service users might welcome the involvement of specialist palliative care social workers when they are facing such difficulties.

CONCLUSION

We know that 'the public' do not seem to know much about social work, and the people who took part in our project generally began with little understanding and often very negative preconceptions of social work. However, what they valued from specialist palliative care social work practice were goals, qualities and skills that historically have been seen as key to social work, particularly those concerned with enabling autonomy and supporting self-determination. The service users we spoke with did not identify any skills which they saw as being in any way 'specialist' to specialist palliative care social work. Again this may reflect the limited public understanding of such practice, but it may also be a reflection of the complex and subtle nature of this and other branches of social work practice.

From what service users say, it seems that specialist palliative care social work still encompasses and is very much rooted in what has long been seen as the best practices of traditional social work. These practices include the ability to see people as whole people and not just as a set of problems, the capacity to locate them in their broader social structures, the ability to understand the complexities and connections of their lives, and the knowledge and skills to support people in the ways that they want; thus enabling people to build on their own strengths whilst recognizing the strengths of their families and communities. It would be difficult to overstate the importance that service users attached to the quality of the relationship with the social worker.

There was strong evidence of competence across all areas of social work practice and a willingness on the part of social workers to learn. This competence was built on a strong social work value base and a clear philosophy of palliative care which prizes patient and family involvement, holistic care and multidisciplinary working, with the emphasis on self-defined quality of life. Service users emphasized a number of elements of the support which specialist palliative care social workers offered which were important to them. These were, notably, friendship, informality and 'ordinariness'. Such elements of friendship, informality and 'ordinariness' seem to have gained little attention in social work literature and education, yet they tell us a great deal about how service users feel social workers can work effectively with them.

SUMMARY

Both groups of service users, patients and people facing bereavement, seemed to value specialist palliative care social work equally. In this chapter we explore two of the elements that service users seem most to value in specialist palliative care social work practice. These are:

- the relationship with the social worker
- the social worker's holistic approach to practice.

The relationship with the social worker

The emphasis that service users place on the relationship with the social worker and the continuity of that relationship has not been reflected in recent developments in social work and social care, which have tended to minimize its importance, emphasizing instead the technical and referral role of the social work practitioner as care manager.

Service users frequently express their valuing of the social work role in terms of 'friendship'. They do not seem to mean by this that they do not understand that the role is a professional one with boundaries. Instead they highlight the benefits of flexibility, reciprocity, warmth and the balancing of power between service user and practitioner. The complexities of their understandings are explored and some of the potential problems examined.

A holistic approach to practice

Palliative care has emphasized the holistic nature of its approach to meeting service users' needs. Service users' comments suggest that the potential for such an approach begins with specialist palliative care social workers' sensitive, informal and ongoing approach to assessment, which contrasts with the increasing move to more formal models in statutory social work and care management. This takes into account both emotional and practical issues.

The way that social workers address both practical and emotional issues and offer a wide-ranging model of practice which addresses the two and takes account of their complex interrelation and interactions emerges as a theme in service users' comments. The trust that develops between service users and practitioners makes it possible for the former to seek support with multiple losses and multiple problems, to have a sense of being able to talk about anything, and to feel that they can, with the social worker's support, hang on to their existing identity and continue to be themselves in very difficult and challenging circumstances.

The strengths of specialist palliative care social work emerged clearly, but there were also areas of concern. In particular, this included the failure of some social workers to spell out their role clearly and in a few cases to offer consistently welfare rights type support which addressed the serious material problems faced by some service users. Both of these shortcomings may impact more heavily on some groups than others, particularly those who are poor and disadvantaged, and thus may compound disadvantage.

It is important to recognize that the humanistic qualities that service users seem to value in specialist palliative care social work are those that have long been associated with good social work practice. They stand in some contrast to recent developments and policy proposals that treat social work and social care practice and provision as being agencies for referral and management.

CHAPTER 11

THEORY AND PRACTICE

In the last chapter, we saw that what service users seem to value from specialist palliative care practice does not necessarily fit well with the current directions in which social work practice is being developed in public and agency policy. It may be additionally helpful at this point to consider specialist palliative care social work in relation to theory. We particularly want to examine it in the context of theoretical work on death and loss, although we also want to consider in general the different approaches to practice adopted by specialist palliative care social workers more critically.

No service user made any specific reference to theory in their comments, although their views and ideas clearly have their own theoretical underpinnings. We want to see to what extent the accounts given by service users of what they perceived as helpful match existing theoretical work, and which theories seem most pertinent. Sometimes professionals are perceived as having rather fixed theoretical ideas which can lead to narrow and stereotyped responses to clients' needs (Walter 1999). We wanted to see if this rang true in any of the interviews and discussions we had with service users.

While social work has sometimes come in for criticism as being atheoretical, there has in fact been a growing emphasis on theory in its literature (Shaw, Arksey and Mullender 2004). However, such theorizing has almost entirely come from academics and others without significant or recent direct experience as practitioners. Moreover, social work practitioners have tended to be marginalized in social work discourse and theoretical debate (Beresford and Croft 2004). Both these factors seem likely to limit the value of such theorizing. They also raise broader questions about the relationship between social work theory and actual practice and the degree to which much social work theory actually connects with or indeed impacts upon social work practitioners.

There has also so far been very limited involvement from service users in the development of social work theory. Yet social care service users, particularly disabled people, especially over the last 25–30 years, have been developing their own discourses and theoretical discussions (Campbell and Oliver 1996). Most influential among these have been the idea of a social approach to or model of disability, and the concept of independent living (Oliver 1996). Both have had major effects on mainstream social policy and thinking. Yet it is debatable how far they have been addressed in social work's own theorizing (see, for example, Dominelli 2004).

NO THEORETICAL TYRANNY

From the accounts of service users that we heard, there was no sense that the social workers they encountered had any rigid theoretical preconceptions about death, dying or bereavement, or that they pathologized reactions to grief, however unusual. In fact we were repeatedly told by service users that they had had their feelings acknowledged, accepted and 'normalized' and this seemed hugely comforting for many people. By 'normalized' we don't mean that the social workers attempted to slot people into some predetermined pattern of 'normal' grieving, nor that they ignored signs of serious mental distress, but rather that they helped people understand that the ferocity of their feelings was in line with their experience and their loss and that it did not mean they were about to lose control totally – which seemed to be a major fear. Many people referred to having thought they were 'going mad' and to their terrible and over-whelming fears of falling apart. Service users said that they had found this process of normalization extremely valuable. It is important to remember that in the past there has been great pressure on health care professionals to see grief in either normal or abnormal terms. These two assertions by Faulkner and Maguire (1994) are typical:

> In most individuals the period of maximum grief will last some eight to twelve weeks...normal grief can be represented in diagrammatic form...it can take a considerable time for the slope to return to normal, though it usually does within the year. (p.140)

> If a patient is found to be clinically anxious or depressed or behaving in such a way as to be in danger then the health professional needs to refer that patient on to more specialist help...this is normally done through the general practitioner and may require some advocacy on the part of the health profes-sional if the general practitioner is unaware of the true nature of the problem. It is not uncommon, for example, for a general practitioner to believe it is normal to be depressed after mutilating surgery. (p.81)

It seemed clear that the specialist palliative care social workers *did* have a theo-retical knowledge base about loss and grief, but that this knowledge was used supportively to reflect on and contextualize people's feelings, not to constrain, police or pigeonhole them. Because social workers were so involved with both the social context (work, family, community) and the psychological context, they seemed particularly well placed to understand the true scale and complex-ity of the changes taking place in people's lives.

Nor were we told about social workers putting pressure on people to share intense feelings if they did not wish to do so, or pushing them towards some kind of 'acceptance', 'moving on' or 'letting go' of the person who had died. Far from this being the case, we repeatedly heard that social workers stayed with service users wherever they were on their own particular journey. This latter finding is at variance with assertions made, for example, by Walter (1999), who discusses the 'clinical lore' that he sees as informing much of the work of bereavement workers. We assume he would include palliative care social workers here, though as social workers are never mentioned, this could be an erroneous assumption. He says that:

> 'Clinical lore' is much more important than research knowledge in the policing of bereaved individuals for clinical lore is the filter through which research knowledge reaches and controls the public. (p.155)

Walter suggests that although current 'clinical lore' acknowledges diversity in ways of grieving, three elements – 'expressivism, resolution, and some notion of normal and abnormal grief – are remarkably resilient' (p.157). He argues that grieving encompasses much more than this and cites the work of the late Susan le Poidevin, telling us that she:

> observed that bereavement can affect people's identity, emotions, the spiritual meaning they give to life, the managing of practical everyday tasks, their physical health, their finances, their lifestyle (e.g. moving house, starting work) and their roles in family and community. (Walter 1999, pp.157–8)

He tells us that le Poidevin maintained that bereavement care should pick up on whichever of these issues are important for the bereaved person. Walter sees bereavement care as moving, in the second half of the twentieth century, away from this holistic vision described by le Poidevin towards a concentration on the emotions of grief.

In contrast, the service users to whom we spoke, both patients and bereaved people, were clearly telling us that the specialist palliative care social workers with whom they came in contact were characterized by their holistic approach. We saw no particular emphasis on 'expressivism'; in fact several people commented with relief that the specialist palliative care social worker had not pushed them towards this, sensing that it was not their 'style'. Neither did we detect any particular emphasis on pushing people towards resolution of grief. Quite the contrary a number of bereaved people told us that one of the most helpful things about their support was that the specialist palliative care social worker had made it clear that they were available to them in the future should they feel the need. There was an acceptance that bereavement took a variable course and some service users were offered support over very long periods whilst others were seen for quite brief periods. There was certainly no sense of the social workers seeing grief within a rigid time frame, though there was a clear sense of people experiencing progress over time in coping with their situation.

PRACTICE: LINKS TO THEORY
The 'dual process model'

Although service users did not make explicit comments about the theoretical knowledge and understanding of the specialist palliative care social workers who worked with them, what did seem to be apparent was that the support they received and valued could be linked back to much of the theoretical work on death and bereavement. For example, there seemed to be a link between the social work support being provided and Stroebe and Schut's (1999) 'dual process model' of bereavement, where the bereaved person is seen as oscillating between two processes. One is orientated towards the experience of loss, the other toward restoration (sorting things out), with both seen as important dimensions of coping. The loss orientation is when the bereaved person confronts their feelings, and the emotional impact of the loss. We heard repeatedly how the specialist palliative care social workers had listened and supported individuals as they told and retold their stories and expressed their feelings, both sad and happy. Equally, we heard how the social workers played an important part in helping service users in restorative work, thinking about, planning and carrying out the tasks, often very practical ones, that lay ahead in their management of their changed world. Groupwork, as our third example in Chapter 4 shows, similarly allowed for both loss orientated and restoration-focused work. Social work, with its inherent dual focus on emotional and practical issues, seems to enable individuals to experience both of these orientations in a supported and facilitated but unforced way.

The dual process model is generally applied to bereavement, but it seemed to us that some of the patients we spoke to were oscillating in a very similar way between needing at times to explore the full range of their feelings and at other times to set these aside as they addressed a range of practical tasks with advancing illness. It might seem misplaced to talk about a process of restoration in relation to people who may shortly be facing the end of their lives. However, there was certainly a restorative feel about many of the accounts, as people described the ways in which the social workers had helped them, for example, to access better accommodation, or had helped them sort out practical problems with debt. It was as if freeing up individuals from these burdens did offer some hope and, to a degree at least, did restore the chance of a better quality of life – even if time was limited.

Bereavement and biography

Walter (1996, 1999) has written about the need bereaved people have to recon-struct their biography, in order to understand the life of the person who has died and by implication their own life:

> bereavement (whether through death, disability, unemployment, relation-ship break up, or whatever) is the state of being caught between the present, a past, and a lost future. Rewriting the past to make sense of the new present is crucial if sense is to be made of change and the future faced. (Walter 1999, p.70)

In his earlier work, Walter put forward the view that this happened largely through the medium of talking about the dead, getting to know them better through conversations with others who also knew them, who knew about their strengths, their weaknesses, the joys and the frustrations of knowing them. Reality testing is an important component of the process as multiple percep-tions of the dead person are incorporated (Walter 1996, p.13). Walter drew on his experience of a personal loss of a close woman friend and said that, for him, this process of biographical reconstruction could only happen with others who knew her – and knew her well. He saw the process as being essentially social and interactive rather than simply supportive of individualized grief. Walter saw bereavement counselling – 'talking about feelings to a stranger' – as 'a rather poor if much appreciated, second best' (Walter 1999, p.19). He may be right in thinking that most people deal best with their bereavement through their inter-actions with family and friends, but the 'stranger' has a role and not always a secondary one. The need to talk to someone else from outside their family or friendship group was very important for some of the service users we spoke to and this need should not be underestimated. It was often the closeness to family members that got in the way as people struggled to support and protect each other and make sense of their own loss at the same time. Some people simply could not manage it.

In his later work Walter (1999) explored this model more thoroughly. In particular he took time to look in some depth at all the factors that in many people's lives might make conversation about the dead person difficult to accomplish. He highlighted social and family fragmentation, longevity and geo-graphical mobility, as well as deaths that may carry stigma, such as those associ-ated with HIV/AIDS. He acknowledged that in widowhood the person may have just lost his or her lifelong confidant and that sometimes friends don't want to talk, or may 'get the conversation wrong' (1999, p.70). While still somewhat dismissive of counselling, he admitted, perhaps reluctantly, that some counsel-lors told him that they did encourage their clients to tell the story of the dead and of the death, and in non-directive counselling the stories get told anyway. He felt that this might be valuable, while calling for more research to substantiate it.

Had Walter spoken to the service users we interviewed, he might have been pleasantly reassured. Here were many examples of individuals working with their specialist palliative care social workers, not only to express their feelings, but also to tell their story and make sense of their past, their present and in some cases their future.

In many cases the social worker had known the dead person as well as the bereaved person, sometimes over a long period, during which time the social worker had been a witness to the person's changing health, body, abilities and mood and may have known something of his or her hopes and fears. Often social workers learned how the dead lived their lives, and learned about their interests, their family connections and their work. For example:

> [the social worker] had known my partner since her first visit here…and then during the last months of her life and then had been there in her last couple of weeks…she knew the context…she knew about the family, she knew about my partner, she knew about how everything was accomplished, she knew what my partner was worried about…she knew a certain amount about our relationship… (Bereaved man, white UK, age group 26–35)

As a member of the multidisciplinary team, the specialist palliative care social worker will also have known about the treatments, medications and procedures that the person went through. While we are not suggesting that this is the same as knowing the person as a member of the family or a close friend, it does mean that the social worker could be a very appropriate person to listen to the telling and retelling of the story. Palliative care social workers are often far from being 'the stranger' of Walter's account. Having played a part in the story, they were in a position to validate its telling, or in some cases even to challenge it. Thus:

> You think things over and then the next time I see [the specialist palliative care social worker], you know, you can speak to her and say something to her about it and she'll say, 'Yes, I can remember that'… Yes it is support, it's somebody who knew the person, both sides of their character if you like. (Bereaved man, white UK, age group 66–75)

More than this, we saw that there were several other ways in which the social workers were incorporating into their role a number of other elements which Walter identified as important. Sometimes, for example, the specialist palliative care social worker helped a service user to capture his or her memories and to bring the dead person back into his or her life in a way that felt okay. In this example, the social worker was working with a young boy:

> Through [the social worker's] help and experience she helped him talk about the thing that he most needed to, his dad, and…she did this book with him about his dad's favourite things and he so enjoyed it, he lightened up…he

> wasn't so cross with everything, he wasn't cross with his dad, he could talk to his dad, talk about his dad... (Bereaved woman, white UK, age group 26–35)

Specialist palliative care social workers and others working with children have written extensively for a number of years about the importance of helping children grieve and much of this work is strongly supportive of Walter's model of biographical reconstruction (see, for example, Hemmings 2001; Oliviere *et al.* 1998; Smith and Pennells 1995).

We saw that the social workers had sometimes helped the bereaved service users plan and organize funerals, capturing the personality of the person who had died, and ensuring that the bereaved person could identify with the 'story being told', something Walter sees as a highly significant part of the process of biographical reconstruction (Walter 1999, p.78).

Some service users told us how the social worker had helped them to make sense of, or at least learn to live with, the differing perspectives of their (deceased) loved one that emerged from conversations that they had with others about them. Walter didn't ponder for long on the anguish that can result from such different perspectives on someone who has died. He mentioned one or two people who had fallen out with his own close friend who had died and 'were alienated from her other friends'. He went on to say 'how they struggled to make sense of things, I know not' (1996, p.13).

One of the service users we spoke to had found coping with different perspectives very difficult after the death of her husband. She said of his son:

> it came out he just hated his dad... I was just absolutely devastated... I couldn't have talked to anybody in the family at all. (Bereaved woman, white UK, age group 46–55)

But she had valued the chance to talk these issues through with the social worker:

> It just kept me going week to week...each week to be there.

The continuity that was offered by many of the social workers again appears to have been important for people. Many talked about the time it took to tell their story. We heard, for example, from a father of young children, about the social worker's willingness to work afresh with the family as the children grew up and needed to think through new angles to their ongoing story.

A significant number of service users, particularly bereaved people, told us how the specialist palliative care social worker had been instrumental in bringing them together with other service users in groups. Walter (1999, p.79) saw mutual-help groups as an important forum for some bereaved people to share their experiences. He felt stories could be told and retold in this setting. Service users in our study saw groups in this way, but they also saw them as playing an important part in the restorative process described by Stroebe and

Schut (1999). For example in the bereavement group which featured in the third example in Chapter 4, we saw how the group looked at:

> What you do to sort of allay pain and working through it, talking about it, what you feel...but also...doing work and activities...I mean new activities, taking on new activities and hobbies and soon... (Service user in discussion group)

More than anything, what service users conveyed to us was that they did not see the specialist palliative care social workers as prescriptive, but rather as genuinely empowering. We were told many times that people felt they could determine their own agenda, follow their own path, in short, feel their own way, however shakily, with the social worker alongside them providing encouragement, knowledge and skills that made the journey more bearable.

Like Currer (2001), however, we found that for some service users there was no moving on. The toll of their experiences was so great that they were simply holding on:

> For them there was merely a grim satisfaction in having people around who would listen to their sadness, anger or distress, and help them to be as comfortable as possible. This too is accompaniment. (Currer 2001, p.147)

This seems a really important issue to think about, but again, like the issue of 'friendship', there seems to be little discussion of it in the social work literature. We heard from a small number of service users that they had been seeing their social worker for years, long after an illness had stabilized or long after the death of a loved one. Regular contact seemed to have stopped, but there was still intermittent contact. The service users we spoke to seemed to find this contact valuable and sustaining. Huntley (2002) writes about the impact of endings on the client in relationship-based social work. He too talks about the paucity of discussion around maintaining contact in the longer term: 'there is confusion and uncertainty within the profession on the ethics and boundaries of such contact' (Huntley 2002, p.64).

Our sense is that many specialist palliative care social workers have at least one or two people or families with whom they keep in touch for very long periods. From personal experience, we are aware of the guilty justifications that practitioners sometimes put forward for doing this. It is likely to be helpful to explore the myriad of reasons why specialist palliative care social workers might sometimes work in this way, rather than see all such cases simply as examples of dependency or as a failure to draw boundaries, face endings and in some cases face hopelessness. Certainly we are not advocating such long-term contact purely to satisfy a personal need in the social worker. It is also important that it does not seriously block the way for more pressing work with new service users. However, it seems to us that sometimes anxieties about 'professionalism' may close down what could be enlightening and perhaps even liberating discussions.

It is important to avoid 'no go' areas in discussion about the reality of social work practice.

THE FLEXIBLE REPERTOIRE OF SOCIAL WORK APPROACHES

As the study's findings show, we gained no sense from service users of practitioners adopting any kind of 'one size fits all' approach to carrying out specialist palliative care social work. No one approach to practice, tied to a particular theoretical model, predominated. Many service users had variously been offered group, family and individual work. They also mentioned a lot of informal low-key contact. This might mean a quick word in the corridor, a brief phone call or a card sent to mark a sad or difficult occasion. But all these, added together, were seen by service users as a vital part of the support that was keeping them going.

Some service users were clear that they wanted a social worker who was prepared to 'chat' to them in a very informal way, often about seemingly irrelevant everyday life. They wanted this to be the approach to the work and they were able to pinpoint specific ways in which this type of informal support had helped them cope with their situation. There was evidence that for these service users this type of conversational or 'chatty' approach worked effectively, even when the person had complex practical problems and difficult family relationships alongside serious physical health problems and distressing losses.

An important component of 'chatting' is the reciprocity that it involves and, as we said earlier, this can be seen as an indicator of balance and equality within the relationship. Chatting about 'this and that' can also be a way of remaining engaged with the day-to-day world and as such contributes to the maintenance of identity and independence. We have struggled to find any discussion in the social work literature of what might be termed 'informal' approaches to working and yet service users mentioned them on several occasions as being helpful. Other service users were equally clear that they wanted a structured and fairly formal counselling approach. It seems important for social workers to be alert to the need for ways of working that feel right to different people.

Home visits

By seeing people at home as well as in inpatient and day-care settings, specialist palliative care social workers were able to offer further flexibility and continuity of care. A number of service users told us how important this was to them. Currer (2001, p.66) points out that the social worker has a 'somewhat separate identity' and can 'bridge the gap between the institution and the life at home'. This seems to be crucial as the time scale needed for addressing emotional and social issues that are important to the patients and their loved ones is often different to that required for respite or symptom control. It is important that the social worker's involvement is not artificially tied to the period of the inpatient stay. Yet we know that with shortage of social workers in specialist palliative care, with some social workers working on their own, the opportunities to carry out home visits can be limited and for some service users this can only mean that their needs are not fully met.

The social workers in our study appeared to have the flexibility and skills to judge what level and type of involvement and support to offer. They seemed comfortable in chopping and changing styles and ways of working. Even more important was that, while offering these different approaches, the specialist palliative care social workers seem to have been able to *be themselves*. Many service users told us that they saw the social workers as very 'natural', 'genuine', 'real' people.

Challenges of groupwork

Overall service users readily embraced groupwork approaches and levels of satisfaction were very high. It was clear that groupwork had led to a real reduction in social isolation for many service users, particularly older people, who might otherwise have faced loneliness and exclusion. Participation in groupwork gave many people the feeling that they had something to share with other service users, a contribution that was helpful for both parties. As Brown (2002, p.164) writes: 'Group work is a uniquely empowering method of social work because all are potentially helpers as well as "helped".'

Many of the service users said that the social worker had facilitated their group in such a way that they felt real ownership of the group agenda and processes, but still felt they had an anchor when it was needed. Some of the most impressive and innovative work that we heard about took place in groupwork settings. However, it does seem important to note some of the difficulties and challenges that emerged with groupwork approaches. Several bereaved people raised common concerns and we drew attention to some of these in Chapter 7.

First, it was clear that most individuals had felt very anxious about joining a group regardless of whether it was a new group or a pre-existing one. We were told by several people of the many months they had taken to pluck up courage to join. We wonder whether sufficient thought is given to the preparatory work that might be needed prior to a group being offered, to enable people to understand what is on offer and to facilitate their joining.

Second, a small number of people mentioned that they had either felt uncomfortable themselves or had witnessed someone else's discomfort because their type of loss seemed irreconcilably different to the loss experienced by the majority in the group. Some service users talked about a 'hierarchy of grief': the death of a parent not being seen as being as significant as the death of a spouse was an example given. Age differences between group members were also mentioned as being difficult to transcend. Brown (2002) talks about the need actively to support any individual who is in a minority to avoid isolation and marginalization and to enable them to get as much out of the group as 'majority' members. Where people had left groups prematurely, these issues of group heterogeneity often seemed to be the reasons that were mentioned. It was clear that it had been very painful for people when they left a group with this feeling that their particular experience had been misunderstood or devalued in some way. It was not always apparent that any additional support had been offered to those leaving groups early. None was mentioned to us, yet clearly there may be a need for such support.

Third, as we illustrated in one of the examples we offered in Chapter 4, a small number of people mentioned the endings of groups as being problematic. Either the ending seemed to be looming up with no discussion about what next, leaving individuals feeling very anxious, or else there was no mention about the group ever ending and this left some individuals feeling uncertain about their ongoing involvement, questioning whether they could keep coming and wondering how new people could ever be fitted in. Such uncertainty is particularly likely to be unsettling for individuals who were already grappling with issues of loss and endings.

It is only to be expected that group endings, and indeed the ending of individual work with a service user, will sometimes provoke ambivalent and powerful feelings, sometimes re-awakening the feelings provoked by the death of their loved one. However, it does seem a clear part of the professional role to address these issues and not let a group end abruptly with little preparation or else go on forever with no mention of the future. To allow this to happen not only raises anxiety, but also means that there is no natural phase for evaluation and review of what the group has meant to people. It stalls thinking about the future and, as we saw, the ending of a group could, with planning, mean that service users go on to establish their own self-directed support or friendship groups. Some writers are uncertain about the wisdom of such a move; for example:

> There often seems to be much ambivalence in the members, insofar that they wish at one level to continue the contact, but at another to be free of it, to develop new and satisfying relationships in the 'outside world'. (Nichols and Jenkinson 1991, p.133)

However, we saw evidence that self-directed groups had provided a source of rich, close and very sustaining relationships that mattered enormously to service users. What is, perhaps, important is that in facilitating the ending of the initial bereavement group, the social worker leaves service users aware of the possibilities open to them. Our study suggests that where this had happened and where service users had worked out their own solutions for ongoing contact, it seemed to have turned out well – at least for the people to whom we spoke.

Another question that emerged in relation to groupwork was why there seemed to be far more groupwork going on with bereaved people than with patients. Certainly we heard of relatively few patients attending groups but we frequently were told about groups for bereaved people. It may be that social workers resist groupwork with patients as they are cautious about the impact of the death of group members on the others, and this was mentioned to us as being hard for some service users. Thus, for example:

> with the group, because we've all got the same thing, cancer, when anybody dies – we had another lady die at Christmas – and it seems like you are losing them all. And I can't express that to anyone in the group. (Woman patient, a member of a group for women with breast cancer, white UK, age group 36–45)

For this reason other patients told us that they had decided to avoid such groups. Professionals may also feel that specific patient groups are unnecessary, as they would duplicate what goes on informally in day centres. We are not sure, but the patients to whom we spoke who met for specific groupwork spoke very highly of the support they gained from each other and from the social worker.

Family work

A key aspect of palliative care social work is working with people's families. Families are now complex and diverse in nature. Furthermore, people's close relationships may extend beyond the family or not even be based on it. In some ways the term 'family work' has now become shorthand for something much more far ranging and complicated.

Having said this, we were left in no doubt that service users had largely found the support that they received as helpful for the whole family, though it has to be said that in some cases the service users saw the support they got from the specialist palliative care social worker as standing in for family support that was not available. This is of particular significance bearing in mind the continuing policy emphasis on 'informal care' based on the family and the suggestion from some commentators that relationship-based support is inherently preferable to professionalized interventions. For instance:

> I mean my dad comes, he breezes in and he breezes out...my mother I don't really have any contact at all, very little contact. I've got a brother and a half-sister; I virtually don't get any contact with them at all...so I don't really get any family support at all. (Woman patient, white UK, age group 26–35)

Sometimes family were available but there was conflict. We heard of social workers bringing conflicting parties together, once again taking on a sort of bridging role:

> So [the social worker] rang them because they'd had this little quarrel, she
> rang to make arrangements for them to come and see him, the two brothers.
> (Bereaved woman, white UK, age group 36–45)

As emerged in the example we gave of Mike and Linda in Chapter 4, there were
times when the social workers had to confront service users with aspects of their
behaviour towards one another that were causing distress. We frequently heard
how there were different patterns of coping within families and the stresses
from accommodating these differences were explored with the social workers.
We were told stories of families where there had been abuse or difficult
behaviour by the parent who was now dying and in need of support, and the
guilt, anger and sadness that this engendered. All these were issues that people
had talked through with the specialist palliative care social worker. Sometimes
the patients themselves told us how badly they felt they had treated other
members of their family and how they had been able to talk to the social worker
about this without feeling judged or diminished.

We were not often told of specialist palliative care social workers working
with the family as a group, though there were some examples of this, as two of
our examples show, and some service users said that it had been offered by the
social worker but resisted by others in the family. When we did hear about
family work it was clear that the social workers had the expertise and skills to
deal with conflict between couples and within families and between the
competing rights of children and parents.

We wondered whether some of the social workers might have liked to work
with the family as a group more often, but believed that they lacked the confidence or skills to do this. As Monroe writes:

> Family anxiety is often mirrored in the professional carers who may be
> frightened about how to respond to the emotional agendas between patient
> and family and worried that seeing them together will get out of control,
> make things worse or simply take too long. (Monroe 1993, p.176)

Service users spoke more often about seeing the social worker alone or just with
their partner. Other family members – brothers and sisters, parents, children –
were frequently seen, but again on an individual basis. It was clear, however,
that the specialist palliative care social workers saw individuals as being part of a
bigger picture and were closely concerned with the needs of the whole family or
group. Service users valued this.

When conflicts simmered on

As we discussed in Chapter 7, a few service users felt that practical matters had
taken precedence and emotional issues relating to conflict or painful past experiences within families had been left unexplored and unresolved. The anger in
those cases could still be felt in our interviews. From service users' stories it was

easy to see how the immediacy of practical tasks and particularly those tasks surrounding a 'risky discharge' could dominate the agenda. It was not at all clear to us whether the social workers would have been able to make progress had they tried to address the underlying emotional issues at the time. We have no way of knowing how the social workers themselves felt about those cases, or how far they had tried to work on both the emotional and practical fronts.

Whilst we cannot know what went on behind the scenes, what does seem clear was the enormous distress surrounding the discharge of someone to his or her home or a nursing home when a family member felt it was unsafe or inappropriate. Early re-admission or other breakdowns in support in these cases suggested that the service users were right to distrust the discharge arrangements. One or two service users said that they felt the social workers had gone along with medically driven discharges. They felt that their 'scripts' and course of action had been predetermined by the medical team.

We are left wondering how much influence specialist palliative care social workers actually have in these circumstances. How easy is it for social workers to stand their ground on matters they may feel deeply about? We have to remember that a specialist palliative care social worker may be the sole representative of the profession within an otherwise medically dominated team. He or she may already be aware that social work is not held in high esteem within the unit, and may be forced to be selective in which battles he or she chooses to fight, as there may be many discharges that are problematic in one way or another. It was also evident, in the cases we highlighted that didn't run smoothly, that the specialist palliative care social workers were very much left playing a bridging role. We saw, for instance, how it was to the social worker that one service user turned when her relative's morphine didn't arrive in the nursing home. This was so clearly a medical need and yet the perception was that the person who might be available to sort out the confusion was the specialist palliative care social worker.

> But perhaps it wasn't [the social worker's] problem but I didn't get any real support and I had nowhere else to go. (Service user in discussion group)

This bridging role comes up in different ways a number of times throughout the study – between family and patient, between home and hospice, between external agencies and palliative care team – and confirms the point made by Oliviere (2001a) when he describes social workers as playing what he terms an 'eccentric' role:

> More often however it is the social workers who occupy an 'eccentric' position, advocating for a community and family perspective, and exploring the tensions of various interfaces which exist in palliative care situations. (p.239)

This seems a real strength of specialist palliative care social work, but it also highlights a dilemma for specialist palliative care social workers that needs careful exploration. If they are to perform this much-needed linking role, they need to have genuine influence and be sure of the back-up of the broader team. In the case mentioned above the social worker's influence appears restricted. How helpful is it for the service user if the specialist palliative care social worker assumes this role of 'picking up the pieces' but then fails to deliver? What is the cost to the service user in terms of loss of trust, and what is the professional cost to the specialist palliative care social worker? We would suggest that this dilemma – the wide range of responsibility and the limited degree of power and authority – is one that has many expressions for the specialist palliative care social worker.

SUMMARY

This chapter explored service users' accounts of their experience of social work practice in relation to existing theoretical discussions. It looked at key theories addressing loss and dying. The support which specialist palliative care social workers offer people seems to be consistent and compatible with much of the current theoretical writing about loss and bereavement. There is no way of knowing from this study whether theory is informing practice, but certainly theory does not seem in any way to be constraining or conflicting with practice.

No one approach to practice tied to a particular theoretical model emerges. Instead specialist palliative care social workers seem to adopt a wide range of approaches according to the needs and preferences of service users. Some of the challenges associated with these approaches are examined, for example in relation to group and family work, and ways of addressing them identified.

The very small number of cases where there were negative feelings about the social worker's role require further attention. These were generally cases where there was an element of a risky discharge. Here social workers might be constrained by dominant medical professionals and agendas. In such instances the specialist palliative care social worker's role had restrictions placed on it, comparable to those operating on the role of a mainstream social worker in statutory services. These constraints put at risk the valued contribution of specialist palliative care social workers to the detriment both of service users and the profession and require careful re-examination.

CHAPTER 12

SPECIALIST PALLIATIVE CARE SOCIAL WORK: A SERVICE IN THE SHADOWS?

The findings from this study suggest that specialist palliative care social work is a service which is highly rated by service users, in contrast to many other areas of social work and some other areas of palliative care. Yet this value attached to it by service users does not seem to be reflected in the status afforded it in the fields of either social work or palliative care. Despite its evidenced strengths, specialist palliative care social work seems to be a service in the shadows. It often seems to have been overlooked in both social work and palliative care discussions and developments. In this chapter we shall explore this issue and what might explain it. What emerges is that the very strengths of specialist palliative care social work – its closeness and responsiveness to service users – may actually serve to reduce its profile and status. We will examine some of the implications of this for social workers and for users of specialist palliative care. Finally, we will consider the relevance of our findings for social work in general.

THE DISTINCTIVE ROLE OF SPECIALIST PALLIATIVE CARE SOCIAL WORK

It became clear through the course of the project that we carried out that service users who accessed specialist palliative care social work felt that it was crucial to their well-being. Without it they seemed to feel that they would have a range of unmet needs. Other research confirms that many of the gaps service users identify in both oncology and generalist palliative care services relate to psychosocial issues (Hill *et al.* 2003; McIllmurray *et al.* 2001). Research into the needs of people with life-limiting illnesses and conditions other than cancer also shows that psychosocial needs are high on people's agendas, though access to palliative care in their case might often be far more restricted (Addington-Hall 1996; Anderson *et al.* 2001).

The comments of service users left us in no doubt that, when specialist palliative care social work had been available, people's journey through their illness and the palliative care system had been made more bearable. They saw specialist palliative care social work as having a distinct role to play which was not easily substituted by other professions. Palliative care social work was characterized by its holistic approach and by social workers' awareness of the connections in people's lives and of the social contexts within which they lived. In particular, it was distinctive because social workers were open to working with people on the issues that mattered to *them* and these were usually a complex mix of social, psychological and practical issues that were interrelated and could not easily be dealt with as separate entities. Other analysts have echoed these findings of a distinctive role for social work within multidisciplinary teams (Herod and Lymbery 2002).

Service users paint a very positive picture of their experience of specialist palliative care social work. It presents a very particular style of professional working; a style which they like, with which they are comfortable, which they feel is skilful and based on sound knowledge. They feel it is effective and yet still has a human face and is compatible with service users' own perceptions of themselves and their needs. Most important, social workers are seen to support people in a way that demonstrates respect for the individual and preserves dignity. There are undoubtedly deficiencies, problems and issues which still need to be addressed and we have highlighted these. However, overall we were left in no doubt that the vast majority of the service users to whom we spoke saw the social worker as playing a very central part in the overall support that they received from palliative care services.

Specialist palliative care social workers can perhaps feel proud that the service they offer is so highly valued. Equally service users similarly should be able to take for granted access to social work as an integral and fundamental part of specialist palliative care provision. However, as our study revealed, this is far from the case.

INCONSISTENT SERVICE PROVISION

Palliative care provision is itself extremely variable in availability and quality. *The Palliative Care Survey 1999* (National Council for Hospice and Specialist Palliative Care Services 2000) showed that: '96% of Health Authorities described their palliative care services as not yet adequate across the board, 15% felt they were struggling in developing all service components' (p.2). The survey highlighted the increased need for palliative care in areas of acute social deprivation and concluded that levels of provision did not appear to reflect differing levels of need. Home care and out-of-hours cover were particularly variable, which of course undermines the current goal of supporting people in their own homes and enabling them to have choice over where they live and die.

The marginal status of social work

Provision of social work within these services is also patchy and not necessarily related to the levels of deprivation experienced in local areas. It is difficult, however, to give a comprehensive or definitive picture of specialist palliative care social work in the UK today. There is a dearth of up-to-date information on, for example, how many posts there are, what level social workers are employed at, and whom they are managed by and accountable to. There is very little literature on the range or scale of work being undertaken by different social workers in different palliative care settings.

There is however no question that social work is seen by some as a core palliative care service. Dix and Glickman writing in 1997 stated:

> Psychosocial care is concerned with the psychological and emotional well-being of the patient and their family/carers, including issues of self esteem, insight into and adaptation to the illness and its consequences, communication, social functioning and relationships. It is an integral aspect of specialist palliative care…appropriately trained and experienced clinical psychologists, social workers and counsellors share skills for providing specialist psychosocial care as well as having expertise specific to each discipline. (p.6)

While they clearly identified the social worker here as having a key role, there is nevertheless an emphasis, which is stressed elsewhere in their paper, on the psychological component of 'psychosocial' with the social part of the term being marginalized. This deficit is acknowledged in a later discussion paper (National Council for Hospice and Specialist Palliative Care Services 2000b), which states:

> The current use of the term 'psychosocial' is primarily defined in terms of psychological aspects of care and thus deflects attention away from social aspects of patient and family experiences.

The discussion paper goes on:

> The broad social contexts within which patients and families live their lives are significant features that need to be addressed in the care of people who are dying, yet many palliative care services do not contain members with expert knowledge of social care. It is recommended that social workers should be included as core members of specialist palliative care teams.

Despite this, it is still apparent that there are many palliative care services without social workers. Lloyd-Williams, Friedman and Rudd (1999) carried out a survey of hospices to determine the provision of specialist psychosocial care. Though their main interest was the input of psychologists and psychiatrists, they also asked about social work provision. They received data from 97 hospices all of which had inpatient beds, and the majority of which had opened within the previous 15 years. Seventy-three of the hospices reported full- or part-time social work support, 18 said that they had social work support 'available if required', though there was no information given on the circumstances under which this support would be harnessed, and six hospices had no social work support at all. Full- or part-time counsellors were available in 42 of these units (with 30 others having counsellors available on request) but the survey failed to define counsellor so the authors agree that this figure may have included nurses, social workers, doctors or volunteer staff using counselling skills. Yet a US study not only made the case for having social workers in hospices, but suggested that they helped to reduce costs (Reese and Raymer 2004).

The Palliative Care Survey 1999 (National Council for Hospice and Specialist Palliative Care Services 2000a) drew together data from several sources to present an overview of the extent of palliative care provision in the UK. Social work provision was only briefly addressed; it did not form a major part of the study, a fact that may in itself have significance. It was reported, however, that in the case of home care services while 'around half of all nurses work in teams with a doctor, only one quarter work in teams that have both doctors and social workers as team members' (p.4).

Thus, far from being universally available as a core service, there are still some hospices and many palliative care teams without a dedicated social work post (information from Association of Palliative Care Social Workers). A substantial proportion of children's hospices, many of which have opened within the last few years, are run without a specialist palliative care social worker employed within the service (Knights 2004). In some adult services, there appear to have been reductions in social work provision, although it is difficult to ascertain whether these are for budgetary or other reasons. We know, for instance, that during the course of this study one of the specialist social workers with whom we liaised left her post and was not replaced, leaving that hospital-based team without a specialist palliative care social worker. Another hospice decided to disband its social work team completely. One of the project's steering groups told us that the specialist social worker post attached to their centre had been cut. There have also been additional cuts in social work services since this project was completed. There are still many palliative care units with only one social worker or only a very small social work team, which could not possibly be expected to offer the full range of services that service users indicate might be needed. Such shortfalls in social work provision might help explain some of the gaps which we uncovered in the services being offered to the participants in our study.

On a more positive note, some hospices have recognized the particular contribution of specialist palliative care social work and have expanded their teams. For example, we know of two hospices that have opted to employ or have been considering employing a specialist palliative care social worker for the first time. They had taken students studying on the specialist palliative care pathway of a professional social work qualification course taught by one of the authors (Lesley Adshead). Unfortunately, this innovative course has since been discontinued, a measure of the continuing insecurity of specialist palliative care social work.

If social work is to gain a core place in all specialist palliative care teams and secure more resources generally, specialist palliative care social workers and their professional organizations will need to make clear the contribution that they have to offer. They will need to be assertive about their own worth. This will require them to demonstrate professional confidence, so that others are left in no doubt about what social work has to offer. We did not feel that this professional confidence was reflected in service users' accounts of specialist palliative care social work, however much they valued it. Other authors have identified similar issues around such professional confidence (Currer 2001).

OTHER PROFESSIONS' PERCEPTIONS OF SOCIAL WORK

As we talked to more service users, our impression that we were hearing about professional work of the highest quality grew. Service users were in almost complete agreement about their appreciation of specialist palliative care social work. It was clear that it had played a crucial role in supporting both patients and people who had been bereaved, through some of the most difficult times of their lives. Yet we began to realize that an important contradiction was emerging. While service user approval of the social work role was strong, recognition from other professions was much harder to discern. Of course we did not speak to other professionals, that was not the purpose of this project. But there is no reason to assume that service users' positive views of specialist palliative care social workers would be especially discrepant with those of other stakeholders or overly sympathetic. After all, service users had some very critical things to say about other palliative care specialisms – as well as about social work generally.

We might also expect that as they work in multidisciplinary teams the social worker's role would be familiar to other professionals. Earnshaw-Smith (1990), however, cautions against this assumption, highlighting an issue raised by multidisciplinary working.

> [It] carries with it the danger of losing the particular and distinguishing features and skills of each profession... The often discussed and sometimes necessary blurring of roles can lead to a loss of appreciation of the excellence, the sharpness of the training and experience that each profession has to offer, and to clouding of thought in considering the precise needs of patient, family and friends. (1990, frontispiece)

However, a number of factors emerged in the study reported in this book which do raise questions about the value placed on specialist palliative care social work by other palliative care institutions and professions. For example:

- A significant proportion of hospices do not employ social workers. Given the value placed on what these social workers do by service users, does this reflect a view that what social workers do can easily be done by other professionals? Is this underpinned by an assumption that specialist palliative care social work is not associated with a distinctive role or set of skills?

- Service users repeatedly mentioned a failure to refer or very late referrals for social work support. It was as if social work was sometimes only considered as an afterthought. Does this reflect a lack of clarity about what social work can offer or a lack of valuing of its contribution? Some of the service users we met specifically asked for a social worker, but were either ignored or told 'it's not necessary'.

- Service users commented that other professionals seemed to know little about social work. Some of the responsibility for this may lie at the door of social work and its institutions for their own failure to communicate social work's role and purpose clearly enough. But could it also suggest that other professionals wrongly feel that they have a good understanding of social work, or do not feel that social work is worth finding out more about? Have they accepted some of the negative media stereotyping that social work has incurred?

- Very negative comments were made to one service user in relation to an individual specialist palliative care social worker, with the implication that she should not bother to see her. Whilst we appreciate that this was an isolated case, we find it hard to imagine this happening in relation to another profession within palliative care.

A BROADER PROBLEM

This seemingly low profile of social work within palliative care may not be unusual but may in fact be part of a much broader problem about the marginality of social work in general. Other studies have found similar patterns. For example, McLeod and Bywaters (1999, p.558) noted that 'hospital social work is still often viewed as a peripheral activity'. Jordan (2001) commented on the fact that social work is now defined in such a restricted manner by the Labour government that it is largely absent from a range of important new social initiatives, and mentioned Sure Start and the New Deal as examples.

> New Labour, in all its reformist rhetoric, seldom uses the term 'social work' and when it does, for activities that are largely narrow and negative, concerned with rationing and risk assessment; it prefers new words and new agencies for its more ambitious, generous and expansionist initiatives. (Jordan 2001, p.527)

But we wondered, from this study's findings, whether there might also be other issues.

A paradox?

The findings from our project have led us to wonder whether professional recognition of specialist palliative care social work may paradoxically be undermined by its very strengths. One of the characteristics of practice that we couldn't help noticing was the lack of professional trappings that accompanied the social work role. Service users, in our study, welcomed this and saw it as a real advantage. Many times over, we were told that the social worker was seen as an ordinary and approachable person – 'not like a professional'.

It is helpful, in relation to this, to consider social work alongside other health and welfare professions, as well as in relation to professions more generally. Unlike many other health-related professionals, specialist palliative care social workers do not wear uniforms. There is none of the technical paraphernalia of doctors, nurses and related staff. There are no specialized machines, no stethoscopes, resuscitation equipment or heart monitors. There are no emergency helicopters, flashing blue lights or special medical jargon that people associate with health services in their day-to-day life, as well as in television dramas. Social work is not associated with deference, high status or financial reward, as other professions – including the law, accountancy and indeed medicine – are. Unlike counselling, social work is not a profession people expect to pay for – and we live in a world where things, including professional practice, are still frequently judged by what they cost. Some social workers do have statutory powers but, of all the professions, their powers must be the ones that are most often challenged as arbitrarily or inadequately exercised.

This leads us to raise the question of whether the essential 'ordinariness' of specialist palliative care social work – the way it can transform, systematize and develop help and support as elements of a complex professional role – has led to it being misunderstood and devalued. In other words, the very things that service users emphasized as special and important are not more generally seen as such. Thus, what service users see as strengths and positives of social work practice may in fact be factors which reduce the likelihood of it being afforded external recognition. We encountered a number of issues and characteristics associated with specialist palliative care social work and which seem to reinforce such a view. These include:

- the strong 'hands-on' aspects of specialist palliative care social work
- commitment to partnership with patients
- the breadth of its remit
- an emphasis on demystification
- accessibility and flexibility
- association with friendship and friendliness
- avoidance of jargon.

All of these may have an adverse effect on how far specialist palliative care social work is seen to demarcate a 'profession' in its own right, with its own distinct body of knowledge, area of expertise, skills, values and competence. It is worth looking at each in more detail to consider questions that they may raise.

THE STRONG 'HANDS ON' ASPECTS OF SPECIALIST PALLIATIVE CARE SOCIAL WORK

Service users' experience highlights that specialist palliative care social work is very 'hands on' and patient focused. The other side of this coin may be that research and writing about this area of activity have tended to be neglected. A glance at the many palliative care and nursing journals reveals much material written by researchers from a nursing or medical background; there is, by comparison, very little written by specialist palliative care social workers and particularly little written by current practitioners, though this does appear to be changing (see, for example, Oliviere and Monroe 2004). This gives the impression that social work has little to share, little which is distinctive, when our findings suggest something different. It is also curious to note that some of the literature that has come from specialist palliative care social workers is not distinguished by any mention of social work in its titles (for example, Oliviere et al. 1998; Sheldon 1997). Yet these texts offer many excellent examples of social work playing a distinctive role within the broader framework of multidisciplinary palliative care.

The decision by these authors to keep 'social work' out of the titles of their work raises some big questions. Do they feel a need to distance their practice from social work in general, with all its negative connotations in people's minds, or do they feel terms like *psychosocial care* are essential for it to be taken seriously? It is interesting to consider whether professionals from other disciplines would be less likely to read a book if it had *social work* in the title. It may be that these authors want to stress the interdisciplinary context of their work. If this is the case then how does social work present a unique face? We would argue that service users were clear that, while there were other professionals whom they equally valued and respected, they saw the social workers as offering them something distinctive and special. We feel it is important that this uniqueness of social work is not lost when it is written about.

If specialist palliative care social workers don't write about their work, it seems unlikely that anyone else will. Examination of the indexes of many influential books on dying and bereavement reveals an absence of any reference to social workers (see, for example, Dickenson, Johnson and Katz 2000; McNamara 2001; Seale and Cartwright 1994). Where they are mentioned, it is usually in passing and referring generally only to accessing welfare benefits. While this is an important part of the specialist palliative care social work role, it denies its fully rounded nature. A typical example of this can be seen in

Ramirez, Addington-Hall and Richards (1998), where in an article entitled 'The Carers', part of the 'ABC of Palliative Care' series in the *British Medical Journal*, social workers are simply listed as a source of support for financial assistance while, under the heading of psychosocial support, GPs, district nurses, Macmillan nurses, and bereavement counsellors are all listed, but there is no mention of social work!

COMMITMENT TO PARTNERSHIP WITH PATIENTS

Service users were emphatic that specialist palliative care social workers worked in effective partnership with them. But might this be interpreted as diminishing their 'expert' status? We observed the satisfaction with which the majority of service users described their first meetings with the social worker. Frequently we were told that the service user 'just talked' and the social worker 'just listened'. We were told how people felt they had worked to their own agenda. However, in many ways a profession builds a strong identity around the notion that it has exclusive knowledge to which only its members are privy. Traditionally professions have been distinguished by their status, power, authority and 'expertise'. This 'expertise' or knowledge is then shared, but often in a highly structured way that leaves the service user very clear as to who is the expert (the professional). In this way, social work may run counter to the very characteristics which are used to demarcate the professionalization of an activity. By helping individuals to develop their own expertise and by genuinely working in ways that service users want, it may be that specialist palliative care social workers are seen as diluting their own specific expertise, rather than this being recognized as a form of expertise in its own right. Yet this participatory approach to the helping role and practice is closely consistent with increasing policy emphasis on 'putting the patient/service user at the centre' of health and care services and enabling them to have increased control and involvement. It is consistent with the demands of service user movements for more equal, two-way relationships between users and providers of support.

THE BREADTH OF ITS REMIT

Specialist palliative care social workers see their remit in very broad terms, but might this make specialist palliative care social work difficult to pin down, define and understand? Service users frequently told us that they had discovered that the social worker had been willing to tackle 'anything'. This was seen as an important strength. But we also heard that there was widespread ignorance about what social workers had to offer. At the beginning of their involvement, many service users had not been clear about the nature of the role. If social workers do not clearly spell out their role and demonstrate the virtues of its breadth, then it is possible that other professionals and service users will remain unclear and confused about what it is that social workers actually do and will be uncertain about referral. It is important that this breadth and flexibility are not left to be interpreted as having some kind of 'Jill of all trades, mistress of none' role and status, but are truly recognized for what they are: the positive and distinctive attributes of the profession that service users found so beneficial.

AN EMPHASIS ON DEMYSTIFICATION

Service users said that specialist palliative care social workers tended to treat patients' and bereaved people's feelings and experiences as 'normal', rather than routinely to pathologize them. But could this response be seen to diminish and demystify what social workers have to offer? Service users told us that this 'normalizing' approach had been important to them, but it did cause us to wonder if this resulted in other professionals misjudging the situation, assuming that people were able to 'cope' and that there was therefore no real need for social work support.

ACCESSIBILITY AND FLEXIBILITY

Service users seemed to value specialist palliative care social workers' flexible ways of working and responded well when boundaries were fairly elastic. It was very often these elastic boundaries that provided the space for creativity. But might their accessibility and their sometimes long involvement with service users lead to specialist palliative care social workers being seen by others as a 'soft touch' with woolly professional boundaries? As we highlighted earlier, there does seem to be a need for more discussion about some of the thorny issues around flexibility and boundaries here. It seems important that specialist palliative care social workers are clear about why they work as they do, own their own ways of working and resist any inappropriate pressures to model their ways of working on other professions, such as nursing or counselling. Again this requires confidence but it also demands that social workers think through the issues so that they can readily articulate the reasons behind their ways of working and if necessary defend them. We are thinking here of practices such as offering home visits, carrying out 'informal' assessments or keeping cases open when other members of the palliative care team may have withdrawn.

ASSOCIATION WITH FRIENDSHIP AND FRIENDLINESS

Service users consistently talked about feeling that the social worker was like a 'friend' and they valued this. We know though that in some other quarters this may be seen as 'unprofessional'. While it is what service users seem to want, it may thus actually diminish the externally perceived status of social workers. The knee-jerk reaction is to be fearful that the social worker is being exposed as somehow unprofessional, unboundaried or merely doing something anybody could do. We fear that this is the response that there has often been, with commentators and theoreticians trying to distance social work from such perceptions and emphasizing instead its theoretical underpinnings and claim to status.

We suggest instead that social work must learn to listen to what service users are saying and try to explore what this means. Social work needs to look behind its anxieties and appreciate just what it is being told. If it fails to do this, then specialist palliative care social workers may cut themselves off from a source that could cast considerable light on what they do – service users. Words like 'friend' and 'friendliness' might more helpfully be understood as communicating the warmth, integrity, lack of judgement and empathy which social care service users internationally highlight repeatedly that they value and want from social workers. This may be pointing not to a shift away from a theory-based practice, but to a different, potentially much more complex, democratic and subtle, theoretical base for professional practice.

AVOIDANCE OF JARGON

In our study, specialist palliative care social workers generally resisted terms like *clinical assessment, intervention* and *therapy*. They tended to avoid using formal and medicalized terminology. However, jargon and specialist words have historically played an important part in health and social care professions. They become part of their distinct equipment and identity. They have often been used to give them a spurious authority.

It was clear listening to service users that they felt little need for this aspect of professionalism. What mattered to them was that they were understood on their own terms and, for this to happen, they had to be able to express themselves comfortably and to be heard. Jargon is so often allowed to become a barrier between service user and service worker and to undermine service users' feelings of competence. In a similar way, formal assessment frameworks and forms can be used as a tool for focusing and limiting demands and for not hearing the actual person. If specialist palliative care social workers have done away with or have not yet succumbed to these professional props, they need to be confident about their alternative way of working. Unfortunately, much other social work has adopted such terminology and the practices that go with it.

SOCIAL WORK'S UNCERTAIN STATUS IN PALLIATIVE CARE

If any of the issues we have identified are considered in isolation, they may not seem particularly significant and of course all are open to debate. However, they have a cumulative significance. Taken together, we would suggest that they may play a serious part in weakening the position of specialist palliative care social work.

A key related issue is the limited role played by social workers in the management of palliative care. What is not clear is whether this is a cause or effect of the problems that we have highlighted. The importance of management in influencing the quality of specialist social work practice service users receive was one of the issues that emerged in our study. We found that whether and when service users were referred to specialist palliative care social work could be adversely and inappropriately affected by management misperceptions of social work. Shortcomings in palliative care management could limit the contribution that specialist palliative care social workers could make to support service users.

Social workers generally have minimal involvement at a managerial level within hospice and specialist palliative care teams. Though not specifically referring to social work, Hockley (1997) feels that the distinctive *hospice approach* could be under threat because of trends that have been identified:

> the best units are those which are led from a multi-disciplinary standpoint... The clear danger is that all that had been built up over the years could be undermined if the multi-disciplinary emphasis is to be watered down because of overly strong medical or nursing direction. (p.95)

In a similar vein, Field (1998) suggests that there is some substance in fears that a process of re-medicalization, with a dilution of hospice ideals, is accompanying the growth of the speciality of palliative medicine. He identifies more hierarchical authority structures in which some nurse managers are finding their influence diminished. He concludes that there is an increasing focus on symptom management rather than on dying, as hospices perform a greater number and wider range of medical procedures than previously (Field 1998, p.203). This would undoubtedly have implications for the place of social work.

We have no real evidence from our study that this is happening on a large scale, but the dominance of the medical model was picked up by at least one service user in the study, who felt there was insufficient recognition for the role of social work.

> It's a shame they don't recognize it. You know, I think it's all doctors, nurses, doctors, nurses... (Bereaved woman, white UK, age group 56–65)

Where there is 'overly strong medical or nursing direction', as Hockley (1997, p.95) puts it, social workers can find themselves in an isolated and exposed position if they challenge decisions that they see as failing to take sufficient account of psychosocial factors. In this situation, without a considerable degree of confidence and certainty on the part of individual workers, the distinctive voice of social work is at risk of being muted. We felt that this might have been an issue in some of the cases we picked out where service users had been unhappy with social work input.

In some senses, specialist palliative care social workers seem to enjoy considerable professional autonomy. In the main they practise free from many of the external controls that bedevil social workers' autonomy in other settings; but how secure is this autonomy and does it represent a freedom without any power? If they are seldom in positions of authority within the organization, can they expect to influence policies and plans effectively, or does their influence depend largely on the good will of those who hold executive positions?

Looking wider still, it is pertinent to ask how much influence social workers have on the broader policy-making bodies that affect palliative care. There seems to be little detailed information about the role specialist palliative care social workers play in the bodies that influence and shape palliative care at either local or national level. It is beyond the scope of this project to give a full answer to this question but there are some indications that influence is limited because representation on such bodies is low. We know for example that there was very limited social work representation on the editorial board and associated groups of the National Institute for Clinical Excellence at the time they drew up the draft guidelines for *Supportive and Palliative Care Guidance* (NICE 2004). This perhaps accounts for the way that the role of the specialist palliative care social worker is given comparatively slight acknowledgement within the guidelines, though social care more generally is given prominence. In the draft and subsequent guidelines, specialist palliative care social workers were not included as core members of the team. Feedback from stakeholders did not alter this situation. Core members are identified as doctor, nurse and administrator. The House of Commons Health Committee (2004) on palliative care, in contrast, however, argued that:

> it is essential that shortfalls in staff involving other health and social care professionals with relevant experience – such as community nurses and social workers – are addressed at the same time. Palliative Care is manifestly a branch of medicine requiring a team approach. (para.115)

A further indication of the marginalization of social work is that representatives with a social work background only have one place on each of the two key national palliative care organizations in the UK: Help the Hospices and the National Council for Palliative Care.

The picture is the same in social work, where people with a background in specialist palliative care social work are underrepresented in its key organizations. Social work discourse rarely draws on or presents experience from palliative care social work, but instead has continued to be preoccupied with child protection, its most contentious and least satisfactory area of activity.

It is not only in practice and not only in palliative care that social workers find themselves either in a minority or else managed or supervised by other disciplines. Lyons and Manion (2003), reporting on two surveys into doctoral research in social work in the UK, speak of 'the relative invisibility of social work research in the form of doctoral studies'. They go on to say:

> people who have qualified and worked as social workers and are researching issues which are central to social work policy and practice, are undertaking their research with supervisors in other disciplines, for example sociology or social policy, in universities not engaged in social work education. (p.1119)

And furthermore:

> Social work is not recognised as a 'research discipline' for the purpose of allo-cating funding to doctoral students…it suggests a lack of government or other targeted funding for the discipline…[and] there are no annual collec-tions or publications of information about completed social work theses. (p.1119)

This has been confirmed more recently in a national project exploring the status of social work research with the Economic and Social Research Council (ESRC) (Shaw *et al.* 2004).

We have tried to show that many of the aspects of specialist palliative care social work that were emphasized as being important to service users are not necessarily appreciated more generally. In one sense, the things that people told us they wanted and valued were very straightforward, simple and easy to under-stand. Perversely, though, practitioners may actually be scared off attempting them. For when we read theoretical books about social work, the style and language are often obscure and inaccessible. As we noted earlier, social work discourse is predominantly constructed by non-practitioners. Social work texts and theorizing have tended to marginalize the inclusion of people with signifi-cant and, particularly, current experience as social work practitioners. It is all too easy for practising social workers, even experienced ones, to be intimidated by such writings; to feel that they haven't grasped the 'real' issues, that they are missing something and that their own experiences of practice are irrelevant. This can readily engender a feeling of inadequacy and embarrassment, which in turn leads to reluctance to share their own experiences, particularly in writing. It is vital not to lose sight of the fact those things that sound very simple to say may not be so simple to do – 'she just listened' conceals a myriad of knowledge, skills and values being put to work.

Listening to what service users have to say will help specialist palliative care social workers to be clearer about what is valued and therefore better placed to understand the particular strengths and weaknesses of what they have to offer. This knowledge could enhance social workers' understanding of the distinctive nature of their role, thereby raising their professional confidence and ability to argue for the place of social work as a core service within specialist palliative care.

THE IMPORTANCE OF EVALUATION

Clearly, if specialist palliative care social work is to build on the experience and views of service users in this way, then these need to be regularly and systematically included as part of a process of evaluation. Our finding – that few service users had been given the opportunity formally to evaluate or offer feedback on the specialist palliative care service – was perhaps one of the most worrying findings of this study. Certainly there were only a few examples of such evaluation being done in a routine and comprehensive way. We came across no instances of individual service users who had been involved in comprehensive and independent evaluation of the service that they received.

It is important that evaluation involving service users is carried out with care and sensitivity and does not itself impose an extra, unhelpful burden on people. This is a point that was made by some of the participants in our study and which has been highlighted in other studies. Small and Rhodes (2000, p.123) wrote:

> There is something potentially controlling and hierarchical about an imperative to be informed, to have a view, to have to play a part in planning and evaluating services. The space for someone to say, 'I don't want to know, I just want to be looked after, I don't want to face that now' is disappearing, at least as a socially approved or accepted space.

While their conclusion may be an overstatement, their central concern holds. However, some service users made it clear to us that they *did* want to be involved in evaluation. It was sometimes a reason they gave for taking part in our project. These people were in effect being denied an opportunity to say what they had valued, to make clear any gaps, to offer suggestions, or to complain. It is essential that service users, who want to, can be involved in evaluating services, but this will mean creating the right conditions for that involvement. For example, issues of access and support need to be properly addressed (Beresford et al. 2005b). There is ample evidence that where this has been done it is possible to involve even very vulnerable people (Hughes et al. 2004).

Failure to seek the views of service users means that specialist palliative care social workers are closed off from a potential source of positive support, reward and validation for their work. Given the apparent uncertainty and lack of confidence of some of them about what they have to offer, this must be a serious omission. Unless their practice is evaluated, they have little evidence to present to other professions, managers and funding bodies about their role within palliative care and its importance to service users. They have little to counter the prevailing and pervasive negative image of social work other than anecdotal evidence. They have nothing concrete, for example, to substantiate the need for further training or to support requests for more social workers.

The centrality of service users' views

This is a crucial point. If specialist palliative care social workers want to make the case for social work as a valued and legitimate role, the evidence from our study is that they can only benefit by drawing on what service users have to say. If it is left to other professions to pass judgement on specialist palliative care social work, then it does not look as though it will be seen as a highly valued profession, since the very skills that it has to offer can be difficult to distinguish and are frequently not recognized or valued – just as service users themselves are not always valued. Regular and systematic evaluation of service users' views and ideas is perhaps the first step along the way towards securing for specialist palliative care social work the recognition that service users seem to think it warrants.

The scale of the challenge should not be underestimated. As Arnon Bar-On (2002, p.1010) writes:

> Regarding social work's bases of power, the challenge is to re-vitalise the profession's image, which too often still epitomises incompetence, shoddiess…and bureaucratic blindness…and so reduces the weight its practitioners' messages are accorded as well as their latent power. Changing this image is a daunting task because without information to the contrary, there is little to convince others that social workers do help…

If specialist palliative care social work is sensitively and regularly evaluated and the views of service users are included in this process, both its evidence base and its profile are likely to be strengthened. There will doubtless be issues to address, but there is also likely to be good news to share. This is important not just for palliative care, but for social work in general. Social work as a whole is not good at sharing its good news (Smith 2003). This has increasingly been recognized at government level. The Department of Health sought to rectify this with an image-building advertising campaign timed to coincide with the introduction of the new social work degree programmes. But advertising campaigns are unlikely to be enough on their own. Social work's bad press is unlikely to dry up. The work of social workers, particularly in the context of child protection, is inextricable from working with and managing risk. In such a complex environment, particularly given social work's historically low status, inadequate funding and organizational problems, misjudgements resulting in tragedy are sometimes likely to occur. It is important to distinguish between social work's own failings, the negative images and labels that are attached to it and its inherently difficult task, and to seek to address all three of these.

Some social workers in the statutory sector may feel that our findings are only relevant to the specific field of palliative care social work which we have examined. However, we would question this assumption. Our focus has been on people facing loss, change, illness, impairment and sometimes material deprivation. These are issues and characteristics shared by many users of social work and social care. Moreover, all the groups of people who come to the attention of other fields of social work, including older people, disabled people, mental health service users, people with learning difficulties and families with children, may also come the way of palliative care social work. The attributes of good practice that are valued in this setting are not narrowly specialist. We would suggest, from what service users say, that they are likely to be helpful in all social work settings. They build on the traditional skills, values and concerns of social work, though we fully appreciate there is not always the freedom to apply them as social work practitioners might like to in every setting. There is all the more reason for re-stating what service users want because these are the very things that have been lost in so much social work, as many writers highlight (Seering 2003; Trevithick 2003).

Studies that have asked service users about other types of services and what they want from their social workers have come up with remarkably similar findings to our own and it is worth detailing some of these to show the consistency. Children interviewed for research into the working of the Children Act (Aldgate and Statham 2001) were clear what the qualities of a social worker or other professional were that enabled them to discuss their feelings and take an active part in effective decision making. They identified:

- reliability
- practical help
- the ability to give support
- time to listen and respond
- seeing children's lives in the round, not just the problems (p.93).

Their findings about what parents want from services have a very familiar ring as well and we just give examples of two:

- parents value services which offer a combination of practical and emotional help
- parents value social workers who are approachable, honest, understanding, reliable and helpful, and who have time to listen (p.81).

Peer research carried out in the Netherlands by homeless adolescents (De Winter and Noom 2003) found that:

> Communication with social workers is not as it should be. They are not listened to; too many social workers remain behind their desks and there is too little personal involvement. (p.326)

Asked in the same study what an ideal social worker would be, they were told: 'Someone who doesn't regard you as a client, but treats you as an ordinary human being and trusts you' (p.336).

A study into the views of young people (Pritchard *et al.* 1998) about their experience of educational social work concluded that: 'The most important finding…was the central importance of their relationship with their educational social worker and the associated practical help and guidance, which was so highly valued' (p.930). Two major national consultations with adult social care service users, carried out in 2005 towards the preparation of the government's White Paper on health and social care (Department of Health 2006), both highlighted the same range of human qualities in social care workers as was emphasized by service users in our project (Beresford *et al.* 2005a; Branfield *et al.* 2005).

As Parton says:

> The central message that comes across time and time again is that it is not the particular model or technique used by the social workers but the quality and value of the experience. (2003, p.3)

This has been a constant theme in the comments of the service users involved in this study. Listening to what they say may offer the key for bringing specialist palliative care social work (and indeed social work more generally) out from the shadows into the light.

SUMMARY

Service users see specialist palliative care social work as an essential part of palliative care provision. They have identified its distinctive role and value the particular contribution it can offer them. Despite their enthusiasm, specialist palliative care social work seems to be beset by internal uncertainty and external misunderstanding. It is a service in the shadows. Evidence of this is offered by the fact that social work does not seem to be prioritized and is not universally available to palliative care service users, and that there is widespread lack of knowledge about what social workers actually do among other professions, which in turn limits referrals.

There seems to be a paradox here. The very strengths of specialist palliative care social work, which service users say are important – its flexibility, informality and 'ordinariness' – are not generally those that attract professional recognition. Other factors such as lack of social work's managerial influence and limited representation on the outside bodies which govern and develop palliative care all work together to diminish the profile of specialist palliative care social work. This low profile is not exclusive to palliative care. Social work in general is often seen as a marginal activity.

It is essential that service users are meaningfully involved in evaluation of specialist palliative care social work if its contribution is to be recognized. So far there is scant evidence that this is happening. This means that specialist palliative care social work is unlikely to improve in the ways that service users want. It also means that the positive findings about specialist palliative care social work are unlikely to be shared. The findings from this study, while focused specifically on specialist palliative care social work, are likely to be relevant for *all* social work. The good news from palliative care provides insights and encouragement for social work in general. It re-affirms that the traditional skills, knowledge and values of social work remain of central importance to service users.

CHAPTER 13

ISSUES FOR THE FUTURE

In this final chapter, we pay particular attention to the implications of the book's findings both for practice and training in palliative care and social work. We also look specifically at issues of user involvement in palliative care and draw together service users' own ideas about what will be helpful for the training and practice of specialist palliative care social workers for the future. We offer our ideas cautiously because it became clear to us during this work that social work services within palliative care are very diverse. In some hospices there are large teams, offering wide-ranging support, while in others there may be just one social worker trying to keep the flag flying. Undoubtedly, in some contexts, where work is far advanced, these suggestions may be superfluous. In others, they may seem beyond reach. However, we hope they will act as a catalyst for further thought, discussion and action. Most important, they may highlight the need to ensure that service users can expect the same high quality of service wherever they are and whoever they are. Ensuring equity has emerged in recent years as one of the key objectives that health and social care services experience especial difficulty achieving. We begin by looking at some of the strengths and limitations of the study upon which this book is based; strengths and weaknesses which in some cases reflect those of palliative care and specialist palliative care social work themselves.

STRENGTHS OF THE STUDY

The study had a number of significant strengths. It was broad based, covering a wide range of palliative care units, which were diverse in terms of type of management, geographical location, class context and the services they offered. They included inpatient, day-care and home care services. We also tried hard to ensure that the sample of service users was as diverse as possible in terms of age, gender, class, ethnicity and type of illness and condition. We were successful in recruiting people at all stages of their illness and bereavement. The service users who took part included people with speech impairments and who communicated differently, people with visual and physical impairments and people with experience of mental health problems.

The study sought to be inclusive and participatory in approach. By this we mean that service users (both palliative care and other service users), through their inclusion on the project's steering groups and advisory group, played an important role in shaping the project. They helped us in identifying important issues to think about, identify gaps and manage uncertainties. Particularly important, they helped us to explore the findings as they emerged. The service users on the advisory group read drafts of the report as they were written and sought clarity, offered feedback and made suggestions in the light of their own experiences. There was feedback through newsletters to participants and we had some positive comment from them on this approach, although it is not easy to know what impact this has on people who may have wanted to 'move on' from an experience. Entwistle, Tritter and Calnan (2002) urge more research into the effects of giving feedback in research. Similarly, as yet we are at an early stage in understanding and having a clear evidence base about the benefits of involving service users in research. The frequently emerging picture from service users who do get involved, however, is that where that involvement feels meaningful rather than tokenistic, it is inherently positive and beneficial. More research is also needed in this area.

The study demonstrated once again that people facing life-threatening illness or bereavement, even some very sick and distressed people, are willing to be involved in research (Barnett 2001). Some of the participants said it had been very important to them to take part and have the opportunity to say things that they felt mattered. We also found, like others, that with proper informa-tion and assurances about confidentiality and anonymity, many people were prepared to be video-recorded and audio-taped (Hargreaves and Peppiatt 2001). Some service users, like those on our advisory group, are also ready for regular and longer-term involvement, demonstrating a considerable degree of commitment and a strong sense of responsibility.

LIMITATIONS OF THE STUDY

The study, however, also had some limitations and it is important to be clear about these. As we have indicated, some of these seem to reflect limitations in specialist palliative care social work and palliative care themselves. Despite the fact that the sample was very diverse there were some difficulties in recruitment, which resulted in gaps in whom we were able to speak to. We found it difficult to involve children and decided quite early on that we would abandon this goal. There had always been concerns on the part of the funders about including children, but our advisory group had challenged these. In the event, given the scale and resources of the project, it became clear that this was a task which it wasn't feasible to take on. Likewise we found it harder to recruit men, and people from minority ethnic groups, although we did ensure a good representa-tion of both in the end. A particular gap that we did not manage to address may be the absence from the study of people from minority ethnic groups who did not speak English. Though we made it clear that we could offer interpreters, this was not taken up. We did not access anyone identified as having learning difficulties, although other work does help to fill this gap (for example, McEnhill 2004). We suspect that some of these difficulties may reflect wider issues about the actual profile and characteristics of those who use palliative care services and palliative care social work services. So it is likely our difficulties reflect broader problems which need to be addressed in palliative care.

A potential area of concern that we recognized from an early stage was that of 'cherry picking' the service users who took part. Our worry was that by recruiting service users through social workers we may have 'cherry picked' those who were more likely to be positive and give us the 'good news' about specialist palliative care social work rather than being critical. Added to this, reluctance to express negative opinions about 'care givers' is already an acknowledged problem in research (Williams, Coyle and Healy 1998). We have already addressed this issue of 'cherry picking' in Appendix 1, so will not focus on it again other than to say that we were strenuous in our efforts to enable participants to make negative comments and included check questions to encourage this. In the event we certainly recruited a small number of service users who were unhappy about the social work support that they had received, so, as will already be clear, the picture was by no means all positive. Furthermore, while participants were generally positive about social work practice, their comments did highlight problems in its organization and management that could limit the effectiveness of such practice.

An unexpected discovery we did make was that where service users felt well disposed to a service, they also seemed to be keen to see it develop, learn and improve. Frequently we recorded in our process notes that service users were determined to think about how services and practice might be even *better*. If there was any general reluctance to be critical about specialist palliative care social work, it was well hidden. At the same time, significantly, we did pick it up very readily in some people's initial reluctance to tell us about their previous views of social work generally. However, with only modest prompting and encouragement, service users opened up on those issues as the interviews progressed.

Our chosen method of recruitment to the study (only including service users who had experience of specialist palliative care social work) meant that it excluded service users who may have been offered specialist palliative care social work but had refused it. While this meant that all participants had direct experience of specialist palliative care social work and therefore spoke from direct knowledge, this also represents a limitation of the project and further research in this area would be helpful.

To ensure that the project was as sensitive and user friendly as possible, we built flexibility into our research method, but this can also create its own problems. We developed a semi-structured interview schedule, which was used as a guide, but the participants were allowed the chance to give their accounts in the way that they wanted to and on one or two occasions the schedule was all but abandoned. This inevitably meant that though people were able to talk about things that mattered to them, they sometimes didn't provide all the information that we would have liked, as time ran out, they got tired or our research issues were simply not their issues. This raises ethical issues as well as methodological ones and there are no real easy answers to the tensions that occasionally exist as here between the goals of researchers and those of research participants (Seymour and Skilbeck 2002). Whilst we ended up with rich accounts of knowledge and experience, sometimes 'precision' was compromised in the sense that, in a few cases, accounts could be difficult to compare and contrast, as they simply were very different. On balance we felt that it was more important to let people offer their accounts in the way that they wanted, rather than restrict them too readily to suit our schedule. We nonetheless learned a great deal from their accounts.

IMPLICATIONS OF THE FINDINGS

The findings discussed in this book have wide implications. There are significant implications for palliative care, specialist palliative care social work and social work more generally.

Issues for hospice and palliative care

We have already rehearsed a number of these issues in our discussion of the findings from the study. These include:

- the relatively small proportion of people who currently at the end of life access specialist palliative care, despite the evident benefits it can offer
- the continuing and possibly increasing strength of the medical model in palliative care and the challenge it poses to the maintenance of the holistic philosophy and goals that have traditionally underpinned this field
- unequal access to specialist palliative care in terms of class, ethnicity, the nature of life-limiting illness and condition, etc.

Hospice and palliative care are still seen as very threatening by many people and there was initial reluctance among service users to accept referral. We don't know how many of those who did not access the service did so because of this. Service users, including some who were themselves employed in health and social care, tended to have one view of hospice care. They saw it as signifying imminent death. One man said that he had always thought of the local hospice as 'the death house'. Late referral seemed to be very common and this helps to perpetuate such an image. Once in the system service users were very rapidly reassured.

As the range of life-limiting illnesses and conditions addressed by hospice and palliative care has begun to grow and medical responses to them have developed, the potential contact that people may have with palliative care has lengthened. The association of palliative care with rapid death is changing – at least objectively. This is throwing up many new issues of its own. Work needs to be undertaken to make clear the full brief of hospice and palliative care work. We recognize that this is already getting considerable attention. Social workers may have a particular contribution to make here, particularly in seeking to reach people from disadvantaged communities, who may currently be under-represented as users of specialist palliative care. Social workers are already likely to be in touch with a network of schools, social agencies, community groups and other contacts in the community and could almost certainly build on this for outreach and educative work. Some service users indicated that they saw this type of educative work as important and said that they would be prepared to play a role in supporting it.

Issues for the role and image of social work

It is important to be aware of the negative image that social work currently carries as the effects of this are both pervasive and corrosive. Two points need to be made from the evidence of this study. This is not only a consequence of negativity from some media and politicians. We should also remain mindful that sometimes this image has been formed because of actual bad experience. This was certainly what some service users in this study said and it is strongly confirmed by other studies of service users' views of social work and social care (for example, Branfield *et al.* 2005). It is not enough to see the adverse image of social work as unrelated to its actual nature or a consequence of unjustified and politically motivated hostility to social work. We must move on from a view of the solution as essentially a matter of improved public relations and media coverage.

There is a need to explain the social work role very carefully to other professionals, to service users and to the wider world, if there is to be genuine understanding and appreciation of what social work can offer. It is likely to be unwise to remain passive on this issue. It is important to assume that many people, including other professionals, have no idea of what specialist palliative care social workers do, to be ready to explain it and to make sure that the more negative images are directly countered.

It is also important to celebrate the positive achievements and outcomes of specialist palliative care social work through discussion, writing and recording; to establish that these social workers have specific attributes, skills and knowledge which is worth sharing. It is crucial for social work to put the message across that, where social workers are given the opportunity to work creatively and in the ways that they and service users want, then the evidence is that the profession is able to deliver. This will then help to strengthen the reputation of social work more generally and will help those who are currently constrained in their roles to argue for the right to work more freely.

Issues for specialist palliative care social work

We are particularly concerned here, of course, with the issues raised by our findings for specialist palliative care social work because this has been the focus of our inquiry. We believe that what service users have to say casts helpful light on specialist palliative care social work – its strengths and problems. It may be helpful to set out these issues and implications arising from the findings in the same way that we organized the book – in terms of people's journey through palliative care and specialist palliative care social work.

REFERRALS TO SPECIALIST PALLIATIVE CARE SOCIAL WORK

This is an area where significant problems emerged. Whatever the merits of specialist palliative care social work practice, they will be negated if people are not able to access them. This is clearly happening with existing structures for referral. Just as there are exclusions and inequalities in referrals to palliative care, so there is a further set of inappropriate barriers operating to deny people the support that many feel they can gain from specialist social work. There is a need to review referral patterns, carry out audit and identify gaps in who is accessing specialist palliative care social work. Our evidence suggests that patients rather than bereaved people may be the most in danger of slipping through the net.

Put simply, at least three agents may be at work in the process of referral to specialist palliative care social work: other palliative care professionals, the social worker themselves and service users. We know that service users are frequently put off social work. So far the indications are that other professions may lack knowledge about social work, or misunderstand or devalue it. This needs to be addressed. But social workers themselves may need to be more proactive in their stance on referral in their agencies.

It may be helpful for specialist palliative care social workers to reflect upon their own skills and see if any gaps reveal a desire to limit the service or mirror their own anxieties about competence in any particular area; for example, in working with adolescents or with people with certain illnesses and conditions. More thought needs to be given to referral pathways. There needs to be consideration of whether there are gatekeepers to the social work service. If there are gatekeepers, are assumptions being made about their knowledge of specialist palliative care social work?

It may also help social workers to think about the value of both formal and informal approaches to service users. We found that informal 'unannounced' approaches worked very well and without them some very distressed people felt they would not have received the support that they wanted.

As yet it seems that service users play a very limited role in referring them-selves to specialist palliative care social work. Given the status and image of social work and the difficult times service users are likely to be going through, this is perhaps not surprising. There seems to be further scope for extending the role of written information and other media in increasing accessibility. Some service users would have liked more written information about social work and how to access it. Others told us that it had been available and they had turned to it when they felt they were not coping. It will be helpful to find ways of offering social work support more than once. Some service users said that they had rejected social work when it was first offered, but were pleased that it was offered again later and they took advantage of the offer.

ASSESSMENT IN SPECIALIST PALLIATIVE CARE SOCIAL WORK

Most of the service users with whom we spoke were happy about the way that the assessment had been carried out. However, a small minority seemed disad-vantaged by the approach most commonly used, which seemed to be informal, without forms and checklists and perhaps to a degree reliant on service users opening up discussions about their needs. Some service users told us they were not clear what they wanted or needed. Perhaps more important, they weren't clear what it was that the social worker could offer. They had felt rather lost in the process. They needed clearer steering.

Further thought needs to be given to assessment methods in specialist pal-liative care social work. This is not to suggest a move to the more mechanical approaches which now seem to predominate in statutory social work, particu-larly with adult service users, and our study pointed against this. At the same time, there are still some large questions to answer. For example, are there ways of capturing the concerns of some service users who do not respond so well to current, more informal methods? Is there a need for more flexibility of approach, which social workers demonstrated in their practice more generally? Would a multi-method approach be more helpful? Could some of the tech-niques and tools from research have a place here? We are thinking of some of the well-validated, self-administered schedules and questionnaires that researchers use to access the concerns of patients. These might be adapted to use in practice, as a supplement to the face-to-face assessment, to ensure that all concerns were covered.

Perhaps most important, it cannot be assumed that service users know what social work can offer. It is clearly still essential to ensure that the social work role is fully explained at the time of assessment. Any preconception that the service user has any understanding of it needs to be challenged.

THE RANGE AND KIND OF SUPPORT OFFERED

One of the strongest findings that emerged from the project was the many different ways of working that specialist palliative care social workers would enlist to support service users effectively. They were also very sensitive to matching the kind of support with what the individual service user wanted or from which he or she might specifically benefit. However, service users still identified some gaps. These related to the provision of welfare rights support, services offered to children and young people and the availability of groupwork, particularly to patients. There was also little evidence in this study of much work with families as a group or of groupwork with people's wider networks. Most work was done with individual family members one at a time. There were exceptions but we did not find many examples of such whole family work.

It might be expected that the wide variety of settings for specialist palliative care social work – small and large, statutory and voluntary and the range of different traditions they come from – might result in unevenness and patchiness of provision. The issue is not about standardization and conformity. Rather it is about ensuring that the provision of specialist palliative care social work is characterized by shared principles, working practices and an agreed remit. It is likely to be helpful to take forward this strategic goal; for social workers to take time to reflect on the support they offer, the approaches that they use and the service users they work with, to determine gaps and omissions in their particular service and any training needs that need to be met. As yet there is no consistency in social work practice in different places and settings – and this, as opposed to standardization, is likely to be helpful.

WORKING WITH DIFFERENT GROUPS OF SERVICE USERS

Our study reinforced the view that there are gaps and inequalities in access to specialist palliative care services. These in turn further restrict access to specialist palliative care social work. Barriers are also operating to restrict access to specialist palliative care social work to those service users who do enter the palliative care system. There needs to be a systematic audit to help ensure that all users of the specialist palliative care service are able to access the specialist palliative care social worker. As we have suggested, children and adolescents may not be having their support needs met in every setting. There seem to be implications for training here so that the confidence and expertise of social workers can be boosted. Some service users commented that their children needed to meet other children in a similar position. There is scope for joint working between palliative care centres, GPs and schools, so that opportunities for bringing together children who have been bereaved are maximized.

Some men particularly seem to find it difficult to accept social work referral and new thinking is likely to be needed here about ways of both offering and delivering a social work service. Some women felt that they carried an extra load supporting the men in their lives and ways need to be found to offer them additional support. The evidence to date indicates that black people and people from minority ethnic groups do not have equal access to palliative care and specialist palliative care social work and social workers need to be proactive in efforts to address this. Social workers also need additional training around the needs of people with diagnoses other than cancer. As palliative care services become more inclusive and are no longer seen as solely concerned with cancer, there will clearly be a growing need for such expertise and understanding.

WHERE THINGS DID NOT GO SMOOTHLY

We would be cautious about making recommendations about areas where social work practice seemed to go wrong. There were very few such cases and we only had one perspective on them. However, it did appear that certain situations produced the conditions for things to go wrong. Problems seemed to be particularly associated with rushed or disputed discharges from the specialist palliative care service. Social workers often do not have the key say in such discharges.

If this situation is to be improved, there needs to be discussion and reflection about the social work role within the broader interdisciplinary group. The specialist palliative care social worker's 'bridging role' seemed to leave them very vulnerable when the services at either end of the bridge – that is, the hospice- and community-based provision – both failed to deliver adequately, as was occasionally the case.

It was evident that when things had gone badly for a service user, they sometimes found that this complicated their bereavement and they were left with difficult feelings but no continuing support. These feelings were sometimes still quite raw in the interviews. Social workers need to find ways of sensitively offering such service users support in their bereavement either directly or through appropriate referral.

No part of palliative care or particular professional roles within it can be considered in isolation. Our focus was on one specialist palliative care profession – social work. But it became clear that other professions and structures not only impacted on specialist palliative care social work, but could also determine the nature of service users' experience of it – and indeed whether they had experience of it at all. Palliative care is truly about multidisciplinary and interdisciplinary working and if this doesn't happen on an informed and sensitive basis there are likely to be problems.

INVOLVING PALLIATIVE CARE SERVICE USERS

One of the particular characteristics of this book is that it is centrally based on what service users have to say. As we commented earlier, this is still very unusual in writings and discussions about health, social care and welfare. Yet it is clearly important because service users have a unique contribution to make in such discussions. They also have a role to play more generally in policy and provision. In our study, service users themselves suggested ways in which they already were involved or felt they could be more involved in specialist palliative care social work. They could see a helpful role for user involvement in a wide range of aspects of specialist palliative care social work. These included:

- user involvement in service evaluation and feedback
- sharing service user knowledge of social work
- providing peer support
- working as volunteers
- user involvement in training.

User involvement in service evaluation and feedback

Service users generally felt that it was important for service user feedback on services to be sought and for there to be user involvement in service evaluation. At the same time, they stressed the need for this to happen in ways that are meaningful and are not burdensome. Service users need to be assured that any feedback they offer is confidential and that there can be no possibility of negative repercussions for people's care. The frequent failure at present to involve service users systematically in providing feedback and evaluation in specialist palliative care social work, at both an individual and collective level, seems to be one of the critical areas to be addressed for improving practice. This is likely to have financial implications if evaluation is to be carried out independently and to involve service users sensitively and widely.

Sharing service user knowledge of social work

A number of service users in our study suggested that it was really important for specialist palliative care social workers to tell people what they do and how helpful it can be. They had a commitment to this, because they felt that they themselves had been under a misapprehension about social work and that they might have missed out very easily on a resource that had turned out to be important for them. One man described himself as having been 'a bigot' about social work. He did not want others to remain in the same ignorance. It was frequently for this reason that people were motivated to take part in the research and it would not be unreasonable to assume that some may have been equally prepared for involvement in other ways; for example, speaking in support of an application for a new social work post, or speaking to independent service eval-uators. Some service users saw for themselves that there was a lack of knowledge and recognition of both palliative care and specialist palliative care social work, and one man said he intended to talk to his MP about this.

One steering group suggested that service users could contribute a great deal to appointment panels for new social workers. They felt they would be able to identify very quickly if a candidate had the personal qualities that mattered to them.

Providing peer support

There was considerable evidence that service users derive a great deal of support from each other. Some, however, would have liked to have had more opportunity to meet others in the same situation or with the same disease or condition and needed help to make this possible. They saw this as a form of involvement. There were a number of examples of service users running groups for themselves, usually after a bereavement group had ended. Again, many service users expressed the opinion that this was enormously helpful to them. There seems to be significant scope for this to happen more often.

Working as volunteers

In some discussions, service users challenge the idea of volunteering as an expression of user involvement. The feeling is that it reflects an extension of (unpaid) responsibility, rather than the devolution of power and control with which they primarily associate participation (Beresford and Croft 1993). However, in this project, service users highlighted a different understanding of volunteering, which led them to include it as an expression of user involvement. Volunteering is often conceived of as one group of (relatively advantaged) people helping another group of (relatively disadvantaged) people. Service users here challenged such assumptions. Many talked about their wish to work as a volunteer at a future time in the hospice and one or two already were doing this. Others were helping their hospice through supporting fundraising events. Another patient had talked about her hospice on the radio and had positively welcomed that opportunity. In these ways they saw volunteering as a means of engaging in palliative care and injecting a service user element into it.

User involvement in training

The area of user involvement in which there was most discussion from service users was user involvement in professional training and practice. It is difficult and perhaps unhelpful to try to separate the two. Service users offered their thoughts about user involvement in training, as well as highlighting the skills and qualities that they valued in professional practice and that they felt training needed to support and encourage.

Disabled people's and other social care service users' organizations have long argued that user involvement in training is one of the most effective ways of improving the culture of health and social care services (Beresford 1994; Levin 2004). Several service users in our study said that they felt one of the most useful ways in which new social workers could learn was by speaking to and mixing with people facing life-limiting illnesses or bereavement. Members of one of the steering groups remembered their current social worker as a student on placement and recalled her readiness to chat to the patients in the day centre and to learn from them. This was one of the qualities that they valued about her.

Service users conveyed a real sense that many people were happy to share their experiences to help social workers learn. Several talked of their willingness to have students sit in on their counselling sessions, or to have students shadow their social worker when she or he was working with them. One woman said she didn't like speaking in groups or giving talks but she had given her journal to her social worker so that it could be shared with others in a helpful way. Other people said they were happy to give talks. One patient told us that she had gone into the local university at the social worker's request to speak to students. She described herself as being well educated and from a professional background and she felt that her direct involvement in training could help the students challenge assumptions and understand that service users could come from all types of backgrounds. She had valued the chance to make this contribution.

There is nothing especially new about patients and service users playing a part in working directly with students. This has long happened routinely in some medical schools with perceived benefits for both students and patients. Studies looking at the impact of this kind of role on patients (Jackson, Blaxter and Lewando-Hundt 2003; Stacy and Spencer 1999) have found that patients had been able to tell students how they saw their illness affecting them, with many stressing the broader social and psychological impact, as well as their medical concerns. They emphasized the effect on the family in many cases. They also highlighted the importance of being listened to.

Patients felt that they benefited because their expertise in their own condition was being acknowledged. They felt empowered by being able to facilitate the learning of young doctors. They thought that they had been able to share, open up and be listened to. Some said that they had learned more about themselves and their condition and others had welcomed the small gifts of appreciation that the students had given them (Stacy and Spencer 1999). But there were some issues that need to be noted and these are likely to apply equally to the involvement of specialist palliative care service users in the training of social work students. Some patients felt they had been ill prepared for the role. They were unclear what was expected of them and the students were not always clear either. In some interviews with patients, carers had done most or all of the talking and this raised doubts as to whether students had always had the opportunity to hear the patient's perspective directly. Some patients noted that when students visited in mixed gender pairs, the women students did the talking and the men students took the notes. Some patients experienced uncertainty and embarrassment about communicating with students from different ethnic backgrounds, for instance not knowing how to pronounce their name. Perhaps most important, some patients felt exploited because of insensitive and patronizing questioning, or because of questions left unanswered about such things as their right to see what the student was writing about them in their report. If patients are to become more involved in palliative care education or training, then all these kind of issues need to be thought through well in advance, just as ethical considerations are thought through for research participants.

Not only is there experience about user involvement in training and education to draw on from medicine and palliative care. Since the introduction of a new social work qualification in 2002, the involvement of service users has been required in all aspects and stages of professional social work education, from student selection, through the shaping of the curriculum and provision of training, to assessment and post-qualification learning (Levin 2004). This has been a comprehensive and systematic development, for which additional funding has been allocated nationally. Service users and their organizations have been involved in shaping it and there is now a growing literature on the subject. There is now a substantial body of experience relating to training for user training, training in user-controlled placements as well as more traditional settings, and training based on the social models of understanding developed by service users, rather than mainstream medicalized individual models. This provides a valuable resource to draw on in supporting the full involvement of palliative care service users in social work education. It raises its own issues because of the particular difficulties faced by such service users, but the emphasis now placed on imaginative approaches to user involvement in social work provides insights for enabling their involvement in all kinds of ways.

A basis for positive practice

We asked service users what they thought was helpful for training specialist palliative care social workers. Taken together their comments provide a picture of what they value in professional practice. There was a remarkable degree of consistency in their concerns. It is important to remember that these concerns are based on experience – their own experience. We offer their views here. They are not all presented in people's own words because we have tried to amalgamate and summarize a wide range of comments and many people said similar things.

We highlight the issues and themes that service users identified below. These include being:

- sensitive
- close and supportive to service users
- human
- flexible
- informed
- inclusive

and

- providing information
- making connections.

BEING SENSITIVE IS...

- to treat people with individuality and sensitivity
- not to think it is okay just to barge in and ask all sorts of questions
- to be aware that some people may want to talk about end-of-life care even when their condition is stable, they are doing well and they may appear reluctant to talk
- to be aware of people's heightened sensitivity to casual remarks, such as 'You look well' when the person may in fact feel awful
- to be able to adapt to families and their individual ways of coping; to 'fit in' with them
- to let people 'get it all out' without butting in or stopping them
- to be sensitive to the fact that actually the people you are dealing with might know a lot more than you, about a lot of things, so it is important to have humility, self-doubt and sensitivity
- to be aware of the dangers of taking over when people are very sad and vulnerable, making sure it is actually what they want, what they need
- to be aware that the relationships within the family may already be strained and that illness may make things even more difficult.

BEING CLOSE AND SUPPORTIVE TO SERVICE USERS IS...

- to listen, to really listen [to service users]
- to care and be there for the person
- to be strong but gentle
- to be prepared to come into conflict with doctors at times on behalf of a service user

- to get in there as quick as possible, early in the illness
- to try to get to know the 'real' person and what she or he was like before she or he became ill and before any drastic changes might have taken place.

BEING HUMAN IS...

- to be down to earth and use the language that ordinary people use
- to remember that we are all human beings, and we all have our human dignity
- not to be too detached
- to admit to not knowing at times.

BEING FLEXIBLE IS...

- to know when to push and when to hold back
- to try different approaches if one way of working doesn't succeed and understand that with some people it will be a hard slog
- to recognize that everyone responds differently to illness and really to try to understand that
- not to be too cancer orientated; instead, to remember other illnesses.

BEING INFORMED IS...

- to be able to provide a lot of factual and practical information in relation to the individual's specific illness and to know about the available services
- to find out about rare cancers and help the service user get the information they need
- to spend time in the acute hospital services and on the wards and see for themselves what patients might experience when they are attending for treatment
- to have a really good understanding of illnesses and their progression and treatments.

BEING INCLUSIVE IS...

- not to exclude other family members by concentrating communication or services only on the named next of kin.

PROVIDING INFORMATION IS...

- to explain things fully, for example rights to community care and resource limitations.

MAKING CONNECTIONS IS...

- to forge strong links between the hospital and palliative care services so that the hospital team can learn from the approaches used in palliative care
- to go out and tell people what social work is all about, to get the message across
- to understand the ripple effect of grief on all the components and contexts within which someone lives.

Only connect

While service users highlighted these issues and themes in relation to specialist palliative care social work, it is also possible to see their relevance for all palliative care professions and professional practice. One of the broader issues highlighted by service users' views more generally in this book is the importance of recognizing – and sometimes improving – connections and understanding between different palliative care professions and services, as well as with mainstream services. One of the roles of specialist palliative care social work is to support the making of such connections and to help service users to negotiate complex broader service systems. But service users' views about specialist palliative care social work may also offer broader insights. If palliative care is to preserve its traditional commitment to a holistic approach, then it will need actively to learn shared lessons that apply to all disciplines operating within it. More work will need to be done here to explore what service users want from other palliative care professionals. Meanwhile we may hazard a guess that many of the qualities service users are looking for and value in specialist social work may equally apply to all related roles and professions in palliative care: medical, social, spiritual and psychological.

IMPLICATIONS FOR THE FUTURE

From what they said, the service users to whom we spoke, both patients and people experiencing bereavement, had generally not been asked their views about palliative care before. Yet they showed themselves capable of offering coherent proposals for developing user involvement in palliative care for the future, as well as offering through their comments a unique critique of the organization and practice of palliative care, and specialist palliative care social work within it. This is probably the most developed discussion that has emerged so far of a palliative care service from service users' perspectives. It highlights both the feasibility of developing such a perspective and the valuable contribution it has to offer.

We began this book by highlighting the changing context of palliative care and specialist palliative care social work. Both are now being expected to address a much wider range of illnesses and conditions. With medical advances, such conditions, including cancer, are increasingly becoming chronic rather than rapidly terminal. This is having a significant impact on the role and resources of palliative care. In 2005, the National Council for Palliative Care published a *Palliative Care Manifesto*. It was based on three principles:

1. that everyone has a right of access to palliative care services as appropriate to their need

2. that everyone should be able to exercise choice about their place of care at the end of life

3. that everyone is entitled to a good death.

The manifesto highlighted the existing inequity of access to hospice and other specialist palliative care services by diagnosis, age group, geographical area and ethnicity, and made clear the need for much greater investment in palliative care (National Council for Palliative Care 2005).

Medical developments which extend life are also raising new and complex issues relating to the end of life. As we said, major discussions are now taking place about death, dying and rights relating to them, particularly in relation to people with degenerative and debilitating conditions. There are now high-profile public and political debates about the quality of life and 'life not worth living', particularly in relation to these. There is pressure for new legislation to support euthanasia and assisted suicide. While this book was being written, the *Daily Mail* reported a new study of end-of-life decisions (ELDs) made by UK medical practitioners. The *Daily Mail* said that the survey suggested that when patients are nearing death, 'doctors "help" most of them on their way' (*Daily Mail* 2006). It raised the issue that, although in many cases this 'help' is 'benign', there are nevertheless an estimated 3,000 deaths that have resulted from illegal euthanasia.

However, the national survey undertaken by Professor Seale on which the *Daily Mail* reported offered very different findings to what the tabloid suggested. He concluded that the proportion of UK deaths involving all three forms of doctor-assisted dying (voluntary euthanasia, physician-assisted suicide and ending life without an explicit request from a patient) was extremely low. Rates were lower or not significantly different from those in a number of European and other countries where comparisons could be made. Non-treatment decisions (NTDs involving withdrawing or withholding treatments that potentially prolong life) were relatively higher than in four out of six European countries (Seale 2006). Seale's conclusion was that the:

lower relative rate of ELDs involving doctor assisted dying in the UK, and the relatively high rate of NTDs, suggests a culture of medical decision making informed by a palliative care philosophy. Historically the UK developed palliative care approaches earlier than the other countries in which the survey had been done, supporting this interpretation. (Seale 2006, p.6)

The existence of specialist palliative care not only makes possible, as Seale's findings indicate, a different mindset for those making ELDs as medical practitioners. It also offers alternatives to service users who are directly experiencing the difficulties. We know, from carrying out our own study, that some people had experienced desperation when facing life-limiting illnesses and conditions. We encountered both patients and people who had been bereaved, who talked seriously about suicide. But such thoughts did not take place in a policy or practice vacuum. The people to whom we spoke had all accessed the specialist palliative care system. They particularly highlighted the role of specialist palliative care social work in helping them deal with such difficulties. Their comments in our study highlight the crucial role such social work can play in managing the very real psychosocial difficulties facing them. This contribution is likely to have increasing significance as time goes by and end-of-life issues are likely to become even more complex. Blanket demands for a right to death can obscure just what is needed to support people's rights to a good quality of life. Entitlements for all to specialist palliative care, including specialist palliative care social work, can be expected to be key to this. The views of service users are likely to have much to offer in helping us all negotiate these complex issues, which may face any one of us, with appropriate support to help.

SUMMARY

In this chapter the strengths and weaknesses of the study on which the book is based were reviewed. The study included a diverse range of service users using a wide range of palliative care services in different parts of the country. It confirmed that many palliative care service users are interested in being involved in research and evaluation, both as participants and in its process, and that with sufficient support and employing imaginative approaches, this is possible. However, it was difficult to involve some groups of service users, and in some cases this seemed to reflect their unequal access to palliative care and specialist palliative care social work.

The chapter also reviews some of the key issues emerging from the study and their implications for palliative care, specialist palliative care social work and social work more generally. These include issues for:

- referral
- working with different groups of service users
- areas where there are organizational and professional problems.

The chapter focuses particularly on the development of user involvement in palliative care and specialist palliative care social work. It focuses particularly on five key expressions of involvement:

1. user involvement in service evaluation and feedback

2. sharing service user knowledge of social work

3. providing peer support

4. working as volunteers

5. user involvement in training.

It examines the qualities and issues that service users see as making for good practice, raises the question of whether these may also apply for other palliative care professional disciplines and points to the need to follow this up from service users' perspectives. It considers the significance of the psychosocial support role of social work in developing circumstances where issues of the right to death and the right to a good quality of life are likely to become increasingly significant.

HOW WE CARRIED OUT THE RESEARCH

Involving patients or service users in palliative care and palliative care research raises complex practical, methodological and ethical issues. Generally, so far, there has been relatively little attempt to involve palliative care service users in research and evaluation. But this omission raises its own ethical and methodological issues. It flies in the face of increasing current pressures to involve patients, public and service users in research and evaluation, as well as in policy and practice. It also imposes an arbitrary limit on the knowledge base of palliative care policy and practice and on the ways in which that knowledge is collected and developed. The project on which the findings in this book were based – the Involve Project – was an attempt to take forward user involvement in this complex area of research. In this appendix we look in more detail at how we undertook the research and the research approach on which it was based.

INTRODUCTION TO THE PROJECT

The Involve Project was a three-year national research project, supported by the Joseph Rowntree Foundation. It gained its name before the government NHS research and development body commissioned to increase public and user involvement in research, Consumers in NHS Research, changed its name to Involve. The project set out to explore what service users wanted from specialist palliative care social work. Its focus was service users' perspectives on such social work; to establish what it was like for them, what they thought of it and what ideas they had about it. Thus it was concerned with both the process and outcomes of practice for service users and with developing user-defined outcome measures. In this sense, it can be seen as relating to the 'quality' debate about health and social care, but coming from a different standpoint to the dominant service- and policy-based discussion.

In undertaking the project we sought to include, but also to distinguish between, two main groups of service users of specialist palliative care social work. These are people facing life-limiting illnesses and conditions, and people experiencing bereavement. The study has explored the perspectives of both groups. It is important to make clear that we were asking each group about their own direct experiences. That is to say, we talked with bereaved people about their personal experience of palliative care social work both before and after the death. We were not asking them to act as surrogate for their relative who had died, and report on what they thought about how their relative had found palliative care social work, though inevitably bereaved people did talk about their loved one's experiences as well as their own. Similarly, people with life-threatening conditions did talk about their relatives' and friends' experiences; but our primary concern was with their accounts of their own experience. This is an important distinction to draw, given that sometimes people facing bereavement are also conceived of as 'carers' and historically there have been problems with carers' views about service users being sought and accepted in place of the latter's own direct accounts.

We started with a series of central questions to which we hoped to gain answers. These included:

- What do service users see as constituting good practice in palliative care social work?
- In a context of limited resources, what priorities do service users highlight?
- How can palliative care social work support the empowerment of service users?
- How can service users be more involved in the construction and practice of palliative care social work?
- How might professional training be improved, building on service users' views and experience?
- What are the lessons to be gained from service users' knowledge and experience for improved collaboration between health and social services in palliative care?
- What insight does this offer for social work as a profession and user involvement more generally?

The project included the range of settings for such specialist palliative care social work, including independent hospices, NHS hospice units, hospital oncology units and palliative care day centres. The project was a large scale qualitative study, based on interviews and group discussions with the two groups of service users we have identified: those who were living with a life-threatening illness or condition and those who had been bereaved. It is important to recognize that direct services are provided for both these groups within palliative care and specialist palliative care social work. The research sought to find out through in-depth, qualitative methods the observations and views of both these groups. People were interviewed either as individuals or through group discussions, using a semi-structured schedule.

A total of 111 people were interviewed in the project: 61 were bereaved, and 52 had life-limiting illnesses and conditions (two people were both bereaved and patients). Seventy-two people were interviewed individually (of these, 42 were patients and 32 were bereaved people; 47 were women, 25 were men) and there were seven group discussions, including a total of 39 people. Two groups were made up of patients and five of bereaved people. Five of the groups were mixed sex and two were single sex – one all male and one all female. The project included 39 men and 72 women; 9 per cent of participants identified themselves as black and/or members of minority ethnic groups. Service users came from 26 different specialist palliative care settings. These were located in urban, suburban, rural, small town and coastal settings in England, Scotland, Wales and Northern Ireland.

The aim of the project was to provide an opportunity for service users to identify what actually happens in specialist palliative care social work; their definitions of the key issues; their views about good practice, what works and what doesn't; and what outcomes they desire from their involvement with specialist palliative care social work. Based on this, the overall aim was to inform the knowledge base of palliative care social work, to develop policy and practice and to improve training and education.

A PARTICIPATORY APPROACH: SERVICE USER INVOLVEMENT IN THE RESEARCH PROCESS

The project employed a participatory research approach and service users were involved in both the design and management of the project. We aimed to involve specialist palliative care service users in all stages of the project. None of the researchers was a palliative care service user, although the lead author has long-term experience as a mental health service user and also has a long-term involvement in the broader service user movement, which is now beginning to include people who use palliative care services. Clearly what we are discussing in this appendix is an example of user involvement in the process of the research carried out, rather than user-controlled research (Turner and Beresford 2005).

We aimed to involve specialist palliative care service users in all aspects of the Involve Project. Service users were included in the Advisory Group, which the Joseph Rowntree Foundation require all their projects to have. This included two users of specialist palliative care services (people with life-limiting conditions), as well as other social care service users. At every stage the Advisory Group was able to comment on research strategies and design. For example, they were asked to scrutinize the interview schedule to ensure that it was as sensitively worded as possible before it was piloted with other service users and it was revised in the light of their comments.

We also set up three steering groups of palliative care service users to meet throughout the project and we produced regular newsletters to keep everyone we interviewed, whether as individuals or as groups, informed and involved in the progress of the work.

It might be helpful to focus on how we involved service users in the steering groups and some of the issues that this raised. Initially there were three steering groups: two made up of a mix of service users facing life-limiting illnesses and conditions and people who had been bereaved, and one consisting solely of patients. The steering groups were set up in three different locations: a voluntary hospice in a deprived metropolitan area, a voluntary hospice in a rural area and a voluntary hospice on the south coast for people living with HIV/AIDS. In two of the hospices, we enlisted the help of the social worker in setting up the group and, in the hospice for the people with HIV/AIDS, the group was brought together by the chair of the clients' forum.

The aim was for the steering groups to meet approximately four times throughout the project, although we recognized that each group may not always be made up of the same people, as inevitably some service users would die. The aim of the steering groups was to make possible some continuity of involvement, even though their membership might change. In the event, one of the groups met twice and the other two only once, but we went on to have a steering group meeting with a group of patients in a voluntary day hospice in the Midlands who had previously been interviewed as part of the project.

As part of the steering group discussions we asked people about their views and experiences of palliative care social work and for their suggestions as to how the project should go about getting the views of other service users. We also asked for their feedback on how the work was progressing; for example, at the first meeting we asked for comments and feedback on the interview schedule we had drawn up for individual and group discussion.

We produced information for the steering groups, which we asked to be given out to each person attending beforehand. This leaflet provided a contact name and address. We made clear at each meeting that if people had any further comments or worries, or felt upset about anything, they could contact the named person after the meeting. We also wrote to everyone who came to each meeting, thanking them for taking part and again giving a contact name and address. One steering group member did subsequently contact us in this way. The hospices ensured transport was arranged and provided suitable facilities and refreshments, for which they were reimbursed.

ISSUES FOR USER INVOLVEMENT RAISED BY THE STEERING GROUPS

The process of involving service users in the steering groups raised a number of significant issues in relation to developing supportive an ethical user involvement.

It quickly became clear that the service users who took part in the steering groups were very interested in the project and genuinely wanted to offer comments and suggestions. Several people commented on how good it felt to be involved and to be able to offer some of their 'expertise', not just to be defined as a 'patient'. We were struck by how anxious people were to continue their involvement and how much they emphasized they wanted to be kept in touch. One woman who was moving to Scotland, to be nearer her family, asked to be kept in touch with what happened. We had no sense of people wanting to rush off or of feeling the whole exercise was peripheral or a waste of time.

The members of the steering group from the hospice in the Midlands, who had previously been interviewed as part of a patient group, said how pleased they were to know what was happening with the project and to have a chance to be involved again. Apart from one woman, who was too ill to attend, all of those who took part in the first discussion held as part of the research came to the steering group meeting.

Although a lot of painful issues were raised by and for people, the steering groups seemed to 'gel' very quickly. However, a crucial ethical issue about mixing people with life-limiting conditions and bereaved people in the same group was raised by one group member, a man facing a terminal illness. He contacted our worker after the first meeting and said that he knew he was dying of his brain tumour and he had welcomed the opportunity to talk in the group about that and the support he was receiving from the specialist palliative care social worker. But he was concerned that the bereaved people in the group might have been feeling upset if, for example, they had related his experiences to the person they loved who had died.

This was a very important point and the facilitators had noticed that during the discussion one woman, who had been bereaved, did seem to find it more upsetting than other group members. She said she found it very difficult to talk and she also did not stay on for lunch. In the event we were not able to meet again with this particular group, but if we had done so this issue would have to have been addressed beforehand with group members and it may have been appropriate to meet with bereaved people and people with life-limiting illnesses as two separate groups.

The steering groups were an essential part of the project and were essentially 'business' meetings which had an important agenda in terms of the research. People knew this when they came and clearly were happy to focus on the research project, but we recognized it was also very important to be respectful of the personal experiences and accounts that participants had to tell. In groups like these, it takes quite a while for introductions to be made and for people to settle down with a cup of tea and feel comfortable. Often those taking part were raising painful and difficult issues. It was not always easy or appropriate to move people on from 'telling their story' or when they were talking about how they approached the idea of their own death. These complex and difficult issues made the steering groups complex and demanding to facilitate. In the event, a lot of very helpful and useful work was done and judging by the feedback we got people clearly enjoyed participating.

Another issue we encountered in terms of service user involvement was that of gatekeeping. In one hospice, although the social worker was willing to help, the hospice management insisted that, until it had been cleared by the ethics committee, we could not invite service users to take part in the steering group. Yet of course we were not seeking to involve them as research 'participants' but in a co-researcher role. People imbued with traditional understandings of research and research relationships (and the role of the service user/patient within them) often seem to find this distinction difficult to recognize. The social worker had to make a presentation to the ethics committee on our behalf, using the material we sent her – and this overcame objections.

We also encountered difficulties setting up a second meeting of the steering group at this and another hospice. We were reliant on the continuing help of social workers to use their facilities and to let us know if any of the service users who had been involved in the first steering group had subsequently died, so that we did not send out letters which could cause distress to their family or friends. In the event we did not hear back from the two hospices. We do not know if this was because of other pressing priorities or organizational changes taking place. In the event we were not subsequently able to revisit these hospices, although we were able to maintain positive relationships with staff involved.

In contrast it was remarkably easy to arrange a second meeting at the hospice for people living with HIV/AIDS. Our original (service user) contact had moved on, but there was no difficulty in setting up the group again, which included some of the original members. No one who had attended the first meeting of the group had died and this might have made it easier for it to meet again. But we also wondered if this was because, being a centre for people with HIV/AIDS, which had its own clients' forum, it had a much more developed philosophy of involving people in decision making and of treating clients/patients as equals – as people with a right to know what they are being asked and to have the choice to say yes or no for themselves.

RECRUITING SERVICE USERS

A particular set of practical constraints operated to influence how we were able to recruit palliative care service users in this project. These related both to the nature of palliative care service users' circumstances and experience and the state of self-organization of palliative care service users at the time this research was carried out. These constraints meant that we could not access palliative care service users directly.

We ruled out trying to recruit specialist palliative care service users through sampling medical records or the populations of specialist palliative care services generally. This was unlikely to be speedy or sensitive enough or even always appropriate, to enable us to identify a meaningful sample of the two groups of users of specialist palliative care social work in which we were interested, especially given the limited life expectancy of some patients.

A method we have frequently used to recruit a diverse range of service users to research and evaluation projects has been using the networks and advertising of user-controlled organizations; for example, of disabled people and mental health service users. While there are some self-help and mutual-aid groups of palliative care service users affected by life-limiting illnesses and conditions, when we began this project there were few if any ongoing organizations of such service users, comparable to those of disabled people, older people, people with learning difficulties, mental health service users/survivors and other such groups. To the best of our knowledge this situation hasn't greatly changed since. We know of only one project (the research of Philip Cotterell), for instance, where a local group of palliative care service users was centrally involved in the analysis of research data (Cotterell et al. 2005 and 2006). This meant that it was not possible for us to access service users effectively through their own independent organizations, which is a model that we and others have as a preferred route to involving service users.

Therefore, in this case, in order to access as wide a range of users of specialist palliative care service users as possible, we enlisted the help of specialist palliative care social workers. They were very supportive and without their help this project would not have been possible. We recruited the service users whom we interviewed in the project through the network of social workers who belong to the Association of Palliative Care Social Workers. The majority of specialist palliative care social workers belong to this association. We asked social workers to distribute our information leaflets amongst service users they thought might be eligible to take part. The leaflets set out the project aims and clarified what involvement would entail for service users. The basic eligibility for inclusion was that the person had used the services of the specialist palliative care social worker and was either a patient living with a life-threatening illness or a bereaved person. We chose this method of recruitment both pragmatically as we needed to be able to identify easily people who had used the services of specialist palliative care social workers but, more important, we felt it was essential that the person who recruited the service user should already know their individual situation and be in a position to offer further support should any distress or concern arise out of the interview process itself.

At an early stage, we were aware that there could be a problem of service users being 'cherry picked' to include in our sample, which might result in unrepresentative views; particularly views which were more positive about specialist palliative care social workers than should have been the case. We adopted two approaches to try to ensure that this did not happen. First, we stressed to participating social workers that we were seeking participants who reflected the

overall service user population and monitored carefully the particular participants that they pointed us to. We also stressed our concern to access a diverse
range of service users, along the criteria that we have indicated in this book. We
made the final choice of participants (subject to their agreement). While we
were wary of the possibility of bias in their selection, at no point did this concern
seem to be justified.

Whilst this is undoubtedly an issue, we were reassured on a number of
counts. Some of the social workers wrote to *all* their service users, explaining
why they felt the project was an important one, and asking people to contact
them if they wanted to know more. We were shown examples of such letters.
Others displayed our leaflets in the hospice or day centre and asked people to let
them know if they were interested. Some told us they had been very careful to
include, in the people they approached, service users who they suspected might
not have been so happy with their services. Some of the social workers
approached all the members of an existing patient or bereavement group to ask
if anyone would like to be interviewed individually or take part in a discussion
group, thus reducing the chances of 'cherry picking'.

We felt that these factors went some way towards meeting this limitation of
the study but undoubtedly it is an issue. On balance we felt recruitment through
the social worker was important as this type of research could potentially be
unsettling for people and we felt that the social worker input was an important
part of our safeguard for individuals, which we would not wish to sacrifice.

We also took an additional precaution. We included a number of check
questions in the schedule that we gave to participants to enable us to offer them
different opportunities to express any concerns or reservations that they might
have. Interviewers made a point of encouraging such negative responses. We
wanted to establish what service users felt about the quality of practice they
received from specialist palliative care social workers. We paid particular
attention in the project to exploring any negative views service users might have.
We wanted to identify and avoid any tendency there might be to what has been
called the 'grateful patient syndrome', where people at a difficult time in their
life might be overly positive about any help they receive, however limited its
usefulness.

In the event, however, although we encouraged people to tell us about any
negative views they might have about their experience of specialist palliative
care social work, most participants found this question very hard to answer,
generally because they felt their experiences had been so overwhelmingly
positive. There was no evidence that this resulted from the process by which
service users were included in the project. We explored this carefully. Most participants expressed very positive views about specialist palliative care social
work. Although they struggled hard, only a few to whom we spoke could think
of any negative experiences. What was interesting, however, was that while

people's reports on specialist palliative care social work were generally positive, a picture did begin to emerge of potential problems in the way that it was structured and managed. Thus while people may have made only limited negative comments individually, taken together their comments could offer broader critical insights.

We were further reassured by the service users themselves. They showed that they were fully aware that to improve palliative care social work they might need to be critical or to point out omissions. This comment was typical:

> I don't want to sit here and just give all positives. I'm trying to think of a negative! (Man patient, white UK, age group 26–35 years)

The sample

Drawing on the latest issue of the *Hospice Year Book* produced by Help the Hospices, the full range of specialist hospice and palliative care services in the UK were identified. Drawing on the networks of the Association of Palliative Care Social Workers, contacts were made with social work services. Interested sites were sent information, which was produced in association with service users, and then received follow-up calls from interviewing members of the project team, checking out any additional information they wanted and questions they wished to ask.

Demographic profile

We sought to ensure that our sample was as diverse as possible in order to reflect adequately differences of sex, age, ethnicity, class, culture, marital status and domestic responsibilities, as well as services used and medical conditions experienced. This was discussed with the social work contact person to check with service users whether they would be willing to participate in the project. If this was agreed, then practical arrangements for meeting with people were set in train.

Our aim was that the sample should reflect the real diversity of people using specialist palliative care, although it would not necessarily be representative in statistical terms. We had originally planned to include bereaved children in our sample but recruitment for this proved very difficult and, given the resource limitations of the project, it was decided to concentrate on adults. We also wanted to ensure that disabled people and people with experience of using mental health services were included. We recruited from all parts of the UK including urban, suburban and rural locations.

Type of illness or condition

We made sure that patients with a range of illnesses were included as there have been criticisms that palliative care services are focusing too closely on the needs of people with cancer to the potential detriment of people with other conditions, who may have particular and different needs (Seymour and Clark 2002).

Although it was decided that we would not specifically ask service users for a diagnosis, as this was seen as being potentially intrusive, almost all the individuals spontaneously gave a diagnosis for themselves or the person who had died, and this was noted; it was clear, however, that a very small number of service users did avoid talking about their illness in specific terms and the decision not to ask for diagnosis certainly seemed appropriate in the light of this.

Type of setting

We wanted to make sure that we had drawn service users from a range of palliative care settings (reflecting different management structures and service providers) and that we had included people who had seen the specialist palliative care social worker in a range of locations (that is, in day care, on the ward, in their own homes).

Recruitment difficulties

As we recruited and began interviewing, we constantly reviewed our sample to ensure that it was as inclusive as possible along all these dimensions. We found that it was far harder to recruit men than women and also to recruit service users from minority ethnic groups. It was also more difficult to recruit service users to take part in group discussions. We therefore highlighted these gaps in our second phase of recruitment and managed to overcome some of the imbalances. As we have said, our sample was not statistically representative of all users of palliative care. By asking that social workers exclude service users whose conditions were rapidly changing we inevitably ruled out some individuals with the most advanced illness. We did, however, talk to people who were very sick but nevertheless comfortable and stable enough to be interviewed and whose death came within very few weeks of the interview. So our sample was not entirely without representatives who were at a very advanced stage in their illness.

WHO WERE THE SERVICE USERS WE INTERVIEWED?

As shown in Table A1.1, we saw 111 service users: 39 men and 72 women. Ages ranged from 18 years to over 80 years, with three quarters of those interviewed being aged between 46 and 75 years. Only in the age group 46–55 years did the number of men interviewed exceed the number of women interviewed.

As shown in Table A1.2, we interviewed 52 patients, of whom 35 were women and 17 men, and 61 bereaved people, of whom 39 were women and 22 men.

Of the patients we interviewed 37 (71%) were aged 65 or under and 13 (25%) were aged 45 or under. Table A1.3 presents this information.

Table A1.1: Profile of service users interviewed by age and gender

Sex	Age groups								
	15–18	19–25	26–35	36–45	46–55	56–65	66–75	75+	Total
Male	0	1	3	2	13	9	8	3	39
Female	1	1	6	10	12	16	16	10	72
Total	1	2	9	12	25	25	24	13	111

Table A1.2: Profile of service users interviewed by type and gender

Sex	Number of patients	Bereaved	Total
Male	17	22	39
Female	35	39	74
Total	52	61	113

Note: Two people were both patients and bereaved, therefore numbers do not add up to 111, the total number interviewed.

Table A1.3: Profile of service users interviewed by type and age

	Age groups								
	15–18	19–25	26–35	36–45	46–55	56–65	66–75	75+	Total
Number of patients	0	1	6	6	11	13	9	6	52
Bereaved	1	1	3	6	16	12	15	7	61
Total	1	2	9	12	27	25	24	13	113

Diagnosis

As we have noted, we did not specifically ask participants for their diagnosis, but most people volunteered this information. In the majority of cases the person was living with or had died from cancer, but we know that at least nine people with other diseases (motor neurone disease, multiple sclerosis, cardiac disease and respiratory diseases) were included in the sample. We were not aware of anyone living with HIV/AIDS within the sample but some of the steering groups were held at a specialist centre for people living with HIV/AIDS so the perspectives of this group of service users were included in the overall design of the project. Nationally, 5 per cent of patients of palliative care services are diagnosed with illnesses other than cancer (Hospice Information Service 2003) so the percentage of patients with non-cancer diagnoses in our sample (8%) was slightly higher than the average. This was because we had specifically over-sampled this group in order to ensure that their views were heard.

Type of bereavement

The bereaved people included in the project had experienced the loss of a range of individuals, including partners, adult children, brothers and sisters; step-brothers and stepsisters, parents and parents-in-law; and other relatives. Length of bereavement varied between a few weeks to several years (eight years in one case).

Ethnicity

The majority of service users, 101 (91%), described themselves as being from a white, UK background. The other ten (9%) of respondents identified them-selves as being from British Pakistani, black Caribbean, European Dutch, Indian, Jewish, Asian other, black African, black British, German and Armenian backgrounds. Nationally, in figures published for 2000–2001, 97 per cent of palliative care service users report themselves as 'white' (Minimum Data Sets Project).[1] We had slightly over-sampled people from minority ethnic groups in order to gather as diverse a range of views as possible.

Our process notes recorded that some people, both black and white, appeared to find the question about ethnicity uncomfortable. They either did not know how to categorize themselves readily, or did not wish to be categorized at all. There was, however, no apparent discomfort about answering specific questions about whether culture or religion had been respected and needs met.

Family status

Twelve per cent of our service users were single people, 31 per cent were married or living with a partner, 8 per cent were divorced or separated and 49 per cent were widowed. Fifteen service users (13%) had children of school age. Of these parents, six were patients and the rest bereaved.

---

1   Minimum Data Sets Project (National Council for Hospice and Specialist Palliative Care) collects statistics on the use of palliative care services in the UK on an annual basis.

Occupational background

We asked people about their current or previous occupation and analysis showed that service users came from an extremely broad range of occupational backgrounds, including managerial, professional, academic, industrial and manufacturing, caring, retail and skilled and unskilled labour. We did not specifically include questions in the interview schedule about level or type of income. However, it was clear from individual accounts that a substantial proportion of service users were dependent solely or in part on state benefits, regardless of previous occupational background.

Disability and use of mental health services

We were concerned that service users who had experience of disability or use of mental health services were included in our sample and therefore we asked all the service users whether they were registered disabled, perceived themselves as disabled or had experience of using mental health services.

Thirty (27%) of the participants were registered as disabled but only 26 of these people said that they actually perceived themselves as disabled, and a further six respondents perceived themselves as disabled but were not actually registered. Seventeen (15%) of the respondents had experience of using mental health services. There were missing data for this question because many people did not know whether they were registered as disabled or were uncertain how they saw themselves.

The specialist palliative care services they used

The service users were drawn from 26 specialist palliative care settings, including voluntary hospices (20), NHS hospices and hospital palliative care teams (three), Marie Curie Centres (two) and Sue Ryder Care Centres (one). This represents approximately 12.5 per cent of the total palliative care units in the UK at the time of the study (Hospice Information Service 2002a).

Location

Sampling sites included large urban, suburban, small town, rural and coastal settings. We included sites in England, Scotland, Northern Ireland and Wales.

ETHICAL ISSUES AROUND INVOLVING SERVICE USERS

Involving service users in palliative care research raises its own particular ethical issues and challenges (see, for example, Aranda 1995). When we undertook this project, we had to be sure that it was right to talk to people at all who might be extremely ill and already trying to cope with life-threatening illness or bereavement, when the research might not be of direct benefit to them. We know that some people died not long after we interviewed them. Clearly there are also ethical issues around involving bereaved people who may be very vulnerable as they undergo the emotional upheavals and the practical difficulties that often come after a bereavement. The project was granted formal ethical approval through the multiple research ethics committee process (MREC), with in some cases additional permissions from local research ethics committees (LRECs).

In one hospice the hospice management committee insisted that we could not invite service users to take part in the steering group until it had been agreed by the hospice's own ethics committee. The social worker had to make a presentation to the ethics committee on our behalf, using the material we sent her, and this was successful. But beyond procedures, many more ethical issues needed to be addressed.

Existing research into user involvement in palliative care suggested that it was appropriate to seek the views of this group of service users (Addington-Hall and McCarthy 2001; Barnett 2001). Two of us (Peter Beresford and Suzy Croft) in addition had previously been involved in setting up a national seminar on user involvement in palliative care which was held at St Christopher's Hospice in London in July 1999 (Beresford et al. 2000). The seminar was planned and organized by a group of service users and professionals in the fields of palliative care and user involvement. Some 70 people, mainly service users, attended that seminar and said very clearly that they wanted to be involved and were prepared to give up time and energy so that services could be improved, if not for themselves, then at least for future service users.

The seminar showed clearly that people who are very ill can be involved effectively, if suitable support is put in place and the event is structured appropriately and sensitively. Our starting point was, therefore, that it was not just appropriate but important to involve users of palliative care services in this type of research and this was borne out by what was later expressed in the steering groups.

We also thought through the ethical implications of a number of related issues. These included, for example:

- *Recruitment*: to avoid overloading or burdening potential participants who may have other priorities or be experiencing extreme distress.

- *Information needs*: providing full, clear and accessible information in advance, stressing the voluntary nature of involvement in the project, to ensure that participants could have opportunities as real for 'informed consent' as possible.

- *Meeting support needs*: ensuring supportive and accessible conditions for involvement so that people who wish to participate are able to, even if, for example, they are very ill, have limited energy or experience discomfort.

- *Feedback and further involvement*: providing suitable contact details if people wanted follow-up support and/or to be kept in touch.

Recruitment

As we have indicated, we decided to use specialist palliative care social workers to help us find service users to interview. We wanted to be sure, as far as possible, that service users were not at a stage in their illness or bereavement where it would be insensitive, inappropriate or unhelpful to approach them. We asked social workers not to recruit anyone if their condition was rapidly changing or they had cognitive problems that might rule out a proper understanding of consent (although we did not in any way discourage the participation of people who had learning difficulties or experience of using mental health services). We also suggested that they avoid service users who had been involved recently in other research, as we did not want to overload people.

Information needs

We were aware that some service users might feel obliged to take part if asked by a social worker to whom they felt grateful, so we paid particular attention to the possibility of this in the written information that was given to service users prior to the interview. Significantly, our information sheets for service users were designed by palliative care service users. They not only spelled out the aims of the project, but also made it clear that their involvement was entirely voluntary and they could withdraw at any time without explanation and without their care being affected.

The information sheet provided a contact name and address so service users could phone and ask for further information or support should they wish. It was also made clear to them that they could also make contact with us after an interview had taken place if they wanted to ask questions or make further comments or criticisms, or if they needed support. The information sheet emphasized that the project was independent of the service they used and any workers working with them. We had discussed terminology beforehand. The information sheets avoided terms such as *terminal illness* and *dying* as we knew that some participants preferred not to address or refer to that part of their illness in that kind of way. Similarly our information sheets were written in jargon-free language and we explained terms such as *palliative care* that might not be familiar to people.

Social workers and service users were made aware that information about the project was available in a range of formats and languages. A specific information sheet was written for children and young people.

We did not see provision of an information sheet, however comprehensive, as a substitute for explaining the project fully to participants when we met them and we tried then to check that each service user had really understood what the project was about prior to starting the interview and was genuinely happy to proceed.

CONFIDENTIALITY AND CONSENT

Our information sheet made it clear that information would not be fed back from the service user to the social worker unless the participant expressly requested this. It was also made clear that no participant would be identified by name in future publications. We highlighted the emphasis we placed on effective confidentiality and anonymity.

The consent form also separately asked for consent for the interview to be tape-recorded. We had a further information sheet and consent form relating specifically to video-recording of interviews, although in the event we did little such recording because of the practical problems involved. This sheet pointed out that it was impossible to offer the same degree of protection for subjects who had been video-recorded with regard to possible identification though it was made clear that actors' voices could be used or faces could be obscured. It was also made clear that the videos would only be used for the development of training materials and that tapes and videos would be stored securely and destroyed at the end of the project.

THE INTERVIEWING PROCESS

The interview schedule was deliberately drafted in such a way as to avoid asking intrusive or searching questions. We did not ask anyone about the nature of his or her illness or condition, but rather invited service users to tell their story about their involvement with palliative care and palliative care social work in their own words. We used a semi-structured interview schedule, which service users were involved in designing, which included a high proportion of open-ended questions.

In this way we hoped control over the interview lay with the service user as far as possible. As we recognized that some service users might want to talk about painful and difficult experiences all the interviews were carried out by people either with experience as specialist palliative care social workers themselves, or others with similar training and backgrounds, such as service user advocacy and support. It was made clear that interviewees could stop and rest at any time or stop the interview altogether if they wished. Interviewers were briefed to ask service users if they wanted to pause interviews if there were signs of tiredness, distress or unease.

We felt it was vital that service users could use the interview to talk at length and in detail about what was important to them, without the interviewer becoming too directive. We encouraged participants to take off in directions of their own choosing in interviews and group discussions. Interviewing and facilitation required particular skill to maintain a balance between our need to address certain questions and opportunities for service users to retain control of the process.

Meeting people's support needs

For all the groups and individuals who took part, we tried to ensure that their involvement in the project was as comfortable as possible and that any costs of taking part, whether financial, emotional, practical or physical, were minimal. For example, all travelling and support expenses were paid for people to take part. We interviewed people at their own choice of venue and offered refreshment where appropriate. The project paid hospices and other services to provide participants with refreshments.

We were aware that participants' feelings might be stirred by the interviews. This was a further reason for recruiting participants through the specialist palliative care social workers. We knew that they would be on hand to offer extra support after an interview, should someone feel they needed it. We gave contact details, so participants could get back in touch with us if they wanted and we could offer professional palliative care support skills, or direct people to other sources of support if they did not want to turn to the specialist palliative care social worker. But their availability represented an additional and ongoing resource.

One social worker commented that the whole process had been quite a learning experience for her. She felt that some of the people interviewed had needed 'a bit of nurturing afterwards', as for example, in one case, the person's bereavement came flooding back. Another social worker asked us to be aware, before we interviewed two women with whom she had been working, that they both felt they had been 'healed by God'. She rightly wanted to make sure the interviewer would be especially sensitive to the fact that not everyone can or does talk about dying when they are very ill.

We also wrote a card to each participant after an interview or group discussion, again giving a name and contact number and making clear we were available to be contacted. In fact one participant wrote to the person who had interviewed her to let her know of some good news she had had about her illness and treatment.

Feedback and further involvement

It was seen as very important that we let the service users who participated in the project know what we had learned from them and to know how this information might be put to use in the future. This was done through the newsletter, as mentioned above, which was distributed to service users who were interviewed and to members of the steering groups.

THE INTERVIEWS

Interviews took place in whatever setting was most comfortable for and preferred by the service user. Sometimes patients were seen in their bed on the palliative care unit, sometimes in a quiet room set aside in the hospice or unit, sometimes at home. Group interviews were held on the units, in a room allocated for the purpose and where confidentiality could be provided. Interviews and discussions lasted about an hour on average, although they varied in length from between 45 minutes to one and a half hours. Most of the interviews covered all the issues included in the schedules; a few did not because of time constraints in individual cases and people's particular interests.

We chose to conduct both one-to-one interviews and group discussions, as we wanted service users to have the chance of being interviewed in the setting most comfortable for them. We felt some people would prefer the opportunity of a private, face-to-face interview, which could take place in their own home if they wished, while others would prefer the support they got from discussing their experiences in a group with other service users. We therefore did not allocate people to one or other type of interview but left this up to the service user and the social worker to discuss and negotiate. Sometimes the social worker asked a group that was already in existence if they wished to be interviewed as a group for this study, but other groups came together purely for the research. Some of the people who chose to be interviewed individually were nevertheless talking entirely about their experiences of social work in groupwork settings.

Permission was requested to tape-record all the interviews and this was granted by all except one participant. That person went ahead with the interview and allowed written notes to be made instead. A small number of video-recordings of interviews were made with specific permission for this.

What we asked service users

The interview schedule is shown in Appendix 2. This was used to guide and structure both one-to-one and group interviews. Whilst we hoped to cover all the areas in the schedule, the service users determined the exact direction and pace of the interview. We were concerned that they were given the opportunity to give their accounts as fully as they wished and in their own words.

The interview schedule focused on the following areas:

- how the person was referred to the palliative care service and specifically to the social work service
- the nature of the social work support the person had received and how the person's needs were identified
- views about social work/social workers prior to this experience, and about the social work service the person had received within the palliative care setting
- level of involvement with the social work process; for example, having the opportunity to give his or her own views on the type of support needed and offering feedback

- views on the strengths and weaknesses of specialist palliative care social work and gaps in provision
- whether the specialist palliative care social worker was respectful of individual differences and individual needs; for example, in respect to age, religion, ethnicity, culture, sexuality and class
- views on what might be helpful in training new social workers.

The interviewing process was a developmental one in as much as later interviews may have probed more fully in areas that appeared to be relevant to themes generated by the preliminary analysis of earliest interview data. All the interviews were fully transcribed and these transcriptions are our primary data set for analysis. Transcriptions were also made of each of the steering group discussions and these have been a secondary data set.

Process notes

After each interview and group discussion, the interviewer made process notes recording his or her reflections about how the interview had gone, the circumstance of the interview, whether anything surprising or unusual had occurred, impressions of key points and any other observations. In particular any apparent distress was noted.

These process notes were used as an adjunct to the primary data set and they enabled us to make some early links across different interviews. They were particularly valuable when consideration was given to the impact of involvement in this kind of research on individuals who are already coping with distressing circumstances in their daily lives. They also allowed us to record our glimpses into the ways in which service users' involvement (as for instance their involvement in this research) could be supported by the social worker.

ANALYSIS

The interviews, discussion groups and steering groups provided rich and detailed data. Our approach to analysis was based on a grounded theory approach, identifying themes from what people said rather than starting with a pre-set range of issues and themes (Glaser and Strauss 1967). Traditionally research has tended to try to fit the answers/comments respondents offer to questions into predetermined categories for the purpose of analysis. Our approach was based on the view that the views and ideas of participants in the project were the most important ones, rather than our own. Ideas which developed were 'grounded' in the ideas and thoughts of participants. Instead of imposing a theoretical framework on what people said, we aimed to let them generate their own frameworks.

In collating and analysing material we used a constant comparative approach (Glaser and Strauss 1967). First, we read the process notes that were made by the interviewers at the time and noted any key impressions. Second, we read each transcript closely, as soon as possible after the interview or group discussion, again noting any key points that emerged. We then considered whether these key points had recurred across the interviews and discussions, and where there was a consistency we classified these as themes to be explored more fully in later interviews and in discussion with steering group members. We then explored each of these themes in more detail to look at the different concepts within each theme, to determine if there were any instructive links and to see whether each theme was consistent across different categories of service users; age, sex, ethnicity, type of illness or nature of bereavement, type of setting and type of social work approach were all considered. We also returned to the points that were key for individual service users but which were not found consistently in other interviews and discussions. We tried to explore these individual experiences to see whether they might be more generally instructive and in particular whether they might be highlighting omissions in specialist palliative care social work support for any particular group of service users.

Both the steering groups and service users involved in the Advisory Group played a part in the analysis of findings through receiving reports of data emerging from the project and offering their own insights in its interpretation. Our discussions with steering group members played a particularly important part in undertaking analysis. They allowed us to reflect our findings and our interpretations back to a wide range of palliative care service users themselves to check out validity and reliability from their perspective. We could fully develop these discussions with steering group members, and this enabled us to fine tune our understanding in a way that would not have been possible in individual interviews or discussion groups. Time constraints alone would not have allowed us this degree of probing with individuals.

THE INTERVIEW SCHEDULE

INTRODUCTION

Hello, my name is .... Thank you very much for agreeing to meet with me. Could I just tell you a bit more about the project that I'm involved with and that I am asking you to help us with? The aim of this project is to enable service users to have a chance to say what they think about the service they receive from social workers who specialize in working in hospices and palliative care like [*name of social worker*] and what they would like in the future.

Have you had chance to read the information sheet about the project? Was there anything that you weren't clear about or that you wanted to ask me?

This session will probably last between one and one-and-a-half hours but if that's too long that is no problem, we can either have a break or finish whenever you want to. Is that okay? Can I just add there are no right or wrong answers; we just want to hear what you think. If at any time there is anything you don't understand or anything you want to ask, please feel free to do so; or there might be other things you want to add.

Could I just tell you a bit more about the terms on which we are asking for your help? I think I should tell you that the project and I are quite independent and separate from the team working with you and everything you say will be completely confidential and anonymous and no names will be used. Nothing you say, unless you want it to, will be passed on to people working with you. Is that okay?

To make sure that we have an accurate record of what you say we would like to tape-record [*or video-record*] this interview. Do you have any questions or comments about that? [*in cases of objection proceed without recording*]

I have the consent form to take part in the project here. Could you read it through and sign that for me? [*plus additional consent form if video-recording*] Is that okay? I will give you a copy of the consent form(s) and information sheet to keep and if you would like one we can send you a copy of the tape/video afterwards as well. We will also try and keep people in touch with what we are doing; for example we have a newsletter that goes out.

I should also say we are quite happy if at any stage you want to withdraw from this project or stop the interview. Is that okay?

Have I made everything clear? Are there any questions you would like to ask? Are you happy to start? [*put tape-recorder on*]

SECTION ONE: CURRENT PALLIATIVE CARE SERVICE

1. Can you tell me how you came to use this service [*insert service they are in*]?

SECTION TWO: SPECIALIST PALLIATIVE CARE SOCIAL WORK

In this part of the interview we would like to ask you a bit more about specialist hospice and palliative care social work. We mean people like [*named social worker*]. Do you know what I mean?

1. Have you had contact with a specialist palliative care social worker e.g. [*insert name*]?
   ☐ Yes   ☐ No   ☐ Don't know

2. Could you tell me how you came to see this person?

3. Could you tell me a bit more about what this contact involved?

   ☐ counselling/individual support

   ☐ practical help, e.g. with furniture, clothes etc.

   ☐ representation or advocacy, e.g. someone helping you, speaking on your behalf or to help you get what you want

   ☐ help with getting money and/or benefits

   ☐ help in contacting and/or getting help from other organizations

   ☐ being with other patients or service users in a group

   ☐ support for family or friends

   ☐ any other kind of help offered...

4. Did you have any views about social work/social workers before you had this experience?

SECTION THREE: WHAT HAPPENS IN SPECIALIST PALLIATIVE CARE SOCIAL WORK

1. Getting to see the social worker (referral)

   • What are your views about the way in which you first had contact with the social worker?

2. Working out what support you needed (assessment)

   • How was it decided what the social worker would do to help you?

3. The social work received (intervention)

   • What do you feel about the work the social worker has done with you?

SECTION FOUR: USER INVOLVEMENT

I'd like now to ask you some questions about the involvement you have had with the social worker.

1. Have you been asked to give any feedback on what happened with the social worker? For example, to give your views so the service could be improved.

   If yes... How did you do that?
   If no... Would you have liked to have been asked to give your views?

2. Do you feel your views were taken into account by the social worker?

3. Did you feel you had a real say in the process with him or her?

4. Did you feel that you had a real chance to talk with the social worker about the things that worried you?

SECTION FIVE: SERVICE USERS' VIEWS OF SPECIALIST PALLIATIVE CARE SOCIAL WORK

In this section we would like to ask you how you think specialist palliative care social work can be most useful to people.

1. Can you tell me what you have found most helpful in palliative care social work; for example, its strengths and what is of value?

2. Could you tell me what you have found to be least helpful; for example, its weaknesses and limitations?

3. Is there anything else that you think it would be helpful for specialist palliative care social workers to offer service users?

4. Has the specialist palliative care social work service made you feel more in control?

5. Do you feel that the specialist palliative care social work service respected and valued you as an individual; for example, in relation to your culture, your age, sexuality or class?

6. Are there ways in which you feel you might have been more involved in the way you received specialist palliative care social work support?

7. In the light of your experience what do you think would be helpful in training new palliative care social workers?

SECTION SIX: SOME QUESTIONS ABOUT YOURSELF

In this section we'd just like to ask you a few questions about yourself to make sure our information is accurate and because we want to involve as wide a range of people as possible.

Gender

    ☐ Male   ☐ Female

Can I ask which age category you are in?

    ☐ 0–4   ☐ 5–9   ☐ 10–14

    ☐ 15–18   ☐ 19–25   ☐ 26–35

    ☐ 36–45   ☐ 46–55   ☐ 56–65

    ☐ 66–75   ☐ 75+

How would you describe your domestic status?

    ☐ Single   ☐ Divorced/separated

    ☐ Widowed   ☐ Married/living together

Do you have any children?

    ☐ Yes   ☐ No

Ages

    ☐ 0–4   ☐ 5–9   ☐ 10–14

    ☐ 15–18   ☐ 19+

How would you describe your ethnic origin?

    ☐ Black Caribbean   ☐ Black African   ☐ Black other

    ☐ Indian   ☐ Pakistani   ☐ Bangladeshi

    ☐ Chinese   ☐ Asian other   ☐ White

    ☐ Irish   ☐ Jewish

    ☐ Other (How would you describe yourself?) ....

Are you registered as a disabled person?

    ☐ Yes   ☐ No

Do you consider yourself disabled?

    ☐ Yes   ☐ No

Do you have experience of mental health difficulties or using mental health services?

    ☐ Yes   ☐ No

Could I ask you what your current/previous occupation is?

Is there anything else you would like to say about yourself?

SECTION SEVEN: CONCLUSION

1. Could I ask if there are any other comments, ideas or suggestions you would like to offer?

2. Are there any questions you would like to ask me?

Can I just thank you for all this help with the interview? We will keep in touch with you and I will shortly send you a copy of this tape if you would like one.

☐ Yes   ☐ No

If at any time you would like to make contact with us, if there are any problems or issues that have been highlighted today or you would like someone to talk to, please contact [*researcher's name and telephone contact details*]

NOTES FOR INTERVIEWER
Section 2 Question 3

1. Ask person what this contact involved. Let them tell their story. Then give prompts.

2. Where an interviewee raises an issue we routinely ask them if they want to say a little bit more about that.

REFERENCES

Adams, R., Dominelli, L. and Payne, M. (2002) *Social Work: Themes, Issues and Critical Debates.* Second edition. Basingstoke: Palgrave.

Addington-Hall, J.M. (1996) Heart disease and stroke: Lessons from cancer care. In: G. Ford (ed.) *Interfaces in Medicine: Managing Terminal Illness.* London: Royal College of Physicians.

Addington-Hall, J.M. and McCarthy, M. (1995) Dying from cancer: Results of a national population-based investigation. *Palliative Medicine,* 7: 295–305.

Addington-Hall, J.M. and McCarthy, M. (2001) Survey research in palliative care using bereaved relatives. In D: Field, D. Clark, J. Corner and C. Davis (eds) *Researching Palliative Care.* Buckingham: Open University Press.

Aldgate, J. and Statham, J. (2001) *The Children Act Now: Messages from Research.* Report for the Department of Health. London: The Stationery Office. Accessed on 18/01/04 at www.dh.gov.uk/scg/childrenactnow.htm

Allan, G. (1996) *Kinship and Friendship in Modern Britain.* Oxford: Oxford University Press.

Allen, K. (2001) *Communication and Consultation: Exploring Ways for Staff to Involve People with Dementia in Developing Services.* Bristol: Policy Press, in association with the Joseph Rowntree Foundation.

Anderson, H., Ward, C., Eardley, A., Gomm, S.A., Connolly, M., Coppinger, T., Corgie, D., Williams, J.L. and Makin, W.P. (2001) The concerns of patients under palliative care and a heart failure clinic are not being met. *Palliative Medicine,* 15: 279–86.

APCSW (2006) *Introduction to Palliative Care Social Work.* London: The Association of Specialist Palliative Care Social Workers.

Aranda, S. (1995) Conducting research with the dying: ethical considerations and experience. *International Journal of Palliative Nursing,* 1 (1): 41–7.

Arnstein, S. (1969) A ladder of citizen participation in the USA. *Journal of the American Institute of Planners,* 35 (4): 216–24.

Bailey, C. and Corner, J. (2003) Care and the older person with cancer. *European Journal of Cancer Care,* 12(2): 176–82 (doi: 10.1046/j.1365-2354.2003.00372.x).

Balloch, S., Beresford, P., Evans, C., Harding, T., Heidensohn, M. and Turner, M. (1998) Advocacy, empowerment and the development of user-led outcomes. In: Y.C. Craig (ed.) *Advocacy, Counselling and Mediation in Casework.* London: Jessica Kingsley Publishers.

Barnes, C. (2003) What a difference a decade makes: Reflections on doing 'emancipatory' disability research. *Disability & Society,* 18 (1): 3–17.

Barnes, C. and Mercer, G. (eds) (1997) *Doing Disability Research.* Leeds: The Disability Press.

Barnett, M. (2001) Interviewing terminally ill people: Is it fair to take their time? *Palliative Medicine,* 15: 157–8.

Bar-On, A. (2002) Restoring power to social work practice. *British Journal of Social Work,* 32: 997–1014.

Barton, L. and Oliver, M. (eds) (1997) *Disability Studies: Past, Present and Future.* Leeds: The Disability Press.

Baxter, L., Thorne, L. and Mitchell, A. (2001) *Small Voices, Big Noises. Lay Involvement in Health Research: Lessons From Other Fields.* Eastleigh: Involve.

Becket, C. (2003) Military metaphors in the spoken language of social work. *British Journal of Social Work,* 33 (5): 625–39.

Beresford, P. (1994) *Changing the Culture, Involving Service Users in Social Work Education.* London: Central Council of Education and Training in Social Work, Paper 32.2.

Beresford, P. (2003a) Involving service users: The best route to improving service quality. Guest column. *Newsletter of the Observatory for the Development of Social Services in Europe*, Frankfurt, 2–4.

Beresford, P. (2003b) *It's Our Lives: A Short Theory of Knowledge, Distance and Experience*. London: Citizen Press in association with Shaping Our Lives.

Beresford, P. (2004) Qualität Sozialer Dienstleistungen: Zur zunehmenden Bedeutung von Nutzerbeteiligung. In: C. Otto Beckmann, H. Richter and M. Schrodter (eds) *Qualität in der sozialen Arbeit: Zwischen Nutzerinteresse und Kostenkontrolle*. Wiesbaden: VS Verlag für Sozialwissenschaften.

Beresford, P., Broughton, F., Croft, S., Fouquet, S., Oliviere, S. and Rhodes, P. (2000) *Improving Quality, Developing User Involvement*. Twickenham, Middlesex: Centre for Citizen Participation, Brunel University.

Beresford, P. and Croft, S. (1993) *Citizen Involvement: A Practical Guide for Change*. Basingstoke: Macmillan.

Beresford, P. and Croft, S. (2004) Service users and practitioners reunited: The key component for social work reform. The future of social work: Special issue. *British Journal of Social Work*, 34 (January): 53–68.

Beresford, P., Croft, S., Evans, C. and Harding, T. (1997) Quality in personal social services: The developing role of user involvement in the UK. In: A. Evers, R. Haverinen, K. Leichsenring and G. Wistow (eds) *Developing Quality in Personal Social Services: Concepts, Cases and Comments*. Aldershot: Ashgate, in association with the European Centre, Vienna.

Beresford, P., Croft, S. and Oliviere, D. (2001) *Our Lives, Not Our Illness: User Involvement in Palliative Care*. Briefing Paper 6. London: National Council for Hospice and Specialist Palliative Care Services.

Beresford, P., Shamash, O., Forrest, V., Turner, M. and Branfield, F. (2005a) *Developing Social Care: Service Users' Vision for Adult Support*. Adult Services Report 07. London: Social Care Institute for Excellence in association with Shaping Our Lives.

Beresford, P., Croft, S., Adshead, L., Walker, J. and Wilman, K. (2005b) Involving service users in palliative care: From theory to practice. In: P. Firth, G. Luff and D. Oliviere (eds) *Loss, Change and Bereavement in Palliative Care*. Facing Death Series. Maidenhead: Open University Press.

Biestek, F. (1961) *The Casework Relationship*. London: Unwin University Books.

Blieszner, R. and Adams, R.G. (1992) *Adult Friendship*. Newbury Park: Sage.

Bliss, J. (1998) District nurses and social workers' understanding of each other's role. *British Journal of Community Nursing*, 3 (7): 330–6.

Bliss, J., Cowley, S. and While, A. (2000) Interprofessional working in palliative care in the community: A review of the literature. *Journal of Interprofessional Care*, 14 (3): 281–90.

Branfield, F., Beresford, P., Danagher, N. and Webb, R. (2005) *Independence, Wellbeing and Choice: A Response to the Green Paper on Adult Social Care: Report of a Consultation with Service Users*. London: National Centre for Independent Living and Shaping Our Lives.

Bright, R. (1996) *Grief and Powerlessness: Helping People Regain Control of their Lives*. London: Jessica Kingsley Publishers.

Brown, A. (2002) Groupwork. In: M. Davies (ed.) *The Blackwell Companion to Social Work*. Second edition. Oxford: Blackwell.

Bywaters, P. (1991) Case finding and screening for social work in acute general hospitals. *British Journal of Social Work*, 21 (1): 19–31.

Campbell, P. (1996) The history of the user movement in the United Kingdom. In: T. Heller, J. Reynolds, R. Gomm, R. Muston and S. Pattison (eds) *Mental Health Matters: A Reader*. London: Macmillan.

Campbell, J. and Oliver, M. (1996) *Disability Politics: Understanding our Past, Changing our Future*. London: Routledge.

Carr, S. (2004) *Has Service User Participation Made a Difference to Social Care Services?* Position Paper 3. London: Social Care Institute for Excellence.

Clark, D. (2001) What is qualitative research and what can it contribute to palliative care? In D. Field, D. Clark, J. Corner and C. Davis (eds) *Researching Palliative Care*. Buckingham: Open University Press.

Clausen, H., Kendall, M., Murray, S., Worth, A., Boyd, K. and Benton, F. (2005) Would palliative care patients benefit from social workers' retaining the traditional 'casework' role rather than working as care managers? A prospective serial qualitative interview study. *British Journal of Social Work*, 35 (March): 277–85.

Cohen, S., Boston, P., Mount, B. and Porterfield, P. (2001) Changes in quality of life following admission to palliative care units. *Palliative Medicine*, 15 (5): 363–71.

Cooke, B. and Kothari, U. (2001) *Participation: The New Tyranny?* London: Zed Books.

Coppick, V. and Hopton, J. (2000) *Critical Perspectives on Mental Health*. London: Routledge.

Corby, B., Millar, M. and Pope, A. (2002) Assessing children in need assessments: A parental perspective. *Practice*, 14 (4): 5–15.

Cotterell, P., Clarke, P., Cowdrey, D., Kapp, J., Paine, M. and Wynn, R. (2005) *Influencing Palliative Care Project: A Participatory Study*. Worthing, UK: Worthing and Southlands Hospitals NHS Trust.

Cotterell, P., Clarke, P., Cowdrey, D., Kapp, J., Paine, M. and Wynn, R. (2006) Becoming involved in research: A service user research advisory group. In: L. Jarrett (ed.) *My Place at the Front of the Queue: Building Identity, Developing Support, Advancing Involvement*. Abingdon: Radcliffe Publishing.

Cox, K. (2004) Sexual identity: Gender and sexual orientation. In: D. Oliviere and B. Monroe (eds) *Death, Dying, and Social Differences*. Oxford: Oxford University Press.

Crossland, C. (1998) Working with widowed men. *Bereavement Care*, 17 (2): 19–20.

Currer, C. (2001) *Responding to Grief: Dying, Bereavement and Social Care*. Basingstoke: Palgrave.

Daily Mail (2006) Are they playing God with patients' lives? 19 January.

Davies, E. and Higginson, I.J. (eds) (2004) *Palliative Care: The Solid Facts*. Copenhagen: The World Health Organization.

Davies, M. (ed.) (2002) *The Blackwell Companion to Social Work*. Second edition. Oxford: Blackwell.

Davies, M. and Connolly, J. (1995) The social worker's role in the hospital: Seen through the eyes of other health care professionals. *Health and Social Care in the Community*, 3 (5): 301–9.

De Winter, M. and Noom, M. (2003) The quality of services to homeless young people. *British Journal of Social Work*, 33 (3): 325–37.

Deakin, N. (1994) *The Politics of Welfare*. Second edition. Hemel Hempstead: Harvester Wheatsheaf.

Dearden, C. and Becker, S. (1997) *Young Carers in the UK: A Profile*. London: Carers National Association.

Dearden, C. and Becker, S. (2000) *Growing Up Caring: Vulnerability and Transition to Childhood – Young Carers' Experiences*. York: Youth Work Press for the Joseph Rowntree Foundation.

Department of Health (1995) *A Policy Framework for Commissioning Cancer Services: A Report by the Expert Advisory Group on Cancer to the Chief Medical Officers of England and Wales*. The Calman Hine Report. London: DOH.

Department of Health (2000) *The National Cancer Plan*. London: DOH.

Department of Health (2005) *Independence, Well-Being and Choice: Our Vision for the Future of Social Care for Adults in England*. Green Paper. London: The Stationery Office.

Department of Health (2006) *Our Health, Our Care, Our Say: A New Direction for Community Services*. White Paper. London: The Stationery Office.

Department of Health/NHS (2003) *Building on the Best: Choice, Responsiveness and Equity in the NHS*. Strategy Paper. London: The Stationery Office.

Dickenson, D., Johnson, M. and Katz, J. (eds) (2000) *Death, Dying and Bereavement*. London: Open University/Sage.

Dix, O. and Glickman, M. (1997) *Feeling Better: Psychosocial Care in Specialist Palliative Care*. Occasional Paper 13. London: National Council for Hospice and Specialist Palliative Care.

Dominelli, L. (2004) *Theory and Practice for a Changing Profession*. Cambridge: Polity Press.

Dowson, S. (1990) *Keeping It Safe: Self-Advocacy by People with Learning Difficulties and the Professional Response*. London: Values Into Action.

Drakeford, M. (1998) Last rights? Funerals, poverty and social exclusion. *Journal of Social Policy*, 27 (4): 507–24.

Duck, S. (1991) *Friends, for Life: The Psychology of Personal Relationships*. Revised second edition. Hemel Hempstead: Harvester Wheatsheaf.

Eagle, L.M. and De Vries, K. (2005) Exploration of the decision making process for inpatient hospice admissions. *Journal of Advanced Nursing*, 52 (6): 584–91.

Earnshaw-Smith, E.A. (1990) Editorial comment. *Palliative Medicine*, 4 (2): frontispiece.

Egan, G. (2002) *The Skilled Helper*. Seventh edition. Pacific Grove, CA: Brooks/Cole.

Elkington, H., White, P., Addington-Hall, J., Higgs, R., Edmonds, P. and Pettinari, C. (2004) The last year of life of COPD patients: A qualitative study of symptoms and services. *Respiratory Medicine*, 98 (5): 439–445.

Entwistle, V., Tritter, J.Q. and Calnan, M. (2002) Researching experiences of cancer: The importance of methodology. *European Journal of Cancer Care*, 11 (3): 232–7.

Evers, A., Haverinen, R., Leichsenring, K. and Wistow, G. (eds) (1997) *Developing Quality in Personal Social Services: Concepts, Cases and Comments*. Aldershot: Ashgate, in association with the European Centre, Vienna.

Fairbairn, G.J. (2002) Ethics, empathy and storytelling in professional development. *Learning in Health and Social Care*, 1 (1): 22–32.

Faulkner, A. (2004) *Ethics of Survivor Research: Guidelines for the Ethical Conduct of Research Carried Out by Mental Health Service Users and Survivors*. Bristol: Policy Press.

Faulkner, A. and Layzell, S. (2000) *Strategies for Living: A Report of User-Led Research into People's Strategies for Living with Mental Distress*. London: Mental Health Foundation.

Faulkner, A. and Maguire, P. (1994) *Talking to Cancer Patients and their Relatives*. Oxford: Oxford University Press.

Field, D. (1998) *Sociological Perspectives on Health, Illness and Health Care*. Oxford: Blackwell.

Fowler, H.W. and Fowler, F.G. (eds) (1970) *The Concise Oxford Dictionary of Current English*. Fifth edition. Oxford: Clarendon Press.

Franklin, J. (1996) *The Association of Hospice Social Workers is 10 Years Old*. Edinburgh: Annual Conference of the Association of Hospice Social Workers.

General Social Care Council (2002) *Codes of Practice for Social Care Workers and Employers*. London: GSCC.

Gilbert, K. (2002) Narrative approaches to grief research. *Death Studies*, 26 (3): 223–39.

Glaser, B.G. and Strauss, A.L. (1967) *The Discovery of Grounded Theory: Strategies for Qualitative Research*. London and Chicago: Aldine.

Gore, J.M., Brophy, C.J. and Greenstone, M.A. (2000) How well do we care for patients with end stage chronic obstructive pulmonary disease (COPD)? A comparison of palliative care and quality of life in COPD and lung cancer. *Thorax*, 55 (12): 1000–6.

Gott, M. (2004) User involvement and palliative care: Rhetoric or reality? In: S. Payne, J. Seymour and C. Ingleton (eds) *Palliative Care Nursing: Principles and Evidence for Practice*. Maidenhead: Open University Press.

Gott, M., Ahmedzai, S.H. and Wood, C. (2001) How many inpatients at an acute hospital have palliative care need? Comparing the perspectives of medical and nursing staff. *Palliative Medicine*, 15 (6): 451–60.

Goy, E.R., Schultz, A. and Ganzini, L. (2003) Psychological and psychiatric aspects of palliative care: An annotated bibliography. *Palliative and Supportive Care*, 1: 181–8 (doi: 10.1017/S1478951503030293).

Griggs, L. (2000) Assessment in community care. In: M. Davies (ed.) *The Blackwell Encyclopaedia of Social Work*. Oxford: Blackwell.

Hanley, B., for the Toronto Seminar Group (2005) *Research as Empowerment, Report of a Series of Seminars Organised by the Toronto Group*. York: Joseph Rowntree Foundation.

Harding, T. and Beresford, P. (1996) *The Standards We Expect: What Service Users and Carers Want from Social Services Workers*. London: National Institute for Social Work.

Hargreaves, P.N. and Peppiatt, R. (2001) Is video-taping of consultations acceptable to patients attending a hospice day centre? *Palliative Medicine*, 15 (1): 49–54.

Harlow, E. (2003) New managerialism, social service departments and social work practice today. *Practice*, 15 (2): 29–44.

Harrison, L. and Harrington, R. (2001) Adolescents' bereavement experiences. Prevalence, association with depressive symptoms, and use of services. *Journal of Adolescence*, 24: 159–69 (doi: 10.1006/jado.2001.0379).

Hawkins, L., Fook, J. and Ryan, M. (2001) Social workers' use of the language of social justice. *British Journal of Social Work*, 31 (1): 1–13.

Hayek, F.A. (1982) *The Constitution of Liberty*. London: Routledge and Kegan Paul.

Heaven, C.M. and Maguire, P. (1997) Disclosure of concerns by hospice patients and their identification by nurses. *Palliative Medicine*, 11: 283–90.

Hemmings, P. (2001) Button sculpting. *Bereavement Care*, 20 (2): 29.

Herod, J. and Lymbery, M. (2002) The social work role in multi-disciplinary teams. *Practice,* 14 (4): 17–27.

Hill, D. and Penso, D. (1995) *Opening Doors: Improving Access to Hospice and Specialist Care Services by Members of Black and Ethnic Minority Communities.* Occasional Paper 7. London: National Council for Hospice and Specialist Palliative Care Services.

Hill, K.M., Amir, Z., Muers, M.F., Connolly, C.K. and Round, C.E. (2003) Do newly diagnosed lung cancer patients feel their concerns are being met? *European Journal of Cancer Care,* 12 (1): 35–45.

Hockley, J. (1997) The evolution of the hospice approach. In: D. Clark, J. Hockley and S. Ahmedzai (eds) *New Themes in Palliative Care.* Buckingham: Open University Press.

Hogg, J., Northfield, J. and Turnbull, J. (2001) *Cancer and People with Learning Disabilities.* Kidderminser: BILD Publications.

Hospice Information Service (2002a) *Directory Hospice and Palliative Care Services in the United Kingdom and Ireland.* London: Hospice Information Service.

Hospice Information Service (2002b) *Minimum Data Sets – National Survey 2000–2001.* www.hospiceinformation.org.uk

Hospice Information Service (2003) *Minimum Data Sets – National Survey 1999–2000.* www.hospiceinformation.org.uk

Hospice Information (2003) *Hospice Directory 2003: Hospice and Palliative Care Services in the UK and Ireland.* London: Hospice Information.

Hospice Information (2005) *Hospice and Palliative Care Directory United Kingdom and Ireland 2005.* London: Hospice Information.

House of Commons Health Committee (2004) *Palliative Care.* Fourth report of Session 2003–04 vol. 1 (HC 454-1). London: Stationery Office.

Howe, D. (1996) Surface and depth in social work practice. In: N. Parton (ed.) *Social Theory, Social Change and Social Work.* London: Routledge.

Hughes, R.A., Down, K., Sinha, A., Higginson, I. and Leigh, P.N. (2004) Building user involvement in motor neurone disease: Key lessons. *Journal of Interprofessional Care,* 18 (1): 80–1.

Huntley, M. (2002) Relationship based social work – how do endings impact on the client? *Practice,* 14 (2): 59–66.

IFSW (2001) Definition of social work. www.ifsw.org/en/p38000208.html (accessed 6/6/06).

Ingleton, C., Skilbeck, J. and Clark, D. (2001) Needs assessment for palliative care: three projects compared. *Palliative Medicine,* 15 (5): 398–404.

Jackson, A., Blaxter, L. and Lewando-Hundt, G. (2003) Participating in medical education: Views of patients and carers living in deprived communities. *Medical Education,* 37 (6): 532–8.

Jackson, S. (2000) Assessment in community care. In: M. Davies (ed.) *The Blackwell Encyclopaedia of Social Work.* Oxford: Blackwell.

Jerome, D. (1981) The significance of friendship for women in later life. *Ageing and Society,* 1: 175–97.

Jones, C. (2002) Poverty and social exclusion. In: M. Davies (ed.) *The Blackwell Companion to Social Work.* Second edition. Oxford: Blackwell.

Jordan, B. (1997) Social work and society. In: M. Davies (ed.) *The Blackwell Companion to Social Work.* Oxford: Blackwell.

Jordan, B. (2001) Tough love: Social work, social exclusion and the third way. *British Journal of Social Work,* 31: 527–46.

Karim, K., Bailey, M. and Tunna, K. (2000) Non white ethnicity and the provision of specialist palliative care services: Factors affecting doctors' referral patterns. *Palliative Medicine,* 14 (6): 471–8.

Kayser, K. and Sormanti, M. (2002) Identity and the illness experience: Issues faced by mothers with cancer. *Illness, Crisis and Loss,* 10 (1): 10–26.

Kemshall, H. and Littlechild, R. (eds) (2000) *User Involvement and Participation in Social Care: Research Informing Practice.* London: Jessica Kingsley Publishers.

King, D. (1987) *The New Right.* London: Macmillan.

Knights, T. (2004) An examination of the social work role in specialist children's palliative care settings – Children's hospices. Unpublished study undertaken as part of Diploma in Social Work, Middlesex University.

Koffman, J. and Higginson, I.J. (2001) Accounts of carers' satisfaction with health care at the end of life: A comparison of first generation black Caribbeans and white patients with advanced disease. *Palliative Medicine*, 15 (4): 337–45.

Kraus, F., Levy, J. and Oliviere, D. (2003) Brief report on user involvement at St Christopher's Hospice. *Palliative Medicine*, 17: 375–7.

Langan, M. and Lee, P. (eds) (1989) *Radical Social Work Today: Social Work in the Recession.* London: Hutchinsons.

Laybourn, K. (1997) The guild of help and the community response to poverty 1904–c1914. In: K. Laybourn (ed.) *Social Conditions, Status and Community 1860– c1920.* Stroud: Sutton.

Lemieux, L., Kaiser, S., Pereira, S., Pereira, J. and Meadows, L.M. (2004) Sexuality in palliative care: Patient perspectives. *Palliative Medicine*, 18 (7), 1 October: 630–7.

Levin, E. (2004) *Involving Service Users and Carers in Social Work Education.* Social Care Institute for Excellence, Bristol: Policy Press.

Lidstone, V., Butler, E., Seed, P.T., Sinnott, C., Beynon, T. and Richards, M. (2003) Symptoms and concerns amongst cancer outpatients: Identifying the need for specialist palliative care. *Palliative Medicine*, 17 (7): 588–95.

Lloyd-Williams, M., Friedman, T. and Rudd, N. (1999) A survey of psychosocial service provision within hospices. *Palliative Medicine*, 13: 431–2.

Lowes, L. and Hulatt, I. (eds) (2005) *Involving Service Users in Health and Social Care Research.* London: Routledge.

Lyons, K. and Manion, K. (2003) Social work doctoral studies: Researching research. *British Journal of Social Work*, 33 (8): 1115–21.

MacDonald, D. (1991) Hospice social work: A search for identity. *Health and Social Work*, 16 (4): 274–80.

Marsland, D. (1992) The consequences of paternalist collectivism. *Social Policy and Administration*, 26 (2), June: 144–50.

McAdams, D.P. (1993) *The Stories We Live By.* New York: William Morrow.

McEnhill, L. (2004) Disability. In: D. Oliviere and B. Monroe (eds) *Death, Dying, and Social Differences.* Oxford: Oxford University Press.

McIllmurray, M.B., Thomas, C., Francis, B., Morris, S., Soothill, K. and Al-Hamad, A. (2001) The psychosocial needs of cancer patients: Findings from an observational study. *European Journal of Cancer Care*, 10 (4): 261–9.

McLeod, E. (1995) Patients in interprofessional practice. In: K. Soothill, L. Mackay and C. Webb (eds) *Interprofessional Relations in Health Care.* London: Edward Arnold.

McLeod, E. and Bywaters, P. (1999) Inequalities in physical health. *British Journal of Social Work*, 29 (4): 547–65.

McLeod, E. and Bywaters, P. (2002) Ill-health. In: M. Davies (ed.) *The Blackwell Companion to Social Work.* Second edition. Oxford: Blackwell.

McLeod, E., Bywaters, P. and Cooke, M. (2003) Social work in A & E departments. *British Journal of Social Work*, 33 (6): 787–802.

McNamara, B. (2001) *Fragile Lives: Death, Dying and Care.* Buckingham: Open University Press.

Mercer, G. (2002) Emancipatory disability research. In: C. Barnes, M. Oliver and L. Barton (eds) *Disability Studies Today.* Cambridge: Polity.

Meyer, H.A., Sinnott, C. and Seed, P. (2003) Depressive symptoms in advanced cancer. Part 2, depression over time; the role of the palliative care professional. *Palliative Medicine*, 17 (7): 604–7.

Milner, J. and O'Byrne, P. (2002) *Assessment in Social Work.* Second edition. Basingstoke: Palgrave.

Monroe, B. (1993) Psychosocial dimension of palliation. In: C. Saunders and N. Sykes (eds) *The Management of Terminal Malignant Disease.* Third edition. London: Edward Arnold.

Monroe, B. (1998) Social work in palliative care. In: D. Doyle, G. Hanks and N. MacDonald (eds) *The Oxford Handbook of Palliative Medicine.* Second edition. Oxford: Oxford University Press.

Monroe, B. and Oliviere, D. (2003) *Patient Participation in Palliative Care: A Voice for the Voiceless.* Oxford: Oxford University Press.

Napier, L. (2003) Palliative care social work. In: B. Monroe and D. Oliviere (eds) *Patient Participation in Palliative Care: A Voice for the Voiceless.* Oxford: Oxford University Press.

National Council for Hospice and Specialist Palliative Care Services (2000a) *The Palliative Care Survey 1999*. London: National Council for Hospice and Specialist Palliative Care Services. Accessed 12/02/2004 at www.hospice-spc-council.org/uk

National Council for Hospice and Specialist Palliative Care Services (2000b) 'What do we mean by "psychosocial"?' *Briefing Paper 4*, March.

National Council for Palliative Care (2005) *Palliative Care Manifesto*. London: The National Council for Palliative Care.

National Hospice Council (2001) Support and self-help for people with new diagnosis, user involvement. *Information Exchange* (September).

Newnes, C., Holmes, G. and Dunn, C. (eds) (2001) *This is Madness Too: Critical Perspectives on Mental Health Services*. Ross-on-Wye: PCCS Books.

NICE (The National Institute for Clinical Excellence) (2004) *Supportive and Palliative Care Cancer Service Guidance*. www.nice.org.uk

Nichols, K. and Jenkinson, J. (1991) *Leading a Support Group*. London: Chapman and Hall.

Norris, J.E. and Tindale, J.A. (1994) *Among Generations: The Cycle of Adult Relationships*. New York: Freeman.

Oliver, M. (1996) *Understanding Disability: From Theory to Practice*. Basingstoke: Macmillan.

Oliver, M. and Barnes, C. (1998) *Disabled People and Social Policy: From Exclusion to Inclusion*. London: Longmans.

Oliviere, D. (2000) A voice for the voiceless. *European Journal of Palliative Care*, 7 (3): 102–5.

Oliviere, D. (2001a) The social worker in palliative care – the 'eccentric' role. *Progress in Palliative Care*, 9 (6): 237–41.

Oliviere, D. (2001b) User involvement in palliative care services. *European Journal of Palliative Care*, 8 (6): 238–41.

Oliviere, D., Hargreaves, R. and Monroe, B. (eds) (1998) *Good Practices in Palliative Care*. Aldershot: Ashgate.

Oliviere, D. and Monroe, B. (eds) (2004) *Death, Dying and Social Differences*. Oxford: Oxford University Press.

Packman, J. and Hall, C. (1998) *From Care to Accommodation: Support, Protection and Care in Child Care Services*. London: The Stationery Office.

Parr, S., Byng, S. and Gilpin, S. with Ireland, C. (1998) *Talking About Aphasia*. Maidenhead: Open University Press.

Parry-Jones, B. and Soulsby, J. (2001) Needs-led assessment: The challenges and the reality. *Health and Social Care in the Community*, 9 (6): 414 (doi: 10.1046/j.0966-0410. 2001.00316.x).

Parton, N. (1994) Problematics of government: (Post) modernity and social work. *British Journal of Social Work*, 20 (1): 9–32.

Parton, N. (ed.) (1996) *Social Theory, Social Change and Social Work*. London: Routledge.

Parton, N. (2003) Reconsidering professional practice. *British Journal of Social Work*, 33 (1): 1–16.

Payne, S. (2002) Are we using the users? *International Journal of Palliative Nursing* 8 (5), May: 212.

Payne, S., Gott, M., Small, N., Oliviere, D., Sargeant, A. and Young, E. (2005) *User Involvement in Palliative Care: A Scoping Study*. Final report to St Christopher's Hospice, June. Sheffield: University of Sheffield.

Postle, K. (2001) The social work side is disappearing. I guess it started with us being called care managers. *Practice*, 13 (1): 13–26.

Postle, K. (2002) Working 'between the idea and the reality': Ambiguities and tensions in care managers' work. *British Journal of Social Work*, 32: 335–51.

Pritchard, C., Cotton, A., Bowen, D. and Williams, R. (1998) Young people's views on educational social work. *British Journal of Social Work*, 28: 915–38.

Ramirez, A., Addington-Hall, J. and Richards, M. (1998) ABC of palliative care: The carers. *British Medical Journal*, 316: 208–11.

Reason, J. and Rowan, P. (eds) (1981) *Human Inquiry: A Sourcebook of New Paradigm Research*. Chichester: John Wiley & Sons.

Reese, D.J. and Brown, D.R. (1997) Psychosocial and spiritual care in hospice: Differences between nursing, social work and clergy. *Hospice Journal*, 12 (1): 57–65.

Reese, D.J. and Raymer, M. (2004) Relationships between social work involvement and hospice outcomes: Results of the national social work survey. *Social Work*, 1 July, 49 (3): 415–422.

Regan, S. (2001) When forms fail the reality test. *Community Care*, 25–31 October: 36–7.

Rhodes, P. and Shaw, S. (1999) Informal care and terminal illness. *Health and Social Care in the Community*, 7 (1): 39 (doi: 10.1046/j.1365-2524.1999.00147.x).

Rice, A. (2000) Sexuality in cancer and palliative care 1: Effects of disease and treatment. *International Journal of Palliative Nursing*, 6 (8), September: 392–7.

Richards, S. (2000) Bridging the divide: Elders and the assessment process. *British Journal of Social Work*, 30 (1): 37–49.

Rogers, C.R. (1961) *On Becoming a Person*. London: Constable.

Ryan, P., Ford, R., Beadsmore, A. and Muijen, M. (1999) The Sainsbury Centre case management study. *British Journal of Social Work*, 29: 97–125.

Schalock, R.L. (1995) *Outcome-based Evaluation*. New York: Plenum Press.

Seale, C. (2006) National survey of end-of-life decisions made by UK medical practitioners. *Palliative Medicine*, 20: 1–8.

Seale, C. and Cartwright, A. (1994) *The Year Before Death*. Aldershot: Avebury.

Seering, H. (2003) The continuing relevance of casework ideas to long-term child protection work. *Child and Family Social Work*, 8: 311–20.

Seymour, J. and Clark, D. (2002) Palliative care and policy in England: A review of health plans 1999–2003. *Palliative Medicine*, 16 (1): 5–11.

Seymour, J. and Skilbeck, J. (2002) Ethical considerations in researching users' views. *European Journal of Cancer Care*, 11: 215–19.

Shaping Our Lives National User Network, Black User Group (West London), Ethnic Disabled Group Emerged (Manchester), Footprints and Waltham Forest Black Mental Health Service User Group (North London) and Service Users' Action Forum (Wakefield) (2003) *Shaping Our Lives – From Outset to Outcome: What People Think of the Social Care Services They Use*. York: Joseph Rowntree Foundation/York Publishing.

Shapiro, S., Angus, L. and Davis, C. (1997) Identity and meaning in the experience of cancer. *Journal of Health Psychology*, 2 (4): 539–54.

Shaw, I., Arksey, H. and Mullender, A. (2004) *ESRC Research, Social Work and Social Care. How knowledge works in social care report series*. London: Social Care Institute for Excellence.

Sheldon, F. (1997) *Psychosocial Palliative Care: Good Practice in the Care of the Dying and Bereaved*. Cheltenham: Stanley Thornes.

Shipman, C., Addington-Hall, J., Barclay, B., Briggs, J., Cox, I., Daniels, L. and Millar, D. (2002) How and why do GPs use specialist palliative care services? *Palliative Medicine*, 16: 241–6.

Smaje, C. and Field, D. (1997) Absent minorities? Ethnicity and the use of palliative care services. In: D. Field, J. Hockney and S. Small (eds) *Death, Gender and Ethnicity*. London: Routledge.

Small, N. and Rhodes, P. (2000) *Too Ill to Talk? User Involvement and Palliative Care*. London: Routledge.

Smith, S.C. and Pennells, M. (1995) *Interventions with Bereaved Children*. London: Jessica Kingsley Publishers.

Smith, S.D.M., Nicol, K.M. and Devereux, J. (1999) Encounters with doctors: Quantity and quality. *Palliative Medicine*, 13: 217–23.

Smith, M. (2003) Social workers praised by service users! What the Climbié Report doesn't say. *Practice*, 15 (3): 7–16.

Soothill, K., Morris, S., Thomas, C., Harman, J.C., Francis, B. and McIllmurray, M.B. (2003) The universal, situational and personal needs of cancer patients and their main carers. *European Journal of Oncology Nursing*, 7 (1): 5–15.

Stacy, R. and Spencer, J. (1999) Patients as teachers: A qualitative study of patients' views on their role in a community-based undergraduate project. *Medical Education*, 33 (9): 688–94.

Stanley, N. (1999) User-practitioner transactions in the new culture of community care. *British Journal of Social Work*, 29: 417–35.

Stroebe, M. and Schut, H. (1999) The dual process model of coping with bereavement: Rationale and description. *Death Studies*, 23: 197–224.

Sudbery, J. (2002) Key features of therapeutic social work: The use of relationship. *Journal of Social Work Practice*, 6 (2): 149–62.

Thompson, C. (ed.) (1991) *Changing the Balance*. London: National Council for Voluntary Organisations.

Thompson, N. (1997) Masculinity and loss. In: D. Field, J. Hockey and N. Small (eds) *Death, Gender and Ethnicity*. London: Routledge.

Thompson, N. (2002) Anti-discriminatory practice. In: M. Davies (ed.) *The Blackwell Companion to Social Work*. Second edition. Oxford: Blackwell.

Training Organisation for the Personal Social Services (2004) *The National Occupational Standards for Social Work*. Leeds: TOPPS England. Online at www.toppsengland.net/view.asp?id=140.

Trevithick, P. (2003) Effective relationship-based practice: A theoretical exploration. *Journal of Social Work Practice*, 17 (2): 163–76.

Turner, M. (1997) *Shaping Our Lives: Interim Report*. London: Shaping Our Lives, National Institute for Social Work.

Turner, M. (1998) *Shaping Our Lives: Project Report*. London: Shaping Our Lives, National Institute for Social Work.

Turner, M. (1999) Involvement or over-involvement? Using grounded theory to explore the complexities of the nurse–patient relationship. *European Journal of Oncology Nursing*, 3 (3): 153–60.

Turner, M. and Beresford, P. (2005) *User Controlled Research: Its Meanings and Potential, Final Report*. Shaping Our Lives and the Centre for Citizen Participation, Brunel University. Eastleigh: Involve.

Walker, A. (1996) *Young Carers and their Families*. London: The Stationery Office.

Wallcraft, J. (1998) Survivor-led research in human services: Challenging the dominant medical Paradigm. In: S. Baldwin (ed.) *Needs Assessment and Community Care: Clinical Practice and Policy Making*. Oxford: Butterworth-Heinemann.

Walter, T. (1996) A new model of grief: Bereavement and biography. *Mortality*, 1 (1): 7–25.

Walter, T. (1999) *On Bereavement: The Culture of Grief*. Buckingham: Open University Press.

Weinberg, A., Williamson, J., Challis, D. and Hughes, J. (2003) The working practices of care managers. *British Journal of Social Work*, 33 (7): 901–19.

White, I., Devenney, M., Bhaduri, R., Barnes, M., Beresford, P. and Jones, A. (1988) *Hearing the Voice of the Consumer*. London: Policy Studies Institute.

WHO (2002) *Definition of Palliative Care*. Source: www.who.int.

Wijne, I. (2003) Palliative care needs of people with intellectual disabilities, literature review. *Palliative Medicine*, 17 (8): 55–62.

Williams, B., Coyle, J. and Healy, D. (1998) The meaning of patient satisfaction: an explanation of high reported levels. *Social Science and Medicine*, 47: 1351–9.

Williams, F. (1996) Postmodernism, feminism and the question of difference. In: N. Parton (ed.) *Social Theory, Social Change and Social Work*. London: Routledge.

Winter, R. and Munn-Giddings, C. (eds) (2001) *A Handbook for Action Research in Health and Social Care*. London: Routledge.

Worden, W. (1996) *Children and Grief*. London and New York: The Guilford Press.

SUBJECT INDEX

accessibility of social workers 96–8, 198
  equality issues 146–52
  impact of social work's negative image 133–8
  ways of increasing 213–14
advocacy 71, 112, 159, 166–8
age of service users 106–9, 236–7
anonymity 72, 115, 127, 209, 242
assessment process 61–2, 67
  appropriate use of power 64–5
  different approach for men 148
  informality of 62–3
  issues of concern 65–6, 214–15
  ongoing and supportive 65
  social worker skills 162–4
Association of Hospice Social Workers 27–8
attitudes
  to death and dying 15
  towards palliative care 43–4, 51
  towards social work 25, 133–6
autonomy, professional 200–1
availability of social workers 96–8

benefits see welfare benefits
bereavement
  and biography 178–82
  'dual process model' 177
  theories of grief 175–7
bereavement groups
  benefits of 61, 146
  ending of 184
  reducing isolation 122–3
  structured approach 79–84

bereavement support 145–6
  Fred's story 76–84
  lack of 119
  late referrals 142–3
  offered proactively 55–6
  timing of 58–9
biographical reconstruction 178–82
black service users
  inequality of access 150–1
  poverty issues 113, 164–5
breast cancer patients, support for 109–10, 113

Calman Hine Report 31
cancer 23
  different types of 111–12
  few groups for patients with 185
  less support for men with 109–10
  Mike and Linda's story 73–6
  patient centred services 31–3
  rare types of 113, 211–12, 222
'care management' approach 155, 167
child protection issues 25, 134–5, 201, 204
children
  feedback from 205
  helping to grieve 180
  parental fears 134–5
  and referral 149–50
  work with 107, 123, 215
'choice agenda' 30
'clinical love' 176
code of practice for social care workers 27–8
Commission for Social Care Inspection 30
community care assessments 163–4
community support, breakdown in 117–18

complaints, communicating 125–6
confidentiality 242
consent 37, 242
continuity of support 98–9, 159, 181
counselling
  bereavement support 145–6
  non-directive 94, 178
  skills of social workers 143, 161
  users' experiences of 102
criticisms of specialist palliative care social work 114–19, 128

death and dying
  changing attitudes towards 13–14
  end-of-life decisions 224–5
  'death anxiety' 169
demographic profile of study sample 235
diagnosis 111–12, 113, 237–8
  effects of late 73–4
  and referral 151–2
discharge issues 117–18, 187, 216
doctor-assisted dying 224–5
doctoral research, lack of 201–2
doctors
  and continuity of care 98, 170
  disrespect for patients 106
  and early discharge 118
  lack of time for patients 54, 108, 124–5
  misdiagnosis by 73
  patients' relationship with 62, 157
'dual process model' of bereavement 177

Economic and Social
    Research Council
    (ESRC) 202
emotional support 71,
    101–2, 121, 168–9,
    175–7
employment background of
    service users 111, 239
end-of-life decisions (ELDs)
    224–5
equality issues in referral
    146–52, 215–16
ethical issues 239–43
ethnicity of service users
    110, 238
euthanasia 224–5
evaluation of palliative care
    social work 125–7, 129,
    203–6
expertise
    of patients 219, 230–1
    perceptions of 197
    of social workers 99

family
    difficulty talking to 60–1
    relationship breakdowns
        116
    status of service users 238
    support work 69, 72–6,
        84–6, 123, 137, 185–6
feedback from service users
    125–7, 203–6
financial problems
    making illness harder to
        bear 140
    taking priority over illness
        164–5
financial security, social
    workers improving 124,
    165
flexibility of social workers
    90–2, 182–3, 198, 222
friends, service users relating
    to 60–1
friendship 89, 156–61,
    198–9
friendship groups 123, 184
funding
    of independent hospices
        24
    lack of research 201–2
future implications 223–5

gender of service users
    109–10, 112–13
General Social Care Council
    27, 30
government
    advertising campaigns
        204
    changed approach to
        health and welfare
        28–31
    encouraging user
        involvement 31–2
    funding of hospices 24
    restrictive definition of
        social work 194
'grateful patient syndrome'
    234
grief, theories of 175–6
groupwork
    for bereaved people
        79–84, 180–1
    challenges of 183–5
    positive experience for
        men 109, 148

health and welfare policy
    emphasis on illness and
        care 23–4
    market sector values 28–9
    'quality strategy' 30
Help the Hospices 33
holistic approach 21, 31,
    140, 161–71, 172–3
home visits 99–101, 182–3
hospice movement 21–2, 23,
    31
Hospice Year Book 235
hospices
    change of attitude towards
        43–4
    funding of 24
    lack of social work
        provision 192
    late referral to 44–5
    management of 200
    perceptions of 42–3,
        211–12
    psychosocial care in
        191–2

identity, preserving 158–9
illness, impact on family
    relationships 116

inconsistencies
    in referrals 142–3
    in service provision 190–3
independence, loss of 135–6
Independence, Well-Being and
    Choice: Our Vision for the
    Future of Social Care for
    Adults in England
    (DOH) 167
individuality of treatment
    approach 105–6
informal approach of social
    workers 141–2, 148,
    162–3, 171–2, 182, 214
information, written 148,
    214, 241
Internet, and bereavement
    support for children
    150
interpersonal relationship,
    importance of 155
interviewing service users
    243–5
    ethical issues 242
    interview schedule
        247–51
Involve Project 36–8, 227–8
    analysis of data 245–6
    ethical issues 239–43
    implication of findings
        211–16
    interview schedule
        247–51
    limitations of 209–11
    methodology 228–9
    profiles of service users
        236–9
    recruiting service users
        232–6
    steering groups 229–32
    strengths of 208–9

jargon, avoidance of 199

listening skills of social
    workers 94–5
literature
    for bereaved people 142
    by social workers 196
    for children 150
long-term support 98–9,
    181

loss
    coping with 169, 177
    talking about 178
    theories of 175–6

managerial influence of
    social workers 200
marginalization of social
    work 174, 190–3,
    201–2
medical care
    breakdown in 108,
        117–19
    developments in 23 4
medical issues, support with
    70, 71, 124 5
medical model, dominance
    of 144, 200, 211
medical professionals
    domination of 187
    lack of time for patients
        108, 119
    perception of palliative
        care needs 140
    research on palliative care
        196
    social workers challenging
        73
medically oriented referrals
    139–41
men
    referral patterns 147–8
    reluctance to talk about
        problems 109, 148
minority ethnic groups 110,
    238
    poverty of 164–5
    and referral 150–1
    unequal access to care
        216
multidisciplinary teamwork
    breakdown of 117–19
    and referrals 144

National Council for
    Palliative Care 33, 224
National Health Service
    Cancer Plan 31
National Service
    Frameworks 30
negative stereotyping of
    social work 134, 137–8
NHS and Community Care
    Act (1990) 29

non-cancer patients 111,
    113, 151–2, 237–8
non-treatment decisions
    (NTDs) 224–5
normalization of feelings
    175

older service users,
    treatment of 107–9
outcomes of specialist
    palliative care social
    work 120–5

palliative care
    attitudes towards 43–4,
        51
    changing perceptions 23
    definitions of 21, 27
    fear of 42–3
    historical origins 21–2
    implications of project
        findings 211–12
    lack of social work
        provision 191 3
    management roles 200
    national organizations
        201
    policy-making bodies
        201
    specialist services 22–4
    specialist social work
        26–8
    user involvement in 31–4
Palliative Care Manifesto
    224
Palliative Care Survey 1999,
    The 190, 192
palliative medicine, focus on
    symptom management
    200
paperwork, help with
    108–9, 123–4, 166
parents
    fears of losing children
        134–5
    feedback from 205
participation see user
    involvement
partnership working 93–4,
    197
patients
    end-of-life decisions
        224–5
    inconsistent referral
        142–3, 213

issues with groupwork
    184–5
lack of continuity in
    medical care 170
profile of 236–9
psychosocial needs 166,
    168–9
relationship with service
    user 115–16
relationship with social
    workers 197
working with students
    219–20
peer support 83–4, 122–3,
    218
personal qualities of social
    workers 92–3
policy-making, limited
    influence from social
    workers 201
poverty 164–5, 167–8
powerlessness of social
    workers 187–8
practical issues
    support with 71, 108–9,
        123–4, 164–6
    taking precedence over
        emotional 117, 186–7
proactive approach of social
    workers 55–6, 73,
        141–2, 148
professionalism of social
    workers
    recognition of boundaries
        159–60
    undermined by their ways
        of working 194–9
psychological impact of social
    work support 120–2
psychosocial care 168–9,
    191, 196–7
psychosocial needs
    ignored during referral 140
    not being met 166, 189

qualities of social workers
    valued by service users
        92–3, 205–6
quality standards, improving
    30–1
questions
    aims of Involve project 228
    interview 248–51

reciprocity 90, 157–8
recruitment of service users 232–6
referral process 52–3, 66–7
  auditing, need for 152
  bereavement support 55–6
  early referral, importance of 56–8
  equality issues 146–52
  inconsistent patterns of 55, 142–3
  informal approach 53–5, 141–2
  medically orientated 139–41
  proactive approach 141–2
  reasons for late referral 44–5
  reliance on other professionals 59, 136
  role of other professionals 143–5
  self-referral rate, low 52, 141
  turning down support 58–9
  value of written information 59–60
relationships
  family 115–16
  between patients and service users 115–16
  between social workers and service users 88–92, 154–61, 172, 197
reliability of palliative care social workers 99
religion of service users 110–11
research
  lack of funding for 201–2
  user involvement in 35–6, 209
  see also Involve Project
respect, being treated with 95, 106, 108
responsibility vs. powerlessness of social worker 187–8

Saunders, Dame Cicely 21, 31
self-referral 52, 135–6, 141, 214

sensitivity of social worker 221
service users
  attitudes towards hospice care 43–4
  being given time 95–6
  coping strategies, supporting 120–2
  emotional needs 168–9
  experiences 72–86
    seen as a journey 41–5
  family and friends, difficulty talking to 60–1
  fear of palliative care 42–3
  feedback from 125–7, 203–6, 217
  first contact with social workers 52–5
  forging links between 72
  involvement 29
    in palliative care 31–4
    in research 35–6
    in training 218–23
  issues needing support 69–70
  lack of information about social work 50
  peer support 83–4, 122–3, 218
  perception of social worker's personality 92–3
  perceptions of social work 133–6
  profile of 236–9
  psychological support 120–2
  quality of relationship with social workers 88–92, 154–61
  recruitment of 232–6
  social work interventions 68–9
  treated as individuals 105–6
  turning down support 58–9
  views of social work 45–50, 51
  working as volunteers 218
  working in partnership with social workers 93–4
Shaping Our Lives, user-controlled organization 30–1, 35

social burial 159
social isolation, reduction of 122–3, 183
social work 15–16
  approaches of 25–6
  assessment 61–5
  criticisms of 25
  cuts in services 192
  history of 24–5
  knowledge about 50
  literature 196–7
  marginal status of 190–3
  negative views of 45–50, 51, 134–5, 136
  other names for 137
  other professions' perception of 193–4
  palliative care 26–8
  promoting 212–13
  purpose of 27–8
  relieving poverty 164–6
  theory 174–5
  see also specialist palliative care social work
social workers
  accessibility of 96–8, 198
  assessment pressures 163–4
  bridging role of 187–8
  code of practice for 27–8
  counselling skills of 143, 161
  different approaches of 102
  knowledge of illnesses 111–12
  knowledge of welfare services 167
  listening skills of 94–5
  negative views of 45–50, 51
    perceived by other professionals 136
  non-judgemental attitude 95
  overstretched 143
  personal qualities 92–3
  proactive approach with men 148
  providing support 68–72
  training of 218–23
  undermining own profession 137
  underrepresentation of 201
  see also specialist palliative care social workers

specialist palliative care
   social work 26–8
   adverse criticisms of
      114–19
   assessment methods
      214–15
   evaluation of 125–7,
      203–6
   inconsistent service
      provision 190–3
   lack of external
      recognition 194–9
   outcomes of 120–5
   positive feelings about
      133–4
   referral issues 213–14
   role of 189–90
   wide scope of 101–2,
      164–71, 197–8
   see also social work
specialist palliative care
   social workers 56
   appropriate use of power
      64–5
   assessment by 62–3
   autonomy of 200–1
   and bereavement work
      145
   contact at referral 52–61
   'hands-on' approach
      166–8, 196–7
   quality of relationship
      with service users
      88–92
   role of 135
   support provided 68–72
   user-identified themes for
      training of 220–3
   using other titles 136–8
   see also social workers
standards for social workers
   27–8, 30
statutory social work
   bureaucratic nature of
      166–8
   ignoring emotional needs
      168
steering groups 229–30
   issues raised by 230–2
students, service users
   working with 219–20
suicide, prevention of
   121–2, 169
support
   continuity of 98–9
   turning down 58–9
support groups 76–9

Supportive and Palliative
   Care Guidance (NICE)
   201
Symptoms and Concerns
   Checklist 166

teamwork, breakdown of
   117–19
theory of social work
   174–5, 202
time for service users, social
   worker allowing 95–6
touch, importance of 91
training
   professional organizations
      27–8, 30
   service user concerns
      220–3
   service user feedback
      116, 151–2
   user involvement in
      218–20

UK health policy 23–4
user involvement 29,
   229–30
   cancer services 31, 33
   evaluation and feedback
      217
   positive experiences 33–4
   pressures against 32–3
   providing peer support
      218
   in research 35–6, 240
   reservations raised 34
   sharing knowledge
      217–18
   in training of social
      workers 218–23

volunteers, service users as
   218

welfare benefits, help in
   accessing 70, 71, 111,
   165, 167
women, support groups for
   109–10, 148
written information 148,
   214, 241

young people
   feedback from 205–6
   and referral 149–50
   timing of support 58–9
   work with 107

AUTHOR INDEX

Adams, R. 24, 25
Adams, R.G. 157
Addington-Hall, J.M. 163, 189, 197, 240
Ahmedzai, S.H. 140
Aldgate, J. 205
Allan, G. 157
Allen, K. 34
Anderson, H. 135, 144, 148, 189
Angus, L. 159
APCSW 27
Aranda, S. 239
Arksey, H. 174
Arnstein, S. 34

Bailey, C. 159
Bailey, M. 150
Balloch, S. 31
Bar-On, A. 204
Barnes, C. 35, 36
Barnett, M. 209, 240
Barton, L. 36
Baxter, L. 36
Becker, S. 149
Becket, C. 160
Beresford, P. 30, 31, 32, 33, 36, 159, 174, 203, 206, 218, 219, 229, 240
Biestek, F. 155
Blaxter, L. 219
Blieszner, R. 157
Bliss, J. 141
Branfield, F. 206, 212
Bright, R. 147
Brophy, C.J. 151
Brown, A. 183
Brown, D.R. 169
Bywaters, P. 141, 165, 167, 194

Calnan, M. 209
Campbell, J. 29, 174
Campbell, P. 29
Carr, S. 33
Cartwright, A. 196

Clark, D. 39, 151, 235
Clausen, H. 139
Cohen, S. 134
Connolly, J. 141
Cooke, B. 33–4
Cooke, M. 141
Coppick, V. 171
Corby, B. 164
Corner, J. 159
Cotterell, P. 233
Cowley, S. 141
Cox, K. 105
Coyle, J. 210
Croft, S. 32, 174, 218, 240
Crossland, C. 147
Currer, C. 137, 159, 181, 182, 193

Daily Mail 224
Davies, E. 21
Davies, M. 24, 141
Davis, C. 159
De Vries, K. 140
De Winter, M. 205
Deakin, N. 28
Dearden, C. 149
Department of Health 23, 167, 204, 206
Department of Health/NHS 31
Devereaux, J. 170
Dickenson, D. 196
Dix, O. 191
Dominelli, L. 24, 175
Dowson, S. 34
Drakeford, M. 165
Duck, S. 157
Dunn, C. 171

Eagle, L.M. 140
Earnshaw-Smith, E.A. 193
Egan, G. 161
Elkington, H. 151
Entwistle, V. 209
Evers, A. 30

Fairbairn, G.J. 162
Faulkner, A. 36, 157, 175
Field, D. 150, 200
Fook, J. 160
Fowler, F.G. 21
Fowler, H.W. 21
Franklin, J. 26

Ganzini, L. 171
General Social Care Council 27, 30
Gilbert, K. 162
Glaser, B.G. 245
Glickman, M. 191
Gore, J.M. 151
Gott, M. 31, 140
Goy, E.R. 171
Greenstone, M.A. 151
Griggs, L. 62

Hall, C. 135
Hanley, B. 36
Harding, T. 30, 159
Hargreaves, P.N. 209
Hargreaves, R. 149
Harlow, E. 155, 162, 170
Harrington, R. 149
Harrison, L. 149
Hawkins, L. 16
Hayek, F.A. 28
Healy, D. 210
Heaven, C.M. 144
Hemmings, P. 180
Herod, J. 190
Higginson, I.J. 21, 150
Hill, D. 150
Hill, K.M. 189
Hockley, J. 200
Hogg, J. 147
Holmes, G. 171
Hopton, J. 171
Hospice Information 21, 22, 24
Hospice Information Service 147, 151, 161, 238, 239

House of Commons Health
    Committee 201
Howe, D. 155, 168
Hughes, R.A. 203
Hulatt, I. 35
Huntley, M. 181

IFSW 27
Ingleton, C. 151

Jackson, A. 219
Jackson, S. 62
Jenkinson, J. 184
Jerome, D. 159
Johnson, M. 196
Jones, C. 165, 168
Jordan, B. 25, 194

Karim, K. 150
Katz, J. 196
Kayser, K. 147, 159
Kemshall, H. 35
King, D. 28
Knights, T. 192
Koffman, J. 150
Kothari, U. 34
Kraus, F. 32

Langan, M. 25
Laybourn, K. 25
Layzell, S. 36
Lee, P. 25
Lemieux, L. 105
Levin, E. 219, 220
Levy, J. 32
Lewando-Hundt, G. 219
Lidstone, V. 166
Littlechild, R. 35
Lloyd-Williams, M. 191
Lowes, L. 35
Lymbery, M. 190
Lyons, K. 201

MacDonald, D. 167
Maguire, P. 144, 157, 175
Manion, K. 201
Marsland, D. 28
McAdams, D.P. 162
McCarthy, M. 163, 240
McEnhill, L. 147, 210

McIllmurray, M.B. 189
McLeod, E. 141, 165, 167,
    194
McNamara, B. 196
Mercer, G. 35, 36
Meyer, H.A. 171
Millar, M. 164
Milner, J. 162
Mitchell, A. 36
Monroe, B. 32, 146, 149,
    186, 196
Mullender, A. 174
Munn-Giddings, C. 36

Napier, L. 27
National Council for
    Hospice and Specialist
    Palliative Care Services
    190, 191, 192
National Council for
    Palliative Care 224
National Hospice Council
    32
Newnes, C. 171
NICE (The National
    Institute for Clinical
    Excellence) 201
Nichols, K. 184
Nicol, K.M. 170
Noom, M. 205
Norris, J.E. 159
Northfield, J. 147

O'Byrne, P. 162
Oliver, M. 29, 36, 174
Oliviere, D. 32, 146, 149,
    180, 187, 196

Packman, J. 135
Parr, S. 34
Parry-Jones, B. 163
Parton, N. 24, 206
Payne, M. 24
Payne, S. 32, 155
Pennells, M. 180
Penso, D. 150
Peppiatt, R. 209
Pope, A. 164
Postle, K. 164
Pritchard, C. 206

Ramirez, A. 197
Raymer, M. 192
Reason, J. 36
Reese, D.J. 169, 192
Regan, S. 162
Rhodes, P. 33, 163, 203
Rice, A. 105
Richards, M. 197
Richards, S. 164
Rogers, C.R. 158, 161
Rowan, P. 36
Ryan, M. 160
Ryan, P. 155

Schalock, R.L. 31
Schultz, A. 171
Schut, H. 177, 181
Seale, C. 196, 224, 225
Seed, P. 171
Seering, H. 205
Seymour, J. 211, 235
Shaping Our Lives National
    User Network 31
Shapiro, S. 159
Shaw, I. 174, 202
Shaw, S. 163
Sheldon, F. 196
Shipman, C. 140
Sinnott, C. 171
Skilbeck, J. 151, 211
Smaje, C. 150
Small, N. 32–3, 203
Smith, M. 204
Smith, S.C. 180
Smith, S.D.M. 170
Soothill, K. 165, 166
Sormanti, M. 147, 159
Soulsby, J. 163
Spencer, J. 219
Stacy, R. 219
Stanley, N. 163
Statham, J. 205
Strauss, A.L. 245
Stroebe, M. 177, 180–1
Sudbery, J. 155

Thompson, C. 34
Thompson, N. 147, 162
Thorne, L. 36
Tindale, J.A. 159
Training Organisation for the
    Personal Social Services
    28
Trevithick, P. 205

Tritter, J.Q. 209
Tunna, K. 150
Turnbull, J. 147
Turner, M. 31, 36, 156, 229

Walker, A. 149
Wallcraft, J. 36
Walter, T. 174, 176, 178,
     179, 180
Weinberg, A. 168
While, A. 141
White, I. 34
WHO (World Health
     Organization) 21, 161
Wijne, I. 147
Williams, B. 210
Williams, F. 25
Winter, R. 36
Wood, C. 140
Worden, W. 149